The Things I Want Most

The Things I Want Most

THE EXTRAORDINARY STORY
OF A BOY'S JOURNEY
TO A FAMILY OF HIS OWN

Richard F. Miniter

Bantam Books
New York Toronto London Sydney Auckland

THE THINGS I WANT MOST
A Bantam Book / September 1998

All rights reserved.
Copyright © 1998 by Richard F. Miniter.
Book design by James Sinclair.
No part of this book may be reproduced or transmitted in any form or by any
means, electronic or mechanical, including photocopying, recording, or by
any information storage and retrieval system, without permission in writing from
the publisher. For information address: Bantam Books.

Library of Congress Cataloging-in-Publication Data
Miniter, Richard F.
The things I want most : the extraordinary story of a boy's
journey to a family of his own / Richard F. Miniter.
p. cm.
ISBN 0-553-10933-2
1. Therapeutic foster care—Case studies.   I. Title.
RJ504.55.M56   1998   98-4915
362.1'9892—dc21   CIP

Published simultaneously in the United States and Canada

Bantam Books are published by Bantam Books, a division of Bantam Doubleday
Dell Publishing Group, Inc. Its trademark, consisting of the words "Bantam
Books" and the portrayal of a rooster, is Registered in U.S. Patent and Trademark
Office and in other countries. Marca Registrada. Bantam Books, 1540 Broadway,
New York, New York 10036.

PRINTED IN THE UNITED STATES OF AMERICA

BVG   10   9   8   7   6   5   4   3   2   1

This story is dedicated to Laura Ronning
Taken from the family on July 27, 1991

Contents

The Things I Want Most

This is the true story of a remarkable and profoundly emotionally disturbed boy who descended upon our woefully unprepared family in late summer of 1993.

It is the story of his first year, of his progress, the changes he forced in the family and in himself, and to some considerable degree it is a story of animals, of legends and woodsmoke, and of a special program called Harbour.

The book is based upon numerous letters, documents, and a detailed, day-by-day diary I have of eight of those twelve months. At the request of the Dutchess County, New York, Department of Social Services, the name of the boy and the names of some other individuals have been changed. To provide a clearer illustration of the various lessons the family learned and to explain why we acted the way we did, I've occasionally altered the chronology and frequently indulged in mind reading, for which I apologize. None of the conversations in the book was ever recorded electronically and then transcribed. Many conversations were recorded word for word in my diary at the end of the day, but others were reconstructed in the following year based on diary entries and some questioning, but mostly on the memories of family members.

To other new parents of emotionally disturbed, difficult, or abused children, I can only say "God bless you," because despite being very experienced parents, we survived that first year in part, as my wife Sue says, "because after firing every arrow in our quiver, we threw rocks," but then as our "rocks" grew too heavy to shoulder, we were sustained with prayer, imagination, and by other family members, not the least of whom was the boy himself.

CHAPTER ONE

a family, a fishing pole, a family

"Why would they even show us something like this?"

It was the spring of 1993, and I was asking the question of my wife, Susan. We were alone in an office on the top floor of a house the Mental Health Association had converted to its head-quarters. There, for the better part of the morning, we had been examining a file. And if the file was only half accurate, the child described in it was a monster. In fact, as I read on, one word kept tramping back and forth in my thoughts with heavy boots—*sociopath, sociopath, sociopath*. The person—the child—I was reading about was a sociopath.

At this time in my life I hadn't had any thought at all of help-ing anyone else, much less someone who needed this much effort. But we had been working up to this point ever since Sue had erupted with a sudden, bizarre interest in foster children a few months ago. It wasn't the first occasion in our married life when she had roared off after something. In fact, I often thought of her as a tiny door that opened on an immense furnace. But that extravagant force had usually been directed at some issue in the lives of our own five sons and one daughter or, as they grew, at the building of SCM Tax Prep, her tax preparation and finan-cial planning business.

This, I had thought to myself many times at the start of those months, wasn't her. And it wasn't me, either. I had spent twenty-five years in manufacturing, beginning fresh from four and a half years in the Marine Corps as an expediter for a division of North American Phillips before winding up as a director of manufacturing for a medium-sized corporation in New Jersey. Then, determined to finish a novel I had begun while on a job in South Africa years before, I refused a reassignment, pocketed a check, and decided to see if I could make some sort of a living out of the abandoned and haunted old pile of a country inn in New York's mid–Hudson Valley that we were now calling home. And it all had just started coming together.

It wasn't as simple as I had first thought. But the place was getting finished on the inside, at least; we were renting bed-and-breakfast rooms on a long-term basis to some very quiet guests; I was working temporarily for a tiny, cobbled-together local manufacturer; and the book was finished. Meanwhile, I wasn't wearing a suit, I hadn't been on an airplane for business in a couple of years, and even though I had gained about twenty pounds, my blood pressure was down thirty points. I felt healthy, I still had all of my red hair—it was graying a bit in my mustache and on my temples, but it was still there—and every morning I'd get up with the dogs and climb the beautiful mountain we lived on. In milky, rainy dawns and violet sunrises I hiked every day for an hour through our overgrown hay meadow, past the beaver pond, up into the neighbor's manicured orchard blocks, then by the lakes and far up to where I could grin at the distant silvery stream of cars commuting south on the crowded New York State Thruway.

I had just finished helping myself, and life was good.

Our boys—even though they were large enough now that whenever they were home together, they reminded me of five young stallions, restless and cramped in a wee paddock—still required a lot of our time and energy. Our eldest son, Richard, was off and gone on a mad career as a writer and film producer, but others of them hadn't finished college. Henry was a senior and Frank a second-year man at Norwich, the Military College of Vermont, Brendan was just starting George Mason University in Virginia, and Liam was charting new boundaries in the typical male Miniter indifference toward high school. Our second child and only daughter, Susanne, had graduated from the State University of New York at Albany and was working, but this summer she was getting married and we were holding the reception at the house. It wasn't as if we didn't have things to do.

Yet whenever I raised any of these issues, Sue just paved over my objections with, "Rich, we're just looking into it and we're not making any decisions yet. I just want you to go along for a while. You can always say no later on."

"It's the empty-nest syndrome, isn't it, Sue? All the babies have grown and you miss them."

"No, I just have to take a look at this thing."

And so, confused and doubtful, not quite understanding what was driving her, I followed along.

What Sue hadn't told me—wouldn't tell me until long after our orderly, smug little life had been turned on its head—was that she had been struck much as Paul was smitten on the road to Damascus. She hadn't heard a voice or been knocked off a horse, but she had seen a picture—many pictures—and then been challenged in an extremely personal way.

During tax season Sue typically takes a short break around six or six-thirty in the evening in our inn's old barroom, where she perches on a stool, flicks on the news, and then eats a quick dinner, which I've laid out for her. It is a quiet, private time for her—twenty minutes or a half hour when she can be all by herself, get some nourishment, and recharge her batteries before going at it again for the next four or five hours.

It was in her second-story office that Sue made the leap from a job she commuted to in Manhattan and a part-time business into a flourishing full-time practice, and much as I do now, she revels in the thirty-second commute from our apartment with a second cup of coffee in her hand to the remodeled room where she toils happily with her cat dozing on the copy machine behind her. But the hours have stayed brutal—often eighteen hours a day during the months of January through April, as client after client comes calling.

I'm usually extremely careful to leave her entirely alone during her sole break of the day, but what I didn't understand this year was that other, darker presences were intruding.

Night after night in that early spring, the evening network news was full of pictures of starving children in Africa. Children dying in their mothers' arms, children being buried in shallow graves, children helplessly begging for something—anything—to eat. And meanwhile, there would be Sue, sitting all alone in the dim light, night after night, slicing into her juicy lamb chop and swallowing asparagus and mashed potatoes. Finally, one evening, utterly helpless and angry, she slammed down her knife and fork and jerked the TV directory over to her to find something other than news to watch. But when she riffled through the little booklet it fell open to an advertisement—a plea from an organization called The Harbour Program for experienced parents to provide a structured, nurturing home for abused and neglected children.

Sue had sat there stunned for a long moment, read and reread the advertisement, and then finally folded the page over and tore it out.

Yet later, at bedtime, she didn't explain any of this. All she did say was, "I saw an advertisement in the paper I want us to answer."

"What kind of advertisement?"

"There's a special kind of foster-care program that needs help. It's called Harbour."

"What? Why?"

Harbour is a small, new division of the Mental Health Association in Ulster County, which places difficult-to-manage, often emotionally disturbed children into local families which could, with an intensive system of training and support, provide a therapeutic setting for them. The idea is to introduce these children to a normal family routine and then, working with the biological parents, perhaps safely reunite them with their own families. When Sue called the phone number in the advertisement, the social worker who answered listened to a synopsis of our background and invited us up for a chat.

"No."

"Rich," Sue said, tapping her foot, "an hour of your time."

"No."

"Rich, I'm not going to come back here and try to repeat everything I've heard. I want your reading on this, too."

"No."

Sue gritted her teeth; the word she was trying to get out never came that easily for her. "Please."

"Rats."

The next day we went up to Kingston, had coffee with a nice lady named Debi, and were introduced around. Despite misgivings, I found I liked most of the people we met. I appreciate people with a clear vision or mission, and these people seemed to have one. And it wasn't sewn together out of odd parts, either. What was conveyed to us that day was lucid, simple, and understandable: they wanted to break the dreary loop of abuse, removal, return, and then more abuse, followed by more removals, that all too often seemed to prevail in the current child-care system. They would recruit experienced parents, place a single child with them long-term, and then follow up with a comprehensive system of support.

So, modeling itself on other "therapeutic foster care" programs elsewhere, Harbour was sorting out those children and families in the mid-Hudson region who would benefit most from an intensive system of support from seven-day-a-week, twenty-four-hour-a-day availability of staff, from family specialists with very small caseloads, weekly and intensive visits, a comprehensive system of reporting, a strong and daily emphasis on the positive reinforcement of both parents and children, and perhaps most of all, the example furnished to both parents and children by the long-term placement of the children with stable families. The example of, as The Harbour Program termed them, "professional parents."

Us.

Harbour wasn't a broad-based program. The families selected were few and very carefully chosen, as were the children involved. Harbour was determined that it too would provide a model for further programs and could do that only if it was successful in turning the lives of many of its children around.

In learning all of this, I couldn't avoid feeling complimented when, during that first informal visit, Debi seemed to consider us very impressive parents and suggested we consider joining. Of course there was still a universe of doubt on my part. This first brief introduction to Harbour seemed to confirm Sue's determination to help some new child somewhere, and the visit dampened much of the instinctive aversion I had to mucking about in somebody else's life and, of course, to unsettling my own. Yet I was still deeply suspicious of getting involved in something so very different from anything we had ever done before. Professional parent? Me?

But then I began a very private line of thought. A leafless little thing at first, it started to sprout and flower in my imagination as we made the quiet forty-five-minute drive home. "What if such a child was a girl?" I was sick of boys. In one dimension I thought I was tough. I had been a Marine Corps NCO, a chief of police, had made a living for a lot of years in a rugged field, but raising any one of my five sons was like mining gold in the midst of a rock slide. When it's all over there might be a nugget or two in your pouch, but you're a long way downhill, awfully bruised and broken up. I hadn't, I thought, the stamina for another go. But a girl? I remembered how marvelous my daughter Susanne was when she was growing up. Girls you can buy pretty little dresses for, they have nice friends, their room smells nice, they smell nice, and they always remember your birthday.

So I had a secret agenda operating when Sue suggested we "at least go through the training" and complete Harbour's multi-page application. Then, after a preliminary acceptance, we were scheduled for training classes. We completed them in the evenings, met a "family specialist" we would be working with if we accepted a child, interviewed several other parents in the program, and had our background intensively investigated.

And now, several months later, we were inspecting a child's file. A child The Harbour Program thought we might consider a match.

The Harbour staff hadn't seemed to hold much back in training. The children selected for this special program had emotional, psychological, and/or physical problems. Typically they'd been exposed to family violence, drug use, prostitution; they'd been starved, kept out of school, left alone for long periods. Many of them had failed over and over in earlier placement attempts with standard foster-care programs.

Yet at the same time the Harbour people assured us that a panel of professionals had reviewed the children's case histories and determined they would and could benefit from therapeutic foster care. The general picture Harbour painted of these children was one of withdrawal and hurt—*vulnerable, bruised, torn* were the words used most often, and so Sue and I, particularly Sue, started the file with more than some empathy for this unknown child.

But all that changed very fast as we read. The children we had learned about in training now seemed abstract and theoretical, almost laughably passive. This thing we were getting a picture of was something very different.

It was all there in a very thick stack of densely typed reports: eight years of evaluations, family court orders, social service summaries. The boy was borderline retarded, unmanageably violent, and had to be continually medicated. I counted the number of foster families and institutions that had tried to do something with him, and it summed up to a nice round dozen. When he was young he had been severely neglected—not fed regularly, not bathed, not dressed. He was removed from his mother when he was fifteen months old, then returned at the age of three, whereupon he was beaten into a coma. Now, according to the psychiatric reports, the boy had an extremely low IQ, erratic small-motor coordination, and would not take any direction. He regularly assaulted the staff, wet his bed, and refused to climb out of it in the morning. When he did finally get to his feet, he couldn't walk very well and was suicidal.

It was horrible. This wasn't what Harbour had been talking about all these months. Was it? Besides, Harbour knew what we wanted in a child—they had certainly asked us enough times. We wanted, certainly Sue wanted, a child who could be gently coached into something like a normal life. And it certainly wasn't, I thought sadly, a girl.

"Sue, why would they even show us something like this?"

To my immense relief Sue seemed to throw up her hands, too. "Joanne said he was an attractive boy, and I know these kids need help, but there are limits—we can't deal with something like this. No. Not this—I don't want this." She sighed. "I might feel different if there was even one tiny shred of evidence to suggest this kid wants to be helped. But it's just not there."

I took off my glasses, rubbed my face, and stood up. The file was scattered around the room in odd piles. We had pulled it apart and divided sections of it up between us.

"Okay," I said, "let's put the stuff back."

Sue nodded and stood up to help.

"Rich, what's this?"

Sue was holding a single sheet of blue paper I hadn't seen. Apparently it had slipped out of the file when we took it apart and dropped to the floor. The paper was a sloppily photocopied form labeled across the top, "The Things I Want Most." There were three lines below it numbered one, two, and three. Over and around those lines was a child's sprawling, smudgy handwriting.

With a very uncomfortable feeling I remembered that in the entire file there had been nothing from the boy himself—no direct quotes, no transcripts, no letters—and I was grateful for the lack, glad that I hadn't that sort of connection with this child, even in a thirdhand way. So when I realized what Sue was holding, I said quickly, "Forget about it, put it back. You don't want to read that."

Sue almost did slip it back into the stacks of reports, but then shook her head.

Instead she walked over to the desk lamp and, after a moment or two of hesitation, I joined her.

Sue got it first, with the look of dismay caught in amber pushing aside the piqued curiosity on her face, and then she slowly, raggedly caught her breath. But it was more difficult for me to puzzle out. I had to trace my fingertips again and again over the ragged pencil marks before I realized it said:

The Things I Want Most
1. A Family
2. A Fishing Pole
3. A Family

Just then Joanne Dalbo, the family specialist assigned to work with us, opened the door balancing two cups of coffee in one hand.

"Hey, how did you guys make out?"

Then she saw the strained look on our faces and asked, "What's wrong? Are you okay?"

Sue just turned away and walked over to the window with her arms crossed over her chest.

When Joanne raised her eyebrows in question, I looked back over at Sue. I could tell from the set of her shoulders that she was making up her mind, and a single word popped out of my mouth.

Curiously, I then recalled an odd fact. Whenever a black box is retrieved from the scene of an airplane wreck, the last bit of speech recorded by the pilot before he hits the ground is often that very same word.

Joanne put the coffee down on the desk and then placed her hands on her hips. Attractive, slim, with dark hair and eyes, she was a bright, soft-spoken family specialist working for Harbour while she studied in her spare time for an advanced degree in English literature, and she had a profound interest in careful and precise speech. Now she seemed puzzled and a little bit hurt. "*Shit,*" she repeated. "What does *shit* mean?"

It took us weeks to get to meet Mike. It was Joanne's job to schedule an initial meeting, but she was put off by the Catholic Children's Home, where he was living.

Programs like Harbour have to struggle with all the complexities of child-care placement, including the issue of access to children in a complicated, multilayered system that involves many organizations with variable, often arbitrary, and constantly changing rules and procedures. The Catholic Children's Home was no exception. And, of course, it's difficult to have a good working relationship with an agency or institution you have never encountered before.

In Mike's case, he had been referred to Harbour by the very children's home that had him now, but two issues, one very human and one quite frightening, were complicating access. The first was that, despite having referred many children to Harbour, the children's home was now somewhat doubtful of the program because Harbour had accepted none of them. But the other was the fact that in the time that had elapsed between their referral and Harbour's contact, Mike had tried to hang himself.

The act was labeled as "not a serious suicide attempt," I suppose because he didn't succeed, but the home had decided it was better to hold Harbour at arm's length while he "restabilized."

Meanwhile, we learned some additional facts. We learned that unlike most children in The Harbour Program, integration back into his biological family wasn't an option. He had been freed for adoption, and family court was determined there be no further parental contact.

We also found out that he did have a visiting "resource." It seems an older brother and sister were adopted by a local family three years earlier and that this family had taken Mike into their home as well. Unfortunately, the results were fairly horrific— uncontrollable tantrums, violent behavior, sleeplessness—and eventually he was removed for psychiatric evaluation to Rockland State Hospital. Following that admittance he was placed in the Catholic Children's Home in Rhinebeck and the family's application for adoption denied. But they still visited him from time to time, taking him for weekends and some holidays.

This last point only seemed to stiffen Sue's now-iron resolve to meet the author of that pathetic note. In her mind's eye, or perhaps her mother's heart, she could picture the despair of this child as he watched his brother and sister get on with their lives while he was routinely rejected in the most profound way.

"How can they pick him up and then just cart him back?

How many times has he stood there in the parking lot of the children's home and waved good-bye to his brother and sister?"

In the days that followed, Sue developed a long list of other sad images. I'd see them emerge at mealtimes, while driving in the car, or when visiting friends. In the middle of talking about something completely different she'd suddenly declare, "Mike isn't sleeping, I just know it." "They haven't told him anything about us yet, and he's just as upset and hopeless as he ever was." "He isn't eating. What kind of food do they have there, anyway?" "Who's talking to the doctor about his medication?"

"Sue," I'd protest, "we haven't even met this child, and anyway, the children's home is top drawer, everybody says that. They're not neglecting him. Calm down. Things will sort themselves out."

But one night she woke me up out of a deep sleep. "For God's sake," she said, "I don't think anybody reads to him."

Groggy and confused, I said, "Reads to who, Sue? I don't know what you're talking about."

"Mike," she said back. "I know nobody is reading to him."

The next day at work I telephoned Joanne. "Look," I said, "I think we have a problem here. Every day that passes without a meeting has Sue worrying more and more about that boy. You've got to goose these people along. Can't you even get us in there to see him for a few minutes so that she can get this out of her system?"

Joanne sighed. "I know," she said. "Sue's been calling me continuously, and I've been calling them, but the home keeps putting me off."

"Well," I said, "they're the legal guardians. They can do what they want, I guess, but do what you can, would you? By this time next week Sue's going to be up there in the middle of the night dragging a ladder from window to window."

A few minutes later the phone rang back.

"Rich," said Joanne, "I just connected with something you said."

"What?"

"Guardianship. The home is not really the legal guardian; the Dutchess County Department of Social Services is. In fact there's a caseworker assigned, a woman named Gerri. I've spoken to her before. Maybe I should call her now."

Then she paused before adding, "Rich, I'm worried about Sue. We know that you, and especially Sue, can be great advocates for a child; that's half the reason we want you guys in the program. But Sue is beginning to seem like an emotional type of person who can quickly blow very hot, and so I've got to repeat what I know everybody in Harbour has told you: this is a long-term program and it's best that your emotional dial get set to zero. Some of these kids, and Mike is certainly an extreme example of this, have been in and out of so many placements that they're desensitized. Mike might go through the motions, but it will be a long time, if ever, before he could return the same sort of concern Sue is capable of—a long time before he can bond to you guys. Should you decide to take Mike, you're going to have to face the fact that you're not going to get much of anything back for a great while."

Sage advice. She knew what could happen. But I dismissed it because after twenty-seven years of marriage I knew that there wasn't much chance of changing Sue, and I was convinced Mike wouldn't end up with us. The file was just far too daunting, and I believed that Sue was ignoring all of that while constructing a model of this child in her mind that would be dashed to pieces when they actually met—that when she saw with her own eyes what he actually was, she had to understand that we couldn't have something like that in the house. Our guests would leave, and we depended on that income. Her business wouldn't allow that sort of investment of time, nor would our obligations to our own children.

"Hey," I cracked, "virtue is its own reward." I felt guilty, deceptive, in wanting to avoid this child.

Joanne laughed gently, and I could picture her shaking her head. "Okay, you guys. Here we go."

CHAPTER TWO

are you taking petey?

We met Mike at the children's home. I had envisioned an Army Reserve Center without the jeeps parked in front. Instead I saw a converted nineteenth-century Hudson Valley mansion, a sprawling multistory Tudor with slate roofs and stained-glass mullioned windows set down in carefully landscaped grounds.

And for some reason, that made me very edgy.

Inside was quiet—too quiet—and the interior matched the plush facade. We were ushered into a library room on the ground level with a bank of French doors opening on a bluestone patio that was shaded from the bright summer sun by awnings. The library was lined with oak paneling and hung with dark burgundy draperies. *There are supposed to be eighty kids in here,* I puzzled. *Why isn't there any noise?* There wasn't even a picture of a child on the wall.

Eerie. It reminded me of something. What?

Sue and I sat at the polished wide oval table in the center of the room along with Joanne and the group leader for Mike's team at the home, a straightforward, soft-spoken young man named Kevin.

Kevin spoke first. He wore a shy, awkward smile, not wanting to disappoint us, trying to choose his words carefully.

"Look," he said reluctantly, "I have to confess that I find it hard to agree with the purpose of this meeting. I want all of my children to have a home and a family. But Mike is difficult. He can be very charming when he wants to, but he goes through cycles, weeks sometimes, where he's difficult, almost impossible to deal with. Just getting him out of bed in the morning can take an hour or two. Getting him back to bed at night can take even longer. He needs structure, a lot of structure."

That struck home. *Structure* was a key word in the Harbour training. Some of these kids had never had a regular bedtime, mealtime, or bathtime.

Yet that made me question the sort of structure our own children had had from us. Was it enough? Was there any to speak of? Years before we had built a house on Mountain Road in Rosendale, New York, twenty-five miles north of where we were now. It was a very secluded, wooded location up, as the name implies, on a mountain named Shawangunk. The six children had regular mealtimes and bedtimes, their clothes were washed and their lunches made every morning, but we also practiced something Sue called "benign neglect," and that meant in great measure the children working out their own lives. Susanne, the only girl, played with her go-cart and baby carriage on the front lawn or with an immense Barbie doll collection in her room. If she left the property, it was to walk down the road to her grandmother's. Richard, the eldest, after an initial period when he explored the woods alone, either gravitated to his room where he read, also walked or biked down the road to his grandmother's, and often traveled much farther down to visit friends from school. But the three middle boys, Henry, Frank, and Brendan, ran wild together on Shawangunk. Almost from the time they could walk they were in the woods together, and we never worried very much about them, although a few incidents still manage to dredge up a hefty feeling of guilt.

One of these was the lost locomotive.

The three boys came back one day and said they had found an old railroad engine in the woods. I didn't believe a word of it. I had hunted much of the mountain for years and didn't remember anything at all like that.

But Henry, Frank, and Brendan led me right to it. Standing on a set of rusting rails where it had been abandoned just after the second world war was a cannibalized diesel locomotive, the small type that would be called a yard engine. It must have been used for logging. At one time there had been a narrow-gauge railway along the top of Shawangunk, but the land had long since reverted to hardwood and the roadbed was abandoned.

I was shocked. Not because I hadn't seen it before, but because it was miles from the house. Henry then was about ten, Frank eight, and Brendan six years old. I remembered peering down at them and saying, "You kids shouldn't wander this far from home." But the look I got back from all three would bother me for years. It was a sliding, sidelong appraisal that seemed to say, "You haven't the foggiest idea of what we've been up to and where we've been, and now that we've told you one thing, what do you do? You go and turn adult on us. Soooo, I don't think we'll be telling *you* anything else anytime soon."

"Don't give me that look," I threatened.

"Sure, Dad," the three of them chimed back, smirking at each other.

And that was about the quality of the structure I had supplied for my own children.

Sitting there at the conference table with Joanne, Sue, and Kevin, listening to a lecture on structure, I said to myself, *Richard, even if through some wild chance Sue wants to go further with this mad idea, you're the last person a kid like this needs. You can't do this! Not you!*

I turned to Sue and tried to get her attention, wanting to pull her outside where I could say all of this. But she was intent on Kevin, facing him with much the same look on her face as those three boys years ago in the woods.

Then I looked over at Joanne for help, but she refused to make eye contact. She had been through enough of these meetings that she could read the nuances like a book, and she knew I was getting even more hinky.

The four of us sat there with our own agendas. Sue wanted to rescue somebody, Kevin wanted to protect his charge from a situation he believed primed for failure, I wanted to be anywhere else, and Joanne, certain in her belief that Harbour offered this child one last shot at something like a normal life, was hoping against hope that the potential mother wouldn't tear this poor counselor's head off or the father go AWOL.

I got up to leave the room and breathe some fresh air.

"Rich, where are you going? Rich!"

"To find the goddamned men's room."

But I continued on outside and looked around again. Still no kids in sight, just a hushed campus atmosphere with an occasional adult walking purposefully on the grounds, holding a stack of books and papers. Eighty children? The overhead had to be stupendous. I remembered the numbers I had learned: 40,000 children in the New York State child-care system alone, 400,000 nationwide.

It was then that I realized what this beautiful setting reminded me of—the naval hospital overlooking the Pacific at San Diego. Different architecture but the same theme: quiet, hushed, almost luxurious, set down with lots of light and soothing green space. This was where you took the wounded and maimed, those in pain and gangrenous, crying in shock. This was where you cleaned them up, patched them up, and sent them back out again.

Prior to being introduced to Harbour, I had known that the child-care system existed, but not really why. Fundamentally I believed, still believe in fact, that the government or the court system has no role in a family. Perhaps a priest, maybe even a friend, but not courts or judges or lawyers. Before being introduced to Harbour, I had even dismissed the people working in the system as "feel-gooders"—drones who couldn't or wouldn't do something productive with their lives.

But standing there amid those soft beautiful grounds on that warm early-summer day, nervous and jittery, doubting myself, I started to understand what this all was about. The big *why* made sense if you just thought of these children as casualties rather than as children or clients or cases. Although that understanding did not mean I felt competent enough to deal with one of these walking wounded.

I wasn't a doctor or a therapist or a social worker. I was a private person who didn't want to bother anybody else or, really, bother with anybody else outside my family and close friends. If anything, I had been swept along up to this point by Sue's vehemence and by a desire to have her understand she didn't have any role—*we* didn't have any role to play here. It was true I was touched by the boy's scribbled note and by the stories of other children. But was I moved?

Images of the horror stories we had heard in Harbour's training sessions started blurring through my thoughts like a tape spinning faster and faster. It started with an adult beating a three-year-old child into a coma. Then it flashed into all the other horror stories we had heard in the last couple of months: the rapes, the burnings, the starvation, the murders. I remembered the nonchalance with which caseworkers recited the facts: "Lisa was four when her mother's boyfriend began raping her. Whenever she complained, he would have his German shepherd attack." "Paul was right. They *did* kill his baby sister—it wasn't an accidental scalding. When the pathologist examined the body, he found that the soles of the baby's feet weren't blistered—she had been trying to push herself up out of the boiling water while they held her down." "John doesn't talk. We don't know where he came from. A garbage man heard him crying in a Dumpster."

Thousands of splintered little lives now hidden away, snug, recuperating quietly behind spreading yews and English lawn gardens.

I shuddered.

No. I'm out of here. I'll just tell Sue right now that I want to go home and forget about all of this.

"Rich!" I looked over at the wide carved doors of the main entrance. Sue was standing at one of them, her back to it, angrily holding it open. "Get in here," she hissed. "Kevin's bringing him down."

Thin. My first impression of Mike was that he was thin. He was sitting at the conference table with his back to the door. Jeans and sneakers, tie-dyed shirt, maybe five feet tall with lanky blond hair badly in need of a trim. Through the back of the shirt I could see the outline of his shoulder blades. I could even count the hard, knobby little knuckles of his backbone.

And rigid. The child was sitting up straight, tense, with his gaze fixed on Sue, not shading away a millimeter when I walked around the table and sat. He had blue eyes and the wan face of a street urchin with a severe facial tic. Every ten seconds his face would snap away ninety degrees and then back again as if he were being slapped by an unseen hand. He was both fighting it and trying to pretend it wasn't happening at the same time.

Still feeling dragooned, I had an unkind and selfish thought: *This boy wants the placement, too. Now I'm really outnumbered.*

We had been cautioned about the blind determination of

these children. Perhaps because in trying to keep them safe and set them on a new course the system gave them very little latitude within which to make choices, they often seemed to develop very strong character traits. These children could be unbelievably stubborn and single-minded. Since their only means of control was an intractable personality, they became capable of a ferocious resolve.

Then I had a second unkind thought: *I wonder if he has enough basic intelligence even to understand what it is he's determined to get.*

But after I sourly slouched down in the chair, my ear started to twitch in interest. The boy's diction was actually very good. Some of his syntax was awkward and his voice way too loud, but he was generally pronouncing and using words properly.

What had happened to that 70 IQ?

I straightened up a bit and started to listen.

Sue had quietly taken over from Joanne and Kevin. She prefaced with a description of our family and our home. Then in a gentle and low voice she began to ask a long series of questions.

"We have two dogs and two cats. Do you like animals?"

"I always like animals. I like cats and dogs all the time." He licked his lips, concentrating, keeping eye contact.

"We have five sons and a daughter. But they're older. Have you ever thought about how you get along with older children?"

"I always get along with older children. Sometimes I even get along with younger children. But I always get along with older children."

"We live in the country. Do you like the country?"

"I always like the country. I was born in the country. I love the country."

"Would you come to lunch at our home?"

"I always like lunch. I eat lunch here every day."

"What else do you like to do?"

Silence. The eyes flickered away for the first time and then back again. Mike's tongue came out and quickly licked his lips.

You could see his mind working frantically—what answer did this woman want to hear?

Sue prompted him with a smile. "I hear you're very artistic. Do you like to paint?"

The boy let out his breath. "I always like to paint. I painted a turtle. Here—" Mike pushed across to Sue a small jigsaw puzzle that he had been holding in his lap, waiting for the right moment. It was cut out of thick cardboard and then watercolored.

Sue later said she could vividly picture the boy upstairs in his room, desperately casting around for something, anything, that would impress these people who were coming to see him.

Now, head lowered, she spread the fingers of one hand and put it gently down on the puzzle. "This is lovely, Mike."

Their eyes met and locked.

"What else, Mike? I think I heard you like to fish?"

And so it went. The careful measured back-and-forth between Sue and Mike gradually mesmerizing everyone at the table, the crackle of raw energy involved magnetizing us, gathering us all in. Sue wasn't blind to how tense or blindly determined Mike was. Several times she smilingly told him to relax. "There aren't any wrong answers, Mike. We just want to get to know you." Once she put out her hand and took his, and you could follow the process going on in his mind—she took my hand, so I should squeeze hers—then he did so with a jerky little lurch.

"Hey, that's quite a grip you've got there."

Frightened, calculating eyes. "Too hard?"

I remembered one of the cutting little descriptions of Mike—"He can only hold it together for a little while"—and I wondered if in fact he would lose it before Sue finished. But he did stay together. As the large wall clock on the far side of the room ticked off the long seconds like a metronome marking down an endless summer afternoon, he doggedly kept his head up, answered each and every question, then braced himself for the next.

Sue finally sat back. "Is there anything you would like to ask us, Mike?"

At first he shook his head no, but then he changed his mind. There was something—something he was afraid of. He took a big breath, blinked, and for the first time stuttered. "Are you picking Petey?" he asked in a rush.

Sue looked puzzled, and Kevin spoke up. "Peter is another child in his unit."

Sue shook her head at Mike. "No, honey, we're not."

"Petey said you were looking at him, too. That he already knew you."

"No, honey. I'm sure Petey is a very nice boy. But we read about you. We wanted to come meet you, only you, and see if you'd like to visit us."

Mike stiffly pushed his chair back, stood up, and then walked out the door. A moment later the door slammed back open and Mike said, "Good-bye." Then the door closed again.

Sue slumped back in her chair. "Whew. I feel like I've run twenty miles. Now, what was that last bit about?"

Kevin shrugged. "There's a lot of status on the floor if you have a family outside," he said, his voice choked up, "someone who visits you. Mike is very vulnerable in that way; he gets almost no visitors. Some of the other kids tease him and play jokes on him about it."

"What about the Johnsons?" Sue asked, referring to the couple who had adopted Mike's older brother and sister. "I thought they visited him."

Kevin shrugged again, this time with his hands making a hapless gesture. "Not very often—maybe every three or four months—and the other kids know they're not his real family."

Sue puffed out her cheeks and thought about that for a long

moment. The fingers of her right hand were drumming on the tabletop.

A full minute later Joanne quietly asked, "Does this mean you want to take the next step?"

Sue answered without looking up or thinking. "I invited him to lunch."

Then Joanne looked over at me with her dark eyes questioning. "Rich?"

I looked back over at Sue, who was tense now, her back arching. To a great extent I had been swept along in her wake. But many of my doubts had collapsed in the face of the boy's performance. In fact, toward the end of the interview I was squirming in my seat, angry at the brutal choreographic, at the image of four adults examining a frightened, anxious child in a closed room. We had just put too much pressure for far too long on this boy and I was repulsed at being a party to it. It might be necessary, but it wasn't fair. Not fair by a wide margin, particularly since Mike didn't seem anything at all like the sullen psychotic presence he could have been from that awful file. Instead he was skinny, almost emaciated, nervous, wanting to please, awfully alone, and somewhere in there you could see the kid who wanted a fishing pole. He was also a fighter; I was still feeling the force of him in the room.

But what about that file? All those reports? On the other hand, what about Sue? None of this had gone the way I envisioned, not with the boy, not with her. Particularly not with her. Sue's image of Mike as a sad, wan waif had not crumpled and she hadn't been repelled or put off. In fact, the meeting seemed to reinforce her notions about him.

I had to give up. "Okay, lunch," I said tersely.

Sue relaxed back into her chair, pleased but also wryly amused. "Don't be so kind and expansive; it's not like you."

•   •   •

I came home from work early on a hot, humid July after-noon to attend the lunch for Mike, backed into a parking slot, and paused for a long moment behind the wheel looking out. The place should make a wonderful impression on the boy. I had just cut the large sloping rear lawn in back and the side lawn by the parking lot the day before, and the hundreds of flowers Sue had planted for Susanne's wedding in August lined the walks, bordered the tiny, old stone gatehouse behind the main building, and then disappeared in pink and purple rows around the far side.

I got out of the car, dodged through our maze of sprinklers and, walking past the kitchen door, slipped in the bar entrance. The old barroom, built as a speakeasy during Prohibition, takes up most of the bottom or ground floor of the three-story country inn we were restoring. It opens onto the rear lawn, over-looking an abandoned hay meadow. Inside it was cool and shaded, the high summer sun outside streaming past the win-dows. The dark knotty pine of the walls glowed faintly in the one light Sue had on over the long pine table in the center of the room. One end of the table was set for four, with plates of hard rolls, cold cuts, macaroni salad, sliced tomatoes, potato chips, and a large chocolate layer cake waited at the other end.

"Hi," Sue said, walking out of the kitchen with another plate of something in her hands. She looked preoccupied and edgy. "Rich, can you get four bar glasses, a bottle of Coke, and some ice?"

"Sure."

Just as I finished, Joanne knocked at the kitchen door with Mike in tow. Then, while I made conversation with Joanne, Sue ushered Mike through the house, introduced him to the two dogs, Teddy Bear and Pupsy, walked him outside through the garden, and then, bringing him back into the barroom, made a big fuss over sitting him down, getting a sandwich to-gether, and pouring his Coke.

Mike was better dressed than before, in dark pants and a neat pullover shirt. Still no haircut, but you could tell he'd been thoroughly soaped and shampooed that morning. He looked, of course, like he should pack away a couple hundred lunches, but he barely ate or spoke at first. Instead, all of his attention was focused on the dogs sprawled sleeping with the cat on the sunny grass outside the barroom windows.

"Are you worried about the dogs, Mike?"

He looked at Sue. "Are they all right? What do they eat? Do they have brothers and sisters? Do they sleep all the time? Do they have last names? Are they always outside? Do they come when you call them?"

"Whoa," Sue said, laughing, "eat something and I'll try to answer all your questions."

No wonder this guy is so thin, I thought. Sue did find out that his favorite dessert was mint chocolate chip ice cream with whipped cream, that he liked to swim, do puzzles, and make models, and that he liked the house and the area.

But Joanne later said that on the long drive back he talked only about dogs.

When we broke up, I made motions of going back to work, but Sue stopped me with hands firmly on her hips and the set of a question on her face. I sat back down with a bump, the decision she wanted tugging at my shirttails. The next step with Harbour was a weeklong "preplacement" visit, so it looked like we were finally due for "The Talk."

"The Talk" is a technique Sue and I have developed to resolve disagreement on important subjects. It's something we've distilled from years of changing family circumstances and six smart, manipulative children. It's our way of making firm decisions and then shutting down all further discussion.

The way "The Talk" works is that either Sue or I decide we have to or want to make an important decision about something and then we actually set a date and time at which we will do so. We might discuss the issue in advance and in the process feel out the other's position, but we always agree not to arrive at any firm conclusion until the scheduled time of "The Talk." Then, when we meet, it's a no-holds-barred, take-no-prisoners sort of fight. Both of us muster up all of the points we've assembled and hack it out until just one or the other is left standing. Often, of course, we agree, and "The Talk" lasts just seconds, but often we don't, and one or the other has to prevail over a period of hours. The ground rules state that this has to happen, that a decision must be forthcoming, but even more important, that the discussion must never be reopened afterward. The technique means we rarely hold something in that's truly bothering us. But, perhaps most important, it has over the years proved to be a delightful and endless source of frustration to children who would otherwise play one parent against the other. On important issues the kids have always gotten one of two answers out of us, either, "We haven't discussed that yet," or "Sorry, no, we've already discussed that."

Now Sue said the words: "I want to have 'The Talk.' "

"When?"

"As soon as possible—right this instant, if you can stay home."

I could win a postponement. This wasn't quite how it was done—we always asked for a "Talk" a few days or a week off in the future, never right on top of events. But we had been exhausting the preliminaries for months, and I knew how it would go because in all "The Talks" we've had, neither of us has ever denied the other what it was they truly wanted to do. We might have forced the other to defend it, but we've always conceded the point and then supported it. Always.

Sue seemed absolutely committed to taking Mike, and while I still had serious, sober questions about her initial motivation, the disruption of our lives, the effect of such a step on our children, and my own strength, I was also weary of the issue hanging fire between us, and a curious mix of emotions had begun banging around inside of me as well. Despite the immense reluctance I felt when I thought of taking on another boy, another part of me also missed having the excitement of young boys in the place, and while disappointed—almost bitterly disappointed when I thought that there was never going to be a little girl somewhere at the end of this process—I was stirred by Sue's commitment, I liked the staff in the program, I felt awfully sorry for this kid, and we had the room (in fact, we had seventeen rooms). It wouldn't even mean reducing our precarious cash flow—Harbour would compensate us at a rate that was substantially greater than the standard foster-care board. And again, I was impressed with the child himself—impressed by our first visit, and reassured at lunch.

So I got up and gave her a hug.

She pushed me back at arm's length. "So, is this 'The Talk'?"

"Yeah," I said, chuckling, "I guess so. I have to get back to work."

"You don't want to talk about it."

"Sue, I'm all talked out."

Once the children's home understood Sue was actually serious about Mike, they started raising objections.

The Old English word for *harbor* or *harbour* was *haven*. The Germans still use it, although they pronounce it "hah-ven," as in the famous port of Bremerhaven, which means Bremer or Bremen Harbor. A harbor, as everyone knows, is a place out of the weather where you can safely unload or refit, and The Harbour Program implied a place for children to tie up out of the storm, take on supplies, and refit their lives. A safe haven. But it's still a version of foster care—a new version and, as a therapeutic version, one quite different from the standard pattern, but it's still foster care.

And sadly, foster care isn't 100 percent safe and has the reputation of not doing much in terms of mainstreaming children, especially difficult children. It's not that foster care as a whole isn't chock-full of warm and loving families who do the best they can for their charges. It's just that an abundance of problems stem from its role as emergency or temporary shelter.

Even given the best of motives, child-care workers, who can each have sixty or seventy cases at one time, find it impossible to cope with the flood of children washed up into the system and to monitor foster parents closely. Because the families they're dealing with are often in "crisis," as the terminology has it, children have to be whisked out of one environment and into foster care at all hours of the day or night. Then, once placed in foster care, the children immediately slide backward in priority as the heavy caseload spawns another crisis and yet another placement.

Who goes back and carefully evaluates the child's stay in the foster home? The social workers bitterly complain about that. This situation and the lousy pay are the main reasons there are so many ex-social workers around.

Almost all of the family specialists at Harbour are ex-social workers. During our training each had reams to say about the frustration of the caseload they used to deal with and their continual anxiety over the children they had to shuffle around.

Many foster parents complain about it, too. Children placed in the middle of the night and left with no comprehensive medical records or school information. Older children who are sexual predators; younger children who are sexually vulnerable. Children with special medical needs, diets, routines that nobody can sort out until days or weeks later.

In some ways the system often fails the very young lives it was meant to shelter. About the only thing worse is leaving children where they are. But there is a third alternative, the institution— the child village, group home, residence, children's home, or, as we used to say, the orphanage.

Society at large, the courts, and the child welfare agencies believe almost as an article of faith that orphanages should be the last resort. That first and foremost children belong in families— if not their own, then another. I tend to agree that children are usually much better off with their families, even if the families are homeless and wandering the countryside, as it is usually only in families that children learn the struggle and social skills they need later on in life because paradoxically, parents, particularly mothers, force children into a pattern of long-term effort. Even in something as prosaic as table manners, a useful skill if you intend to eat in public, mothers will insist that the child keep struggling with his knife and fork until he gets it right. In fact, while we laugh about such situations in comedy shows on TV, an unmarried child can be thirty-five years old and his mother will still nag him about holding his fork like a shovel, the way he dresses, or the person he's dating, if she feels he's acting inappropriately. Mothers just don't give up prompting the child to perform. Institutions, on the other hand, tend to diagnose and accommodate and so relieve the child from the effort. If little Johnny can't handle his knife and fork at the normal age for children to master that skill, they won't settle down for a lifelong campaign on the issue. Instead, they'll diagnose him as lacking age-appropriate small motor skills and write a dietary order to the kitchen requiring his food to be cut up for him. And, of course, Johnny never learns.

But people working in institutions come at the issue from a profoundly different point of view. They're concerned with safety. They just deal with too many smashed up children com-

ing out of families and out of foster care, for that matter. Therefore, one of their toughest assignments is sending a child back
into the family or back into the foster-care system.

And that's how the children's home felt about Mike.

And about us.

Foster care, foster care, preadoption placement, psychiatric
placement, foster care. That had been Mike's cycle before he
came to them. Now that they had him walking and talking, going to school and not wetting his pants when he was awake,
now that for three years nobody had hurt Mike, they were loath
to let him go. Particularly into foster care.

The Dutchess County Department of Social Services had
the final say, however, and Social Services had referred Mike to
The Harbour Program. But they could always change their
minds, particularly if the staff of professional therapists and
counselors retained by the home sniffed out the faintest danger
to Mike.

They started with his physical condition.

Mike was about five feet tall and weighed less than seventy
pounds. Either emaciated or deathly thin, take your pick, he
looked like a concentration camp inmate, and the home felt
that he should have a hospital placement for two weeks while
nutritionists and doctors examined him.

Once Sue realized what was happening, that tiny door
opened and the flames roared out.

She had already been frustrated for a long time before the
first visit, while Mike restabilized after a suicide attempt. Now
that she had seen him, now that she had had him to lunch,
she wasn't about to be told that his weight problem had to sta-
bilize also.

"One," she told me, "I can feed children. Two, if they lick his
weight problem—and I doubt they will after three years of
trying—they're going to tell me he has a mineral imbalance,

then that he has to complete a battery of allergy tests, then that he has a hearing problem or needs a new eyeglass prescription or maybe orthopedic shoes.

"No," she said, stabbing her left palm with her right forefinger, "I have to trump this process. What's the name of that social worker at Dutchess DSS who has legal guardianship?"

"Uh, Gerri, I think."

Thus the phone calls began.

The second and main level of our inn contains a large butler's pantry, our private apartment, and what was once a ponderous, dimly lit dining room with dark wooden coffered ceilings, heavy gray peeling wallpaper, and a somber stone fireplace. I had converted this room into a light and fanciful office for Sue's tax and financial planning business with new woodwork and dividers, efficient wiring, raspberry-ice walls with a flowery wallpaper border, and all-white trim. The swinging door to Sue's office opens onto the short hall of the house and is directly across from the stairs down to the barroom and kitchen. I have to walk past it all the time on my way out, in, or downstairs, and invariably during the days that followed her first call to Gerri, I'd overhear snatches of conversation as Sue tried to force the agreement she wanted between Social Services and the children's home.

"All my boys went through a cycle. They thinned out, fattened up, grew some more, and then thinned out again. I can shovel three squares into him as well as they can."

"Believe it or not, we have nutritionists and doctors in Ulster County, too. Where do you think we're living over here, on the other side of the river—Bangladesh?"

"Would you *please* get in your car and come look at my boys? Every one of them was born at between six and seven pounds, and they're all weight lifters today. Just tell me how that happened!"

Then one day, "If he's wasting away to nothing anyway, goddammit, why can't he die happy, playing with a dog?"

I stuck my head into the office on that one. "Isn't that just a tad too dramatic?"

"Hey," she said with her hand over the phone, "I'm tired. What do you expect—Peggy Noonan?"

At that point it looked like she was going to be beaten. Even Harbour was predicting it would be months before the pre-placement visit happened, and the belief hardened in Sue's mind that the home was the enemy. But then, as her dogged seesawing discussion went forward into the following week, Sue's tone suddenly became much quieter.

Kathy, a member of the senior staff at the home, and Sue had become friends, and Sue began to preface her conversations with me with the phrase, "Kathy told me": "Kathy told me that three years ago Mike was still defecating in his pants." "Kathy told me Mike's gait problem gets severe with exercise; that at the end of a walk he can barely get one foot in front of the other." "Kathy told me . . ."

Finally one day Sue went up and met Kathy face-to-face, and when she came back I realized they had become complete co-conspirators. "Kathy says if we really want to do this," Sue related, "the last step is to get past their educational specialist, and here's how we do that. . . ."

A week later Joanne called and announced brightly, "Okay, we're all set up for the week's visit, and if that goes all right we'll set a date for the placement."

I was in the office with Sue at the time, and she spun on her heels with her right fist clenched in front of her face.

"Yes!"

It was a downhill slide from there.

Until we held a family meeting with what was left of us. Richard was out on the West Coast, Henry was up in Norwich, and Frank was spending the summer with his grandmother in the Adirondacks. So the family group included Sue, me, Liam, Brendan, and Susanne, and we were all preoccupied by preparations for Susanne's wedding. It was just four weeks away.

Our house sits on fifteen acres of ground in Clintondale, New York. We had moved down here from the Mountain Road home four years before. Long ago the old place was a functioning inn, but had since been abandoned. With most of our restoration efforts concentrated inside and on getting the grounds cleared of sumac and brambles, we had not repainted the outside. It was still an old gloomy pile, nicely trimmed and finished off years ago, but now with thousands of square feet of cedar shingle to be restained a pleasing gray and all that trim yet to be scraped and painted.

Brendan, Sue, our future son-in-law, David Warren, Susanne's high school sweetheart, and I had been working on it each and every evening after work. By this time we were about half done and anxiously watching the calendar. The wedding was to be on the back lawn on August 14. There was to be a large tent, about 150 guests, a caterer, an open bar in the barroom. We had relatives coming long distances, many of whom had never seen the place, many of whom would be staying over.

It wasn't necessarily the best time in the world to bring a child into the home. Particularly not one who was labeled emotionally disturbed.

But Sue was happy and determined. She was also certain that our children would view this move as a positive event for their mother and father. She was looking forward to telling them.

After dark the family gathered in the barroom. We were all exhausted, sunburned, and spattered with gray stain. We had a cold dinner and then, groaning, I got up stiffly to make drinks while Sue sprang the news.

"I have an announcement to make. It looks like we're taking

Mike. Dad and I had him over for lunch, and he behaved like a little gentleman. Then we had to work out some problems with the home. Next we're going to have him for a week, and then, after the wedding, he'll be coming to live with us."

Silence. Just the muted clink of ice cubes as we sipped our Cokes.

Nineteen-year-old Brendan spoke first, with his expressive eyes large and angry. "That's *it*? Not 'Can we discuss this?' Just 'We're taking him'? Into our home! Jesus, we don't even know this person."

I hadn't expected this. Brendan is the easiest of people, caring and considerate, one whose quiet demeanor and helpful humor always seem to attract the best of people.

Embarrassed, Sue turned to Susanne for support.

She didn't get it.

Susanne is twenty-five years old, tiny, only about five one, a hundred pounds. Usually she is very soft-spoken, quiet, and reasonable. But she is as strong-willed as Sue is, every bit the match for her mother when she wants to be.

Now she weighed in with a baseball bat.

"Mom, you two don't know what you're getting into. I worked after school at the Pediatric Center for a long, long time. These welfare children are a horror. They break things, start fires, they're loud and abusive, they steal. They're dirty."

Sue was taken aback and just sputtered, "He's just a child, Susanne. He hasn't a mother or a father."

"No, he's not just a child, he's something different. Believe me, I know." She was punctuating her voice with her forefinger— "yes, yes, yes"—as Sue shook her head.

Wow, I thought, and I got up to make myself a real drink—a real big drink.

Sue tried to reason with her. "Susanne, honey, David was an orphan, and you're going to marry him in less than a month.

You're in love with the guy. You two have been going out since high school."

"You wait," she said, "you just wait, and don't ever compare David to any of those people."

Then both of us cringed and looked over at sixteen-year-old Liam. Slim, almost gaunt at just under six feet, with blue eyes and brown hair, he was our ascetic, working out constantly, monitoring his diet, profoundly interested in religion. He was a wild card. Besides, we knew from long experience that there are 843 things parents can do to embarrass a sixteen-year-old. We hadn't expected such a vehement reaction from Susanne, or from Brendan, for that matter, but we were absolutely confident we'd get one from him.

Liam just shrugged his shoulders. "I'll play with him and try to get along. Show him how to do things. Look out for him."

Sue's mouth dropped open. Then she bowed her head with exaggerated courtesy. "Thank you, Liam."

I got a lump in my throat as an image of Liam came to mind. When we first moved into this place we were standing together at the break of the hill above the old hay meadow. It was dusk on a clear, cold autumn evening. The maples on the far side had faded from bright orange and red to a dusty ocher, and the darkening sedge in the field was hazy with mist. The sun had been setting west over Shawangunk, and just a few shafts of light remained. One of them reached arrow straight from the top of the mountain ten miles away and lit up a spot in the meadow about three hundred yards away.

I said to Liam quickly, "Can you run out and catch that before it goes?"

The boy ran down the hill in the darkness, through the swampy brush, along the deer run, and far out into the field. In the instant that the light disappeared I saw him there, a far-off, tiny figure jumping around with his arms raised, twinkling golden in the rushing darkness.

The stars were out when he came back.

"Liam," I said, "to me you'll always be the last light in the meadow."

CHAPTER THREE

visiting home

The wedding was only fourteen days away when Joanne drove up with Mike for the week's preplacement visit and I barely noticed, just waving at the two of them from the back lawn. Brendan and I were awfully busy. The caterers wanted some temporary electrical lines run, so I had been stringing wire earlier that morning and trying to avoid the men from the tent company driving tent stakes when I noticed a pungent smell coming from down below, where a contractor was spreading stone for more parking. The leach field from the septic tank had expired.

When I had talked to him the contractor just shook his head. "If I bring more equipment in to open it up, I'll wipe out your new road and grind up the grass."

"I can't do that. I have a wedding here in two weeks. How else can I get it done?"

"Well," the man said, squinting out over the property, "you can let the field set and run a new line from the distribution box, snaking it down along that old lane through the woods."

"Okay," I said doubtfully.

"Not okay," the guy said. "You'd have to find some idiot

who'd dig two hundred feet of trench by hand. I can't get my equipment in there either."

"Brendan!"

So Brendan and I were digging the trench in about one hundred degrees of August heat when Mike showed up with Sue. I cut a good picture with big rubber boots and blown-out dungarees spattered with a lot of dark, grungy matter that kept other people standing upwind.

Sue and Mike went into the house. Brendan and I went back to our shovels. I'd see Mike at dinner.

About an hour later I felt rain. Surprised, I looked up out of the trench at the sky. There wasn't a cloud in it. Then I turned around. Mike was standing on a pile of dirt, sprinkling me with the garden hose.

"Mike," I said, "don't do that."

Then I got the first flavor of the literal mind.

"Sue said I could spray the hose if I wanted to."

"Yes, but not on us, kid. Spray the lawn or the flowers."

"I did spray the flowers."

I stood there in the muddy trench, getting wet down and looking at a child who stood up to my shoulder but was reasoning like a two-year-old. I put a lot of ice into my voice.

"Mike, spray that hose somewhere else."

A blank look. "Why are you working when I'm here?"

"Mike, spray that hose somewhere else."

Reluctantly he moved the spray off me and trudged up the hill, dragging the hose.

From far down the trench Brendan chuckled.

All that hot afternoon I shoveled and watched Mike out of the corner of my eye. He stayed with the hose. He sprayed the lawn, the house, chased butterflies with it. He sprayed straight up in the air and stood under it; he sprayed the dogs, the trees, the walk. He sprayed for about six hours straight.

Brendan watched him, too. "He's retarded, Dad."

I didn't know how to respond to that. I wanted to say "No, he's not," but the longer Mike played with the hose like a two-year-old that long, hot summer afternoon, the more bizarre the behavior appeared.

After dark and after Brendan and I took the hose away from Mike to wash each other down outside and then took long, hot showers, we sat down for a meal of grilled hamburgers and salads. The serving plates were passed around to Mike first as the guest. He heaped up everything he could until the food overflowed from his plate onto the table, meanwhile talking like a machine gun and just as loud.

"I have a family already. I have a dog and a grandmother. My room is upstairs in the attic. I sleep in the same room as my brother, Tom. We have chickens and a goat."

"What home, Mike?" Brendan asked, looking at the food mess that surrounded him.

"Mama Johnson and her mother and dad. That's where I really live. But I was raised on a farm in Pennsylvania; that's where I was born. I remember it."

Sue and I studied each other's reaction. We knew Mike had been born in a trailer park outside Poughkeepsie.

Toward the end of the meal there was one hamburger left on the serving plate and Mike basically hadn't eaten anything. Sue asked me, "Do you want that last hamburger?"

"That's mine," Mike yelled. Embarrassed, Sue handed him the plate. He took it, put it on top of his other hamburger, and squirted about half the ketchup bottle over it.

Brendan raised his eyebrows at me to say, "See?"

But later on I tried a test. We were sitting around the table drinking coffee, and somehow the subject of restaurants and tipping came up. Sue mentioned fifteen percent, and Mike insisted he could do percentages. It was evident, however, that he couldn't—in fact, hadn't the foggiest idea what they were. So while Sue was cleaning up I took Mike into the office and closed the door.

"Look, Mike," I said, "can you write the number one hundred?"

And he did, scrawling it in huge numbers on a piece of paper.

"Good, good. Now, tell me what three percent of one hundred is."

"Fifteen!"

"No. Now listen carefully . . ." and I explained that if you have the number one hundred written down you can move a decimal point two places to the left to get one percent. We did it together several times to calculate one percent of one hundred, two hundred, three hundred, etc. Then I showed him it works with any number. Then that if you know what one percent is, you can multiply that number by the percentage you want—one percent times fifteen is fifteen percent, etc. We did that together over and over again, and then I put all the papers away.

"Now, in your head, Mike, what's ten percent of four hundred thirty-seven?"

"Forty-three point seven."

"What's ten percent of eight hundred?"

"Eighty."

"What's five percent of two hundred?"

"Ten."

I walked back down to the barroom, where Brendan was reading Shelby Foote's Civil War trilogy in a quiet pool of light.

In this, his last summer before college, Brendan seemed to be here more often than not at night. Recently he had become intensely interested in American history, particularly the Civil War period. He seemed to be able to unwind by reading it, and so more and more often in those dwindling summer evenings, I found him downstairs.

Yet he was ever willing to put his head up, smile, and talk with me.

Later, long after he had left for Virginia, I found myself unconsciously drifting down to the barroom in the evening hours and was always foolishly disappointed at finding his place at the long wooden table empty and dark.

I would miss him dreadfully then.

For now, though, he was still here.

"He's not retarded," I said, gesturing upstairs.

"What about the hose?"

"He talked about the hose." I shrugged. "It was the first time in his life he was allowed to turn one on. He had seen them before but never, ever was allowed to touch one."

Brendan considered that, and his features softened. "Well, he's still awfully screwed up, Dad."

"True," I said over the top of my glasses. "Now what are you on?"

Brendan thumped the open book. "The battle of Manassas."

"First or second?"

"Second."

"Ah," I grinned, "Stonewall Jackson and the Carnival and Iron Brigade and Ewell loses his leg. Lee triumphs when Longstreet goes in, Pope comes to grief and the South goes wild."

Brendan's eyes lit up. "I'm going to school a few miles from there."

I was out of contact with Mike for the rest of that first week. We were painting, digging, and then painting again. I also had some travel to do for work, but Sue stayed close to Mike all day every day. Late summer was, for her business, a quiet time. The two of them played board games, Mike helped her in the kitchen, and at night she read to him. I didn't have time to sit down with him at any more meals or try any further experiments. His attention was totally focused on Sue anyway, and when the week ended I realized it only by the sudden lack of an overloud voice in the background.

Then the wedding avalanched in on us. Henry showed up from Vermont, Richard flew east with his girlfriend, Frank came down from the Adirondacks, my sisters and my brother-in-law arrived, my brother and his wife, my nieces, my mother.

And Sue didn't mention Mike once.

It was a picture-book wedding, the weather glorious, Susanne beautiful. We managed to get all six children in a row for photographs before church: Richard handsome and accomplished, then Susanne, Henry and Frank in their Norwich blue dress uniforms, Brendan and Liam looking relaxed but formal. A few minutes later Susanne held my hand with a dazzling smile all the way to the church.

Sue was determined to sing at her daughter's wedding. She stood up front in a stunning white and gold dress singing "Amazing Grace" as Susanne paused at the head of the aisle, holding my arm.

Then she cried.

Later, at the reception, her brothers stood up in a tall row, men now, serious, hushing the crowd. One by one they passed the microphone and talked about their sister, told everyone there how much they loved her. Then I cried, too.

It was outside after midnight, sitting in the ghostly moonlit debris of the wedding reception, that Sue mentioned Mike for the first time in more than a week. "Do you think we can somehow make that kid a part of this?"

I was smoking a cigar with a glass of wine in my hand. My tie was awry, feet up on another chair.

"Dunno. I still have the awful sinking feeling that we haven't the foggiest idea of what we're getting into. What do you think will happen when he has to get into a routine, get up and go to school, do chores, and not be the center of undivided attention?"

I saw her eyes in the moonlight. "Rich, you really don't want to do this, do you?"

Whether I wanted to or not, wheels had been turning in the background. Joanne had completed a written report on the week's visit, passed it on to Dutchess County Social Services, which reviewed the intended placement with staff, and in approving it, passed it on to family court and the law guardian, an attorney that, at least in New York State, every foster child has appointed to represent his or her interests. Then, everybody in the loop having concurred, Harbour was given a green light, and Joanne called us with one last note of caution. "Remember, Mike wants this placement very, very badly. But it's almost wholly a peer pressure issue with him. He sees families on TV, and the other children he's in the system with glorify their own families. But he's never had one of his own. Push comes to shove, a child like this hasn't the faintest idea of how to respond over the long haul."

Two days later Sue drove up and got him.

One of the words used to describe to us the withdrawal of a child controlled by the system from a placement was *extraction*.

Extraction sounds overly dramatic, much as if a submarine was going to surface offshore in the predawn darkness and launch a black rubber raft. Unfortunately for the children involved, the reality isn't all that far from the mark.

Regardless of whether a child has spent one night in a placement, or a year or ten years or his entire life; regardless of whether a placement is "home" to the child, the withdrawal is never a "leaving" as families would think of the term, because the child is never, ever coming back. If there are good-byes and moist-eyed grandmothers or anxious parents in attendance, they gather in shared despair, in promises to write, in hurried last-minute hugs or precautions or tears. And often there is not even that, just the "child-care system" cranking the right piece of paperwork onto the right desk, followed by a quick swoop.

Sometimes the children are taken, have to be taken, in the middle of the night. At other times, circumstances might demand that they be yanked away during school or meals.

I have tried to imagine what the experience is like. Who can grow up knowing that the world might turn inside out at any moment and frequently does? Who can live knowing that any little treasured possession—a teddy bear, a game, a set of blocks—might never be seen again unless it is kept within immediate reach?

Mike had been extracted twelve times before Sue parked next to the front door of the children's home on August 27.

Desperately wanting this extraction to be a lot different from the others, she had one last thing to say to me before she left home.

"I have this image of what's going to happen today, and I want to talk to you about it," she said quietly. "Remember the story of the cat who lived in a man's house in Vermont that had thirteen doors opening on the outside?"

"Yeah," I said, "vaguely. Robert Heinlein, I think."

"Yes," Sue said. "During the winter the cat would go to a door and meow to be let out. The man would open it, and the cat, seeing the cold and snow outside, would walk to another door."

"Right, I remember now. The cat was always looking for the door into summer."

"Do you remember what happened?"

"Yes," I said, forcing my memory, "stupid blind persistence won out. The cat kept it up long enough that eventually a door opened and it was summertime outside."

"Right," Sue said. "I think these children are the same way. Some children are born into the right season. But others aren't, so they have to keep stubbornly going from door to door until they find the door into summer, into the place they really want to be."

"So?"

"So," she said, "when this particular door opens for him, I want it to be really sunny outside."

"Whew," I said, "am I that bad?"

"Sometimes."

Stacked up under the vaulted portico was a sad, tiny pile of boxes and bags. Inside, Mike was patiently sitting on a chair in the reception area, already being ignored by the odd staff member bustling through. After Sue took Mike's hand and told the receptionist who she was, Kathy came down briefly to say a few polite words, Mike scrawled his name into the log at the reception desk, and then the front door of the children's home banged shut behind them.

Done!

Later, Sue said she stood there a long time staring at Mike's pathetic collection before she could actually bring herself to put hands on it. She remembered what Joanne had said, that these children rarely had more than what could be quickly bundled into the backseat of a compact car, but she hadn't really believed it.

We used to think that our five sons and one daughter hadn't had much in the way of personal gear. But Mike had only the sneakers he was wearing, a photo album with a couple dozen pictures in it, artwork from school, one stuffed animal, and some clothes.

"Mike, pick this up and let's get the hell out of here."

Forty-five minutes later I raised my head from a book. There was a noise in the house, a loud voice rocketing from room to room. "I remember this," Mike was shouting. "I remember this, too."

When he slammed into the living room, I stood up to say hello with a smile on my face. I remembered Sue's little story and had even prepared a welcoming speech.

But before I could get a single word out, Mike whirled around me like a ball swung on a cord and disappeared into the next room.

So I closed my mouth.

Sue breezed in, looking harried.

"Did you say hello to Mike?"

"Sort of."

"Well, give me a hand carrying his things in."

Liam had the old library for his bedroom then, a very large, light, and airy room with tall windows overlooking the hay meadow in back. It was adjacent to our bedroom, inside our apartment area on the second floor, and since we wanted to keep Mike on the same level with us, Sue and I asked Liam if he could share. "For a little while," he said.

Sue had gotten Mike a dresser and a bed, hung a bulletin board up, and bought matching Jurassic Park sheets, quilt, and pillowcases. There was even a big Jurassic Park poster on the wall by his bed and a plastic model of Tyrannosaurus rex sitting on his nightstand.

"I can't believe I have Jurassic Park sheets," he was saying when I walked in with his bags. Then he pointedly stopped talking and turned his back. Sue's expression said, "Relax. He has to get used to you." But I was miffed anyway and trudged downstairs to the barroom, where I poured myself a cup of coffee.

It was just the four of us around the big table in the barroom that first evening—Liam, Sue, Mike, and I.

Remembering what had happened with food during his visit, Sue carefully portioned his dinner onto a plate and handed it to the boy. Then, once we all settled ourselves, she started to say grace.

But before she managed two words, Mike abruptly faced her and started to talk in his jangling, overloud voice. And talk.

The three of us sat there embarrassed for a few minutes before we realized it wasn't going to stop. Mike's facial tic was working overtime, and he stayed facing Sue and only Sue. When he did manage to get some food up to his mouth, he chewed with exaggerated lip-smacking movements. Several times he rubbed his hand over his forehead without first wiping his fingers on the napkin, so by the time we were halfway through, his face and hair were streaked with barbecue sauce.

"I have a real family. I know all about families," he said. "Mom Alice Johnson and Dave Johnson my dad and my brother and sister, Tommy and Jane, and my little new baby sister Connie, and Grandma. Connie is a crack baby, and we just adopted her. We have a dog named Squiggles and ten goats and ten chickens, and my room is up in the attic, but I have to share it with Tom. I'm going to live there all the time later on and I'm happy there and probably I'm going to have a horse. Grandma is buying me a present for my birthday and for Christmas. Dave Johnson, my dad, works for the post office every day, and sometimes he takes me with him except for the time I had a problem and had to go to Rockland State Psychiatric Hospital, and then they put me in Poughkeepsie, and then they put me in the children's home, and so I didn't get to ride with Dad, but I have a real family. I was raised on a farm in Pennsylvania, so I know all about Pennsylvania, and Grandma is going to buy me a present."

And on and on it went. After ten minutes my ears started to hurt. All of this had the relentless ring of permanence.

"I can do this thing," Sue said later when we were having a cup of tea alone in the kitchen. She had been reading the exasperated expression on my face.

"What is it we want to do?"

Sue didn't answer right away. Instead, she stared down as if she were a gypsy fortune-teller reading the answer in the bottom of the cup. "Give this kid a shot at a normal life," she finally said. "No, that's wrong. What we want to do is get out of his way and let him work out his own shot at a normal life."

"Well, somehow, we've got to slow him up. You'll never be able to communicate with him otherwise. At least we have to turn the volume down, or I'll be wearing ear protection at the dinner table. Five minutes after he started I was wishing for a nice quiet chain saw or maybe a leaf blower."

But Sue didn't laugh. She just stared back into her tea.

"I can do this thing, Rich."

"Okay, okay."

Looking for something intelligent to say, I asked, "What about the Johnsons? There seems to be a considerable bond there, with the grandmother, too."

Sue scrunched up her face. "That's one of the real mysteries about Mike. I spoke to Mrs. Johnson, and she was very emphatic about wanting to stay in contact. But there's something in that relationship we don't understand, something nobody will talk about. Kathy said they wouldn't visit unless she pushed them a bit. Even then, months and months would go by. Then Joanne said that adoption by the Johnsons wasn't an option, that family court had said no and refused to reopen the issue. Something happened way back when."

"Yeah," I cracked, "they tried to have a peaceful dinner."

We never did find out why family court had said that adopting Mike wasn't an option for the Johnsons. In New York it is a criminal offense (one defined in the mental health law) to reveal the treatment or circumstances of a foster child to individuals not concerned with his or her treatment. In practice, child-care workers seemed to us to manifest this proscription as a reluctance to reveal anything except on a "need-to-know" basis. By law we were allowed only that one first look at Mike's file, although later we were furnished with relevant extracts such as a summary of his placements, his birth record, and so forth.

I looked up then, and Mike was standing in the archway.

He had the two dogs with him, Pupsy and Teddy Bear, and one of them was nuzzling Mike's hand while the other was looking up at him expectantly. A nice picture, but it was all wrong—so wrong I could almost hear the "Twilight Zone" theme music in the background.

Our dogs don't like strangers. No exceptions. They just are very uncomfortable around new people, although they're both essentially good-natured and adapt very well to the coming and going of guests. Teddy Bear is a big black Lab mix who spends a lot of time sleeping in the sun on the back lawn, where he can keep half an eye on the hay meadow, hoping for a woodchuck, and will usually just run off and bark at new people from a distance. Pupsy is smaller and also a mixed breed—looks like a blend of Doberman and something else black—and she almost never barks. Extremely shy, she'll usually slink away and hide the first time she sees someone new. Years ago she wandered onto the property we used to own on Mountain Road in Rosendale and the boys adopted her. It looked then like she had been severely abused, and she's always stayed nervous.

The one point the dogs are trained very well on is staying out of the barroom, and they never try to follow anyone downstairs.

Asking myself the question "How did he get both of them to follow him down?"

I said as gently as I could, "Mike, we don't allow the dogs in the barroom."

Mike ignored what I said and spoke to Sue. "What do I do now, Sue?"

Sue smiled at him. "What you do is take the dogs upstairs like you were told, Mike. Then we'll find something to do together."

"What?"

I repeated myself. "Mike, take the dogs upstairs."

For the first time he looked directly at me and spoke. "You're not my boss, Rich." His eyes were big and blue and looked completely guileless.

I started to rumble, and Sue gave me the little going-away hand gesture that meant, "Easy, take it easy."

"Come on, Mike, I'll go upstairs with you," Sue said.

I remembered that the home had said Mike didn't do well with peer groups; in fact, that he did poorly in any sort of social setting. He did best with only one person at a time—the reports from the children's home were firm on this point.

But that didn't explain the dogs' behavior, which I was still thinking about when Liam came downstairs later and sat next to me. "Dad, this kid is nuts."

"No," I said dryly.

Liam shook my shoulder. "He was upstairs arranging his pillows on his bed. First he put one pillow on top of the other, and then he switched them. Then he switched them again and then again. He kept doing that for about ten minutes before he made moaning sounds and started to pull his hair."

I shrugged. "Everybody gets a little tense at pillow-arrangement time."

Liam looked at me for a long moment and then got up. "I know he's emotionally disturbed, but sometimes I think you and Mom are nuts, too."

"Liam," I said, looking up at him, trying to speak seriously and work out a badly organized thought at the same time, "I really don't know what emotionally disturbed means. After all, emotion is a type of disturbance, and it's usually good. If nothing moved your feelings, you'd be a zombie. It's a dumb label that seems to get tossed around pretty casually, but I think people are trying to describe someone so traumatized by past experience that he's forever affected by it. Like a person who survives a shipping disaster but gets the shakes when he hears a foghorn. Families were Mike's big past disaster, so maybe just being with a family again gives him the shivers. Then, too, he knows everybody has said he can't make it in a family, so maybe he feels a lot of pressure to perform."

Liam held his hands out. "But this family is all right."

"How could he know that?"

Liam shrugged and walked back upstairs.

Mike cries in his sleep.

Why hadn't we noticed that on his visit that week?

We heard muffled cries and walked into the bedroom at midnight. Mike had the covers over his head and was crying out in a loud voice. His knees were up under his belly, and his arms were folded under his chest. Thinking it was some sort of game, I pulled the covers off, but he was really asleep.

We tried to straighten him out so he could rest more comfortably, but it was impossible to move him. His sheets were soaked, not with urine but with perspiration.

Finally, Sue just sat down next to him and rubbed his back for about twenty minutes. Little by little the cries petered down to a whimper.

But at about four in the morning, we heard them start up again.

Sue is justifiably smug about reveille. The children's home stressed the impossibility of getting Mike up in the morning, and they were right. But after the first week she found that if she goes in there with the two dogs, he doesn't give her any problem. She just has them jump up on his bed.

"Come on, Mike," she'll say, "let these dogs outside, they have to go." And then Mike gets up and runs to the front door.

But later there is always a shower argument, and then the noise starts again.

"I don't have to take a shower."

"Mike, you wet your bed last night, so you have to take a shower."

"I don't have tooo . . ."

"Mike!"

"I don't have tooo . . ."

Mike is afraid of the dark. Not just leery or nervous. Terrified.

And not just of the dark, either—he's afraid of shadows and quiet rooms. If the light is off in the downstairs foyer in the day-time, he won't set foot into the half-lit entranceway and try to reach the bathroom door.

When we set him up with his paints and a model on the workbench in the cellar, he followed us right back out.

Sue said, "Mike, I thought you wanted to paint your dinosaur model."

"You help me, Sue."

"No, I have to make dinner. You're a good artist. I know you can do it by yourself."

"No, you help me."

I didn't understand. Later I realized there are banks of fluorescent lights in the cellar, but in the far distance lie shadows and hidden areas.

Joanne came over twice in the first few days. One of the significant ways in which Harbour differs from foster care is the close network of support for families. The family specialist visits every week and takes the child out alone for an hour or two. It's a double check. The family specialists are experienced enough to pick up on nuances that may vibrate from the child, but at the same time, the child is given the model of an older sister or brother or perhaps an aunt, who can offer up third-party advice.

Later, the family specialist sits down with the Harbour parents for a chat.

"Why this constant barrage of talk? Mike never shuts up."

Joanne's dark eyes were measuring our posture, our attitude. Finally, she said, "Most of our children, particularly those who have spent a long time in the system, have perfected a story about themselves. It might be wholly imaginary. But it's a defense mechanism with their peers and adults. Sort of a verbal barrage they've learned to throw up and keep up."

"Will it ever stop so that we can talk to him?"

Joanne had been taking notes. Now she tapped her pencil on the table. "Maybe. But with these children it sometimes goes on a long time."

"How long?"

"A long time."

CHAPTER FOUR

the honeymoon

For two weeks I went to work early and stayed at the plant for ten or twelve hours. Then I came home late, had a loud dinner with Mike and Sue, and listened to Sue struggling to get him into bed.

If I tried to lend a hand, I'd hear the "you're not my boss" routine or get the silently turned-away back in my face.

By this point Sue was struggling to keep a smile up. Mike demanded her attention every waking moment. He would not amuse himself at all. He wanted Sue to play a game with him, make a cake with him, help him with lunch, with breakfast, and all the eternal while he was shouting in his loud, loud voice some variation of the theme he played at dinner. Then, too, he had to be supervised in the bathroom or he wouldn't shower. He would not leave the grounds to take a walk or explore the mountain or kick a ball around by himself for five minutes. When Sue was on the phone with a client, he was right there at her elbow, talking.

And it was always a threesome. Somehow, Mike and the dogs had become inseparable, two dark shadows constantly slipping around his legs, getting in our way, too.

Sue was still determined, but any sense of peace in the house was slipping away. I was really starting to resent this kid. "Doesn't he ever shut up?" This clinging, stream-of-consciousness talk wasn't something I ever would have imagined. I could make a huge allowance for the fact that he was frightened and had to work through that, but when would it end? My experience was that as a rule, boys don't talk—you have to pry information out of them with a crowbar—and they don't hang on you, either. If anything, you usually had to worry about where they were and what they were getting into.

I was raised in Brooklyn, and when I was ten, eleven, or twelve years of age and even older, the notion that boys living outside the city limits were able to escape supervision by having woods and fields available right outside their back door always struck me as horribly unfair, and I was most content on vacation in the country or up at my aunt Alice's hotel in Cold Spring, New York, when I too could vanish under trees, climb rocks, or fish or swim in a lake. Yet here Mike was, snatched out of jail for all practical purposes and set down free on top of a mountain, with miles of new territory to explore, lakes and streams to fish in, two dogs who'd run after him, woods, apple, pear, and cherry orchards all around him, beaver ponds, deer in the meadow, with an occasional old sow bear grumbling her way through the briars. Sue and I should be reporting him missing two or three times a day instead of having to amuse him every waking minute.

This was getting very old very quickly for me.

And Sue appeared awfully tired and frustrated herself on the night she called me into her office. But wary, too.

I looked around. I had taken to staying out of here; this was where Mike usually was talking and talking and talking to Sue. Now I could see that after several weeks the office was in disarray, with files and phone messages piling up. She was getting behind.

"Rich, Tom is moving out."

"Why?" Tom Hanaan had been a guest of ours for more than a year. A quiet sort of guy who kept to himself, he was liked by the other guests and by us, too. A middle-aged man who worked for the state highway department, he had come to us after a bad divorce, and he was always neat and clean and paid on time. In the late evenings he read quietly in his room or took long walks through the orchards. Once or twice a month he and I would have a drink together in the barroom, but most of the time we never saw him. He'd come in the guest entrance, go to his room to shower and change, and then go back out for dinner. On weekends he visited a sister in Albany.

I looked at Sue. "Mike?"

"Yeah," she said, looking down and tapping one hand on her desk, "the noise."

"Okay," I sighed, "I'll get some ads back up, and I have some people on the waiting list."

Sue made a little offhand gesture with her head. "Phyllis complained, too."

I winced. As quiet and circumspect as Tom was, Phyllis was even less of a bother. She'd been in one of the corner rooms for almost two years. In fact, she had moved in while we were still painting and plumbing. She was working on her master's locally and working part-time.

Six of the inn rooms were on the upper level and opened on a large common foyer, and although the old thick plaster walls kept much noise from moving room to room up there, I knew sound carried well from floor to floor. Mike was right under Phyllis.

What we were selling were nicely finished rooms, cooking facilities, a laundry room on the premises, the barroom lounge, offroad parking, coffee and tea in the morning, but most of all cleanliness, security, and quiet. Lots of quiet. And our guests usually stayed with us for a long time in consequence.

"Has she talked about moving, too?"

"She hinted at it."

This time I flinched. I didn't want to be two rooms down. It took a long time to find someone suitable.

Then whatever patience I had left suddenly collapsed and I was very angry with the situation and at Sue for getting us into it, for involving us with Harbour, with this child. She might be willing to stay with this program, but I sure wasn't. In fact, I had a long stream of bitter and sarcastic remarks ready and felt like kicking something, so after shifting back and forth on my feet for a minute or so, trying to calm down, I turned my back and stormed off outside.

The hill the house stood on had been terraced—landscaped, that is—years ago with hundreds and hundreds of feet of dry-laid stone walls, each originally about five or six feet high but now tumbledown and overgrown with wild rose and sumac. One of my interminable projects was a foot-by-foot excavation of these ruins, digging the rough quarried stones out from under a yard or so of soil and knotty roots and relaying the old walls. I always had a spot going that I could work on in odd moments, and now I dragged my long-handled shears, five-foot pry bar, shovel, pick, and oak plank out of the barn, banged them down next to a wall, and mindlessly started digging.

It was dark when I gave up, slumping against the stone, covered head to toe in sticky black soil and more resigned now than angry. Mike was loud, churlish, impossibly demanding of time, hopelessly, endlessly juvenile, and he was costing us money, but I realized that unless and until Sue herself rethought this thing on her own, there just wouldn't be much sense in my saying one damn thing.

Besides, that point couldn't be all that far off. Her business was suffering, and that was very much her baby, too.

· · ·

But then Mike started school, and for a brief time Sue and I switched roles.

Not having firm arrangements made for the school year had been, as Kathy had predicted, the last of the children's home's objections. Sue handled it by explaining that she was self-employed and that if Mike was home with her for a couple of days that was all to the good. Meanwhile, she left it to the professionals at Harbour to work out whatever problem there was with the local school district.

We had never had a special-needs child before, and we had kept our other children out of the public schools as much as we could, so the entire system of "special education" was well beyond our experience. We started from the naive belief that since our local public school district had classrooms and teachers and should know what they were doing with both, it was incumbent upon them to simply tell us what bus he had to get on, what his teacher's name was, and then do what they had to do. In a couple of weeks we'd visit his teacher, find out how he was doing and what she wanted from us, and then follow up on his homework.

"No," Sue's sister Eileen, an experienced public school teacher, laughed when, after the first few days of the school year passed, Sue said something like that to her. "It's just not that simple. He's a special-needs child. They have to formulate an IEP first."

"What's an IEP?"

Eileen then took a deep breath and explained that there were new federal laws involved, laws that required all children diagnosed as having "special needs" to be evaluated by a standing committee of the local school district called the Committee of Special Education. Then, in each case, the laws further required an Individual Educational Plan or IEP be developed, approved, and filed under complex guidelines for appeal.

"Huh," Sue said, puzzled. "Why don't they just test him and put him in the right class?"

"Because the IEP has to stipulate in writing the resources they will make available to him first. The school system doesn't want to get sued by parents who don't like the plan. They are sued all the time over IEPs by parents who want some form of extra-special treatment for special-needs kids."

"How long does an IEP take?"

"Usually not long. It's just that right now Mike is probably standing in line. The number of special-needs children is constantly growing. The definition of handicaps is very elastic, and there are no real criteria. We're not talking here about dyslexics or kids in wheelchairs any longer. Parents of overweight children are now demanding that their children be classified as handicapped and be given an IEP, parents of bored kids or slow learners are going out and having their children diagnosed as having attention deficit disorder (ADD) and demanding classification, and it goes on and on."

"Oh."

And in fact, after Labor Day came and went, The Harbour Program came through; Joanne ran around in another busy series of meetings that got Mike placed. Everybody lives in some local school district, of course, but in New York State there is also an entity called the Board of Cooperative Educational Services, or BOCES, for short. BOCES extends over many school districts and began as centralized vocational training, but eventually expanded into other areas, particularly special education. In a nearby town, BOCES occupied one wing of an elementary school, where it maintained a therapist, secretarial staff, and several classes for special-needs children.

Mike's IEP called for him to be placed in one of these, a 1:4:2 class.

As Joanne explained, 1:4:2 is the ratio of teachers to students to teacher aides. One teacher, four students, two teacher aides.

This was fairly puzzling to Sue and me. Although we didn't know each other then, we both remember St. Patrick's parish school in Brooklyn, where the teacher-student ratio was as high as 1:93. One Dominican nun to ninety-three students, and everybody learned to read and write.

Why did they need three adults for four children?

At first we thought it was for intensive instruction—that all of these resources would bring Mike up to the proper academic level, or at least to the best level he could attain.

But the first thing it got him was tied to a chair.

When Mike came home upset on the afternoon of the second school day, Sue got the story out of him in bits and pieces. Then, the next morning, she stormed up to his classroom, determined to clean somebody's clock.

What she found was a thoughtful, well-groomed, professional, calm, reasonable male teacher who patiently explained that Mike's behavior was so extreme that for his own protection he had to be "restrained."

"Mrs. Miniter," the teacher said, "I've been working with emotionally disturbed children for many years, and Mike is perhaps the most disturbed child I've seen. He assaulted the assistant, threw his materials around, and was flailing wildly. I've learned that we have to firmly establish appropriate rules of behavior straightaway and prevent him from injuring himself or somebody else. We had no choice but to restrain him."

That defused Sue's anger. Our home discipline grew out of certain basic rules, violation of which evoked an immediate response. So what he was saying made sense to her. How could classroom work take place if there was no classroom atmosphere?

"But he's been with us for over two weeks, and he's never assaulted anybody."

The teacher looked down at his desk and drummed his fingers on the table. "Does he talk nonstop at home, the same way he does at school?"

"Yes."

"Mrs. Miniter, the longer he's like that at home, the more disturbed he really is. He's struggling to hold it together, and the longer he struggles, the higher the pressure builds. So you can think of this beginning period with him as a honeymoon. Believe me, it will be over all too soon. Meanwhile, of course, he's not holding it together in school, and we have to do what we have to do."

"Honeymoon? What I've been going through with him is a honeymoon?"

"Mrs. Miniter, to be perfectly honest, you don't know what you're dealing with. You've had six normal, healthy children. Mike is not normal, not healthy. He can't function in any sort of social setting where he is not the sole center of attention. In fact, I'm really surprised that the system would place him in a home like yours. You and your husband are completely untrained. He can hurt himself; he can hurt you. If that happens, The Harbour Program has a lot to answer for."

"What can we do?"

"Have you had any instruction in how to properly restrain children?"

"No," Sue answered doubtfully.

"Well, I'm organizing some classes after school hours. Normally, they would be open only to professionals, but I'll see what I can do to get you admitted."

Later on at home, Sue and I discussed her interview with Mike's teacher.

"Sue, I don't care what you say, this is macabre. You're overreacting. If the longer you just talk and don't assault people at home is proof of how sick you are, then the most disturbed person in the world must be Mother Teresa. I don't believe he can't function in a social setting. I think he just doesn't want to. I do know that if you or I tied up this boy, we'd be arrested and charged with child abuse. Why can't three grown adults handle four children without roping them?"

"Rich, you're making it sound all wrong, and I'm not over-reacting. This man knows these children, and we should at least understand how to deal with him physically if something happens. God knows what I've been doing isn't working—he's not settling down. Maybe he is sick."

I was incredulous. "You're actually worried? Frightened?"

Sue looked at me and smiled. "No, I'm not frightened, but I didn't tell you everything. For instance, after they restrained him, all he would do was scream, 'Let me fucking go,' at the top of his lungs, and he did that for over an hour."

"I don't care. I still don't agree with it."

In fact, that was the first real testimony to Mike's normalcy that I had heard. If somebody tied me to a chair, I'd be whooping and hollering, too.

"Well, I do," Sue persisted. "By the way, I'm keeping him home tomorrow. I decided I want to take him with me when I visit my mother. I want to see what she thinks. Besides, I can't leave him here with you—it just wouldn't work."

Sue was going up to spend a long weekend with her mother in Old Forge, New York, in the Adirondacks.

Sarcastically I said, "Oh, I see, despite what you learned today, you're going to be alone in a car with him for four long hours without your child-restraint training."

Sue gave me the gimlet eye. "Okay, you're right, I don't agree with everything that teacher said about his being a danger to us. When I'm not worn out from having to listen to him, I still have the feeling that Mike is basically a very kind, generous person. But still, that man's the professional, he has all the experience. There's got to be something to what he says."

"Don't be too sure."

"Shut up."

Later on that evening, I heard Mike ask Sue if he could telephone the Johnsons and speak to "Mom" and "Dad" and "Grandma."

Sue said okay, and he dialed from the living room phone. I was listening from the next room.

"Hello," he said into the phone, "Grandma, this is Mike."

There was a pause while he was listening, and then he repeated, "Mike."

Then again, "Mike, this is Mike. Do you remember me?"

"Mike."

"Mike," he finally said in a low voice, but I knew the phone was dead.

He walked past in the hallway and went into the office where Sue was. I heard him telling Sue in his loudspeaker voice all about a long conversation with "Grandma" Johnson, how she was going to buy him a present for Christmas.

I felt like banging my head into the wall.

I caught him in the hallway just before bed. He had the dogs with him and, true to form, tried to duck around me with his eyes averted.

Moved by something, I said, "Hold on," and grabbed his thin arm.

"Look at me, Mike."

Those wide, blue blank eyes slowly came up. "Mike, if anyone ever ties you to a chair again, I don't want you to tell Sue. Tell me, instead. Get to a phone and call me at work."

No response.

"Mike, do you understand? Do you?" I shook him.

"Let me go, that hurts. Why should I call you, anyway?"

"Because I'm going to tie them to a goddamn chair, and believe me, I make better knots."

The eyes looked away again.

After he went on about his business, I questioned myself. Was it the right thing to say? Was I just screwing things up by being a bull about this?

That night he said good night to me for the first time.

Sue and the Noise left for Old Forge while I was at work on Friday morning. Sunday afternoon they were back, with Sue looking relaxed and happy, and Mike oddly quiet.

"What happened? Did you have his voice box surgically removed?"

"We had a good time. My mother enjoyed having him. We took a canoe trip, we went to the Enchanted Forest, but it was closed, so we shopped, saw my sister, ate out, had a busy weekend."

"But Mike?"

"Different."

"How?"

"Quiet, just like you see him now. Well, semiquiet, and he did some listening for a change."

"Okay, come across."

Sue grinned. "I finally decided who the adult was in this relationship. I told him to shut up. We were an hour up the road when I realized that I wasn't going to make it with him shouting in my ear the whole time. So I lost my temper and screamed at him."

"Lost your temper?"

"More like turned into a screaming, cursing, snarling maniac. I mean, I really lost it."

"And he shut up?"

She grinned again, but sadly this time. "More or less. I scared the hell out of him. Anyway, he settled down and began to talk to me like a reasonable little person. I could actually have a conversation."

"And?" I prompted her with my hand.

"Big gaps. He's been talking so much and saying so much of absolutely nothing about himself over the past few weeks that I didn't realize what he doesn't understand. In a strange way he's incredibly naive. I think that's a big part of his problem."

"What do you mean?"

"Well," said Sue, "after I yelled at him I told him he could sleep in the car, meaning that it was a long trip and he could nap on the way up. But about a half hour later he asked me where I was going to sleep over the weekend and I said, in my mother's house, of course."

"Okay . . ." I shrugged.

"Rich, he then asked how far the car was going to be from the house."

"So what?"

Sue leaned forward. "Don't you see what I mean? He thought I was telling him that I'd be in the house over the weekend, but that he'd be sleeping outside in the car."

"That's silly."

"But, Rich," Sue said, "that's the point. Despite this demanding verbal smoke screen of his, what he expects to do is whatever an adult tells him to do. Literally. Live in the corner of a trailer like an animal, submit to the most degrading treatment, even sleep outside in the car in the dark in a strange place—and you know what he's like in the dark."

"Yeah."

"Yeah . . . and more. This kid believes in Santa Claus."

I laughed. "Sue, he'll be twelve years old."

"Rich, the Enchanted Forest was closed, but we saw a big figure of Santa Claus through the gate. Mike talked about Santa Claus on and off all weekend. He believes in him—not in a half-believing, wishful sort of way, but as an article of faith."

"Santa Claus?"

"And probably the Easter Bunny."

versation, although at the time,
heard it.

bus early in the morning, hair
reshly ironed clothes. Patheti-
he tattered name tag from the

read it again, and looked up

hat my name is?"
g."
e, "I know what my name is

me and shaking me and say-
e.'"

ell, did you wake up?"
l, I think. I don't remember

outside and he dashed for

f the drive, I got very angry.
w house, new adults, a new
it had all started with being

repeated it to her, "he needs

much less vulnerable. I could

walking along the stone path
hem together. They were far
l brilliantly green back lawn

in a red protective helmet,

That was unsettling. "What else does he believe in?"

"God knows. He's been in that system for a long time. What else do you learn in a family that you can't learn in an institution? Things we take for granted that our children understand. The fact that you have to go shopping every week, that people work at other jobs besides looking after you. Things you don't even think about, like an older brother telling you Santa Claus isn't real."

"Well, if you can't itemize them, how are you going to fill in the blanks?"

Sue shrugged. "Maybe some of them you can't. Probably he has to do it by himself, for the most part. But he's smart. I think the reason he runs on at the mouth is he understands he doesn't know a lot and he's desperate to cover that up. Remember? Joanne said something like that—it's a defense mechanism.

"The problem is, you can't engage the brain while the mouth is in motion. If he's talking, he's not learning."

"So what are you going to do if he starts up again?"

"You know we wouldn't let one of our own children play machine-gun mouth. I've just been feeling too sorry for the little shit. That's over. He starts again and I throttle him. Look at it this way: we're bigger and stronger. If we could have forced him into a car to sleep outside in the dark, we can force him into a reality check every now and then."

"That's it?"

"No. I have to find him something else to do besides follow me around like a two-year-old. Get him out with some normal folks."

"How?"

"I have an idea."

From the street below we could hear the screams and the thick heavy thud of blows being landed. Looking up to the

second-floor windows, we watched the silhouettes of thirty c
so people fighting.

I turned to her. "Sue, these are not normal folks."

It was Liam's karate class. One of us came down here twice
week, first to drop him off and then again to pick him up.

I continued protesting, "Do you think this is a good plan
Mike is really weak physically, and he has a big problem get
ting along with people and following directions. Some of thes
guys in here are thirty years old and weigh a couple hundre
pounds."

"Hey, it's a social setting, isn't it? Good practice."

"Did you tell The Harbour Program about this? They're go
ing to find out. I think their idea of a social setting is more lik
a family dinner or a movie out."

"Look," Sue snapped, "here comes Liam. You get him an
walk back to the car. I want to talk to the instructor."

"No. I want an answer to one question first."

Sue put one hand on her hip. "What?"

"How are you going to tell the teacher who wants you to re
strain him that you're sending him to karate lessons instead?"

with an artless, revealing little cor
I remember wishing I had never

He was waiting for the school
brushed, skin clean, dressed in f
cally, he still insisted on wearing
first day of school, weeks before.

Now he fussed with the tag,
at me.

"Do you know how I know w

I chuckled, "Yeah, it's on the ta

"No," he said in his loud voic
because my sister told me."

"Told you."

"Yep. I remember her shaking
ing, 'Wake up, Mike; wake up, Mik

Not understanding, I asked, "W

"Later on I did. In the hospit
that good."

Then the school bus beeped
the door.

As I watched the bus pull out c
Twelve times in eleven years, a n
school, new friends, a new life, and
shaken out of unconsciousness.

"No wonder," Sue said when I
that name tag."

But today was different. He was
hear it in the edge of his voice.

I was just home from work and
from the parking lot when I saw t
down the hill on the edge of the sti
practicing karate.

Mike's thin figure was padded u

body guard, and gloves. Liam was hitting him, driving him, and Mike was ranting back in his overloud voice: "You can't hit hard! You hit like a girl!"

"Mike," snapped Liam, "I keep telling you, you don't know enough, and you're not strong enough to take a good hit. And there's plenty of female black belts."

"I know all about karate. I took karate before. You hit like a girl—girl, girl, girl."

Bam! Over Mike went, cartwheeling with his arms and legs flopping.

I walked in the kitchen. It was steamy and good-smelling inside, with pots simmering on the stove, but Sue seemed to be boiling over. She had a harassed look on her face and was banging things around. When I asked what was wrong she said, "He's had his hooks into me all day long. Now he's started to find fault, he's started to get nasty, and he keeps telling me we're lying to him about everything."

"How do you mean?"

"I'll talk to you later," she said, distracted now, sniffing around at the sea of scattered pots and pans.

"What are you making?" I asked, starting to snoop under lids.

"Pasta, meatballs, salad, garlic bread, apple pie, and brownies. Deacon Carroll, Alice, and Garrett are coming over for dinner."

I walked into the barroom and saw the china out on the table. I had forgotten about company.

"Rich, set out the glasses."

"Okay." I walked over to the bar and made sure I had a good bottle of scotch tucked away for Deacon Carroll, who was on medication and usually didn't drink. But I remembered him saying he wouldn't take his pills that morning so that he could have one with us and also, with a broad, wistful hint, that he was partial to scotch.

Rummaging through the bottles and glassware, I had a good

view back outside. Mike had gotten up and was warily circling Liam. I could hear their voices.

"I tripped."

"No, I hit you. I told you you couldn't take a hit."

"I tripped."

Sue walked in carrying salad. "Okay. Can you go out and tell those guys to get cleaned up and changed? They're eating with us."

When I yelled down the hill, Liam nodded okay and Mike didn't. Instead, he shouted back, "Fuck you. I don't have to get cleaned up. We're not having company. I'm staying outside." But Liam shoved him ahead, and the two boys stumbled up the sloping grass and then inside.

I just stood there, stunned, for a moment.

As I came back through the kitchen door, Mike was yelling at Sue, "No, we're not having company. You're lying."

Composing herself, she replied reasonably, "Sure we are, Mike. Now get upstairs and wash."

"No, I don't have to."

Liam's arm snaked back down the stairs and grabbed Mike's shoulder.

When the door slammed upstairs, I whistled and asked Sue, "Okay, what happened to him?"

But Sue ignored me and stuck her head in the refrigerator. She mumbled something about not having enough grated cheese.

"Ah, here it is."

"Sue!"

"All right! Ever since he got up this morning, he's been on my case nonstop. When I told him it was eight o'clock, he said it was seven fifty-nine. When I told him to get Teddy outside, he said no, the dog's real name was Teddy Bear. When I told him his white pullover matches his black pants, he said no, his red shirt matches. I noticed a mark on his arm, said it was an insect bite, and told him to go put peroxide on it, and he said no, it was poison ivy. On and on it went all day long, and half of his language has been filthy. He's even been following me from room to room to tell me what's wrong with the things I'm doing and why he knows I'm not telling the truth about anything."

"Well," I said slowly, "that could be dangerous. What would he do if you told him to get out of the way of an oncoming car?"

Sue started stirring things on the stove. "I know exactly what he'd say. Before I started dinner I took him to the supermarket, and he dashed across the parking lot."

"And?"

Sue looked exasperated, "And a car was coming. He started to argue with me when I yelled at him. The car stopped, he's okay, I have to get this dinner on, I have to stay with the stove—it gives me something to do with my hands besides strangling him. So get out of my way. We'll talk later."

The deacon, Alice, and Garrett arrived a few minutes later, and magically, the simmering jumble in the kitchen materialized into a nicely laid-out meal. I poured a bottle of red table wine, drew the deacon a large whiskey, and then we adults sat.

"So," Deacon Carroll said, his blue eyes twinkling, "we're finally going to meet Mike. How's he doing?"

Sue answered promptly, her lips set in a thin line. "We want to talk to you about setting up some religious instruction."

The deacon took a long sip of amber liquid and chuckled. "Ah. Doing that well, is he?"

A down-to-earth guy in his seventies, the deacon had kept the parish going when we lost to retirement the priest who had been in St. Charles for nearly twenty years, then a transfer who had health problems. Now he was patiently settling in a new young pastor. Despite the now-bleak promise in his days since his wife of over forty years, Dorothy, had been killed in a car accident, the deacon kept doggedly putting one foot in front of the other, steadying others on with his wry sense of humor.

The boys came tumbling down the stairs. Mike looked mussed but clean, with his lank hair wetly brushed.

Sue raised her eyebrows in appreciation. "Thank you, Liam."

"No problem." He grinned and then walked over to take the deacon's hand. Liam and Deacon Carroll had spent many a Saturday afternoon together when the deacon was Liam's altar boy instructor, and now they laughed together as if at some inside joke.

Liam sat, and Mike, his facial tic remorseless, sullenly slouched into the remaining seat.

Sue paused with her wineglass just under her lips. "Mike, this is Deacon Carroll, and this is Mr. and Mrs. Hydecker."

"What's for dinner?"

"Mike," said Sue, her smile strained, "introduce yourself. Say hello, please."

Mike ignored her. "The glasses belong on the other side of the plates."

"Little Miss Etiquette," Liam quipped.

"You always set the table wrong."

"Mike, introduce yourself, please." I tried to put as much iron in my voice as I could.

Mike knocked his water glass over, and Alice stood up to avoid getting water in her lap. Sue leaned over and fussed with a napkin. "Mike, be careful!"

"What's for dinner?"

"I think we'll say grace. Deacon, will you do the honors?"

Deacon Carroll bowed his head, and Mike shouted out, "I'm a Baptist."

Deacon Carroll's head came back up slowly, and his eyes went frosty until he looked again at the strained, thin, twitching little face. Smiling warmly, he said, "Mike, I know many Protestants—"

"I'm a *Baptist,*" Mike interrupted loudly.

The deacon patiently began again. "I know many Baptists, and they are all Christian folk, not shy about offering a blessing at meals, either. So won't you join us? We're all friends here."

Mike just looked back with a blank-eyed stare. Then he started to yell something else, but before he got one more word out his face went dead white and his eyes rolled back.

Alice was startled and put a hand on his shoulder in alarm, but the deacon just dashed a quick look at Liam and bowed his head. "Bless us, O Lord," he began.

When grace was over Sue whispered to me, "What happened?"

"I think Liam kicked him in the shins."

Sue's eyes opened wide, but she managed to smile winningly at Garrett and pass him the garlic bread.

Alice was still looking at Mike with concern. "Mike, I have a little boy just like you."

"No, you don't," he corrected her through clenched teeth.

A couple of long, argumentative, wearing days later, Joanne picked Mike up from school, took him to Burger King for a chat, and brought him home.

When we sat down for tea, Sue began with the issue of Mike's behavior. "I don't know which is worse—the first month of nonstop talking, or this new, nasty brat who picks apart or curses literally everything we say or do."

Joanne shrugged lightly. "It had to come—it always comes—and there's no way we could have prepared you for it. You have to look at the situation from his point of view. You've gone through a shakedown period, and now Mike has to begin relating to you. But he's interacted with literally hundreds of adults already—caseworkers, police, doctors, therapists, teachers, staff workers, foster mothers and fathers. Each one came into his

life, said what they believed to be true at the time, and then rotated away, never to be seen again. You and I had our parents,
our brothers and sisters, and maybe a couple of friends and
neighbors. A small group, maybe five to ten people, who stayed
with us all through childhood. You get to know and trust people that way, develop long-term relationships. These children
have never had that. All of Mike's experience says that you'll be
out of his life in a couple of months no matter what he does, no
matter how good he acts or how happy he is here. So you'll just
have to settle for what you've got right now. I'm sure you'll
work through it. Mike is smart—he'll come around."

Sue shook her head. We had begun with no grand strategy
regarding Mike, other than to treat him as our own child. But
when you bring a child you have not raised into your home
and transfer the very same expectations to him that you've had
of the kids with whom you've had years to establish some mu-
tual and very strong expectations about behavior, block by tiny
block, you're totally bumfoozled when he calls you a "fucking
bitch." You just don't know what to do—at least, the first time
around.

But Joanne put her hand up. "No, Sue, believe me. After a life
like that, they have to believe you're lying to them, want to believe you're not being totally honest. The alternative is to be disappointed, dropped back off an emotional cliff again. I see this
to a greater or lesser extent in all my kids."

Sue shook her head again. "I can see what you're saying—I
even agree with what you're saying—but I don't think it explains all of what's going on with him." She paused to grope for
the words. "This unwillingness to trust is too exaggerated—
almost comically exaggerated in him. Maybe everything is. When
he was talking at us, he didn't talk some of the time, he talked
all the time. When he was quiet, he was quiet all the time. Now,
when he's arguing, he isn't arguing some of the time, he's arguing all the time."

What was the point Sue was dancing around?

Before I could finish the thought, Joanne crossed her arms, put her elbows on the table, and announced, "I have to be frank. We're very worried about what you two did by enrolling him in that martial arts program. You should have discussed it with us first. Mike's not all that strong—he's almost frail. He's emotionally disturbed, and we're not sure this instructor knows how to deal with special-needs children."

Despite my initial misgivings, I had become a proponent of the training. At the very least, it seemed to promote discipline and respect, and Mike appeared to love it. He was certainly eager enough. Getting ready for the trip to karate school was about the only prompt he wasn't calling us on. Part of it, I was certain, was the ninjalike black uniform, but another aspect, perhaps more important, seemed to be the dynamics. It looked like Mike wanted to be part of a regular group of people. Still, I knew that if anybody from Harbour ever visited the school, they'd be appalled at the rigorous discipline, the almost servile ritual respect that had to be paid to the instructor, and the exposure to public ridicule. I shifted uncomfortably in my seat.

But that alone wasn't half of my discomfort because I could sense in the discussion to follow the seeds of insistence upon "resources."

Harbour's approach to adaptive and behavior-management issues within the child's new home was a formal extension of what we had done with our own children, rational and well thought out, and I particularly admired the detailed organization and follow-up involved. A series of meetings developed a written treatment plan that identified the most important areas of development for each child, and although I didn't recognize them at first, these areas were classified in a Medicaid terminology that allowed them to be billed for: Counseling Services (CS), Behavior Management Training (BMT), Health Services (HS), Daily Living Skills Training (DLST), and so on. Then the professional parents were required to address the various areas identified in this treatment plan twice a week, recording a narrative of the sessions that always included some comment about the child's response. All this was posted on a blocked-out form in the parents' "logs," which the family specialist collected at the end of the month.

In addition, The Harbour Program required parents to spend some minimum "positive" time with the child every day. This could be an outing, or just a few minutes working with the child in the kitchen. Parents had to record this experience in yet another form in the logs. Then parents were required to find some one thing to compliment the child on each day, such as doing his or her homework, acting responsibly, taking care of a pet, etc. This event also had to be recorded in a short narrative on the second form. Finally, the professional parents were required to assign a number from one to five, with one being the most positive and five the most negative for the day. This, too, was recorded on the second form.

It was a tedious and time-consuming procedure, but had the enormous benefit of reminding one of what one should be doing anyway, following up on areas within which the child needed help, trying to get a little positive experience into each day, and then tracking the progress.

But I had a completely different opinion of Harbour's second and backup procedure for using "resources," i.e., outside counseling and some additional form of rewards-based behavior modification.

So far, we had been able to avoid hooking Mike up with a therapist. We didn't know very much about the profession. None of our children or our friends or family had ever been in counseling, and it seemed a little too mushy for us, particularly when a number of other parents we met at Harbour's monthly meeting explained that, upon the advent of behavior which might displace a child, Harbour would involve a therapist or counselor who would more often than not establish a daily checklist of required behavior and insist that parents record each and every deviation. The idea was that all the deviations for a day would be summed up, and the child's privileges would be reduced or increased according to an established formula. For example, a child might be allocated one hour of TV time daily, and each check mark for a bad word would result in the subtraction of five minutes from that time. Certain scores might cancel an outing or provide a reward.

Adding or subtracting five-minute increments of TV time? Whose life was long enough for something like that? Besides, the technique seemed to undermine parental authority. The child was, in a very important manner, singled out from the family group to be rewarded or punished separately from other children. What did that have to do with being a family? What did it have to do with the parent being the source of discipline and direction?

I didn't want to argue with Joanne or The Harbour Program about this. I just wanted to keep Mike and ourselves away from any system like that.

So when I coupled these factors in my mind with the fact that Harbour's gentle approach bore about as much similarity to the boot camp operating up in the karate school as a garden hoe did to a bulldozer, I couldn't see how we, or rather Sue, could possibly bridge the gap.

It was accomplished with insouciance. She downplayed the entire issue and instead presented the karate class as a logical extension of Mike's treatment plan. Then she flourished a filled-out form from the karate school that listed short-term and long-term goals Mike had established for himself and written down under the instructor's supervision. They were grouped under various categories:

Goals to Strive For

Personal:

Short	Call the Dogs	Dec. 93
Long	Make Two Friends	April 94

Family:

Short	Write Letters	Nov. 93
Long	Plant a Garden	June 94

Work/School:

Short	Do Work on Time	Dec. 93
Long	Read Books	April 94

Inner Strength:

Short	See What I'm Afraid Of	Jan. 94
Long	Conquer It	July 94

Martial Arts:

Short	Stay Focused	Oct. 93
Long	Become a Black Belt	Oct. 98

Joanne studied the little document. "Well, I'm impressed and touched. But still, there's the issue of schoolwork. Won't his karate schedule interfere?"

Sue played her best card. "No, Rich and I reached an agreement with the instructor, and he discussed it in a one-on-one with Mike. Mike will have to produce his report cards from school, and if his marks fall, he'll have to forgo karate for the next quarter. In other words, he'll be earning his reward."

"I see."

But then Sue overplayed it. "And besides, many people feel there's a strong correlation between martial arts and academic performance; also, that it helps with his social skills. And the improved muscle tone might even contribute to less bed-wetting and better digestion."

Joanne looked Sue squarely in the eye. Sue knew, I knew, and now Joanne knew that she was being conned. But then a curious phenomenon kicked in.

Since that discussion about Mike and karate, I've seen social workers suborn the system when they're confronted by adults who act with good motives as advocates for "system" children. It's as if, having seen so much abuse and neglect, they're ready to excuse almost any action that has as its purpose the good of the child—even if they believe the adults are seriously misdirected, or that important guidelines are being ignored.

The best guy I ever worked for called this "giving meat to eagles," meaning that you break the rules in favor of somebody doing something, anything. But this wasn't manufacturing. It was social work. Social workers have more rules than anybody, and they're dealing with fragile lives. In the order of things, it takes a lot more guts.

I watched it happen as Joanne said, deep in thought, measuring the risks, "Before you do anything else like this on your own, you have to discuss it with us first."

"Oh, sure," Sue said quickly.

Afterward, I started to talk to Sue about the incident, but she quickly cut me off with, "Rich, karate is yesterday's news. We handled it. And that little tempest begs the real question of why Mike's acting the way he does now, and I never got out what I wanted to say to Joanne. There's a wrongness about Mike, and I don't mean emotionally. I mean he's out of focus or too focused." When she said "too focused," she smacked her hand on the table.

"I agree, I suppose. But we signed on the dotted line with Harbour—you agreed to play by their rules. Before we do anything else, we have to work it out with them."

Then she cleared her throat and I started to worry.

"Sue, are you starting something else?"

Long silence. Then she said, "I just can't take any more abuse.

I refuse to be told any longer by some sawed-off eleven-year-old that I'm lying, so I called Dr. Reis."

John Reis, a family practitioner, had been one of Sue's clients for a long time. Puzzled, I waited for what she was going to say next.

"When you feel the muscles in Mike's shoulder, they're as rigid as an iron bar. When you massage them, they loosen up and his facial tic disappears for a while. His voice tones down, too. He even loosens up a bit mentally and doesn't seem so argumentative."

Then she bit her lip and cut to the nub. "Mike's been on medication ever since he arrived and for years before that. Who really knows at this point what it's doing to him or what it's done to him already? I read what he was taking to John, and he said that there shouldn't be any adverse side effects if he stopped, and that the tic, the tension in his muscles, and his extreme behavior could at least partially be a result of the meds. I can accept the fact that he doesn't really believe anything we say—I'm sure Joanne is right about the whys and wherefores of that—but I'm sure that's not the whole reason he's such a Tasmanian devil. Something else keeps him at that low threshold—perhaps the same something that kept him acting like a suicidal spastic in the children's home. Maybe it's the drugs; maybe it isn't. I think we should see."

"Well, it's an interesting supposition," I said. But then I understood what she was really telling me, and I put my hand over my face. "When," I mumbled through my fingers, "did you stop his medication?"

CHAPTER SIX

trooping the autumn colors

Mike doesn't cry at night when the dogs are on his bed. When the whimpers begin, Teddy Bear or Pupsy nuzzles a snout under his arm, and he goes quiet.

I've seen it happen a dozen times by now, and it almost frightens me. It's as if the dogs know something we don't, or know how to do something we don't.

Sue said it one way when she was watching the three of them troop along outside her office window. "Somehow, they're on his page."

But I think of it differently. I feel the little beast that's riding Mike's back has a certain degree of malignant intelligence. It knows it can't win an argument with dogs, so it doesn't try.

Mike never tries to correct them. Whatever they want him to do is okay in his book. When he's outside with them and calls them, if they saunter off in a different direction, he changes direction and follows along. If they come with him when he calls, that's okay, too.

"Drug-free in ninety-three," Sue cracked as she dialed Joanne's office phone number.

"Sue," I protested.

"Relax, I'm doing it your way. We'll follow the rules, get a doctor to pull the medication."

"After the fact?"

"We'll get a doctor to pull the medication," she repeated.

Joanne answered the phone, and after about two minutes of chat, Sue told her she was worried about Mike's physical condition.

"He's not eating right."

"No?" Joanne responded.

"No. The children's home wanted to get him to a nutritionist and I pooh-poohed the idea. But now I wonder if we shouldn't get him to see a doctor and see what he thinks."

"Well, sure," Joanne said doubtfully, "but he is scheduled to see Dr. Jacobsen."

Dr. Jacobsen is the psychiatrist with the Mental Health Association.

"Yes," said Sue, "but that's not for three weeks, and we do need a family doctor for him—someone we can call if he gets sick. No family doctor will see him on short notice unless he's already examined him. So maybe we should kill two birds with one stone—get him a family doctor and see if the practitioner wants to recommend a nutritionist."

"Okay."

With her token team effort out of the way, Sue shopped around for a family physician. Not so easy. If you're on Medicaid, it seems, the government's health care system wants you to go to a clinic in a city. At least that's what Sue came to believe when she found out most of the doctors in rural practice—those in Ulster County, for example—won't touch Medicaid.

But she did find three in the next county down. The first one was an aged, upright GP named O'Mara living way back in Pine Bush.

The morning of the appointment Sue laid out a silk blouse,

burgundy business suit, ivory jewelry, long black leather coat, and high heels. After all those years she spent in suits and dresses and high heels, Sue delights in dressing down, working away at her big executive desk in jeans and a sweatshirt, floppy old slippers, and a thick sweater. But today she wanted to make an impression.

Still, she didn't get off to a good start with this old fellow. Mike made an epic scene in the doctor's examining room, talking wildly and loudly about his real mother, his brother and sister who were living in a different family, shouting about Rockland State Psychiatric Hospital. And, of course, correcting everything the doctor had to say. Just generally acting like a nut.

And the way Sue was dressed had the opposite effect she intended.

The doctor almost sneered at her as he fingered the Medicaid card. "Miss Miniter, just how many children do you have?"

"Six others."

"I don't suppose, of course, that Michael's father is still in the picture?"

"No," said Sue, puzzled.

"I didn't think so. Now, are the rest of your children normal? Are there any other full siblings?"

"Huh?"

"How many different fathers did your children have?"

"What!"

"I asked, how many fathers?"

Sue exploded, "I heard what you said. I just can't believe you asked that—and it's *Mrs.* Miniter. I've been married twenty-seven years to the same man. *All* of my children have had the same father!"

Now the doctor looked confused and extremely embarrassed. "Then, what is Mike? He has a different last name."

"Mike is a foster child. Who did you think he was?"

The doctor was taken aback. The only thing he could think

of to say was even more stupidly awkward. "You don't look like a foster mother."

Sue's eyes went blank and hard, her pupils little black arrow-heads. "And just what does a foster mother look like?"

"Mrs. Miniter, Mike is severely disturbed. I don't know you—I've never seen you or Mike before. I thought he came from a badly confused family situation, and I wanted to see if there were any other full brothers or sisters who had any history of emotional problems."

"Well, look," Sue said, trying to calm down and remember what she was there for, "Mike's not having the best day. That's true. But what I want to know is, how is he physically?"

The doctor huffed a little bit. "I don't have his medical records, and I haven't done any workups, but he appears fine—maybe a little too thin. Is that why you're here—just that?"

"No," said Sue, trying to force a smile. She extracted a form from her pocketbook. "He was released from the children's home close to two months ago, and the physician there had prescribed some medication."

She handed over the page from Mike's file.

Dr. O'Mara read it and said, "Oh, yes, I see. You want a new prescription."

"No," said Sue again, "Dr. John Reis in Kingston suggested we wean him off; that perhaps a lot of his muscle tension and maybe his facial tic will ameliorate; that perhaps, at the least, we could establish a baseline for new dosages if we got him off it for a while."

"Oh, I know John," Dr. O'Mara said. Then he looked sharply at Sue. "Did Dr. Reis examine him?"

This was the crucial point of the talk, as far as Sue was concerned, but she was ready. "He consulted as a professional courtesy. But his practice doesn't take Medicaid patients, and Kingston is a long way. He suggested we develop a relationship with a local physician who'd be in a better position to keep an eye on things."

Dr. O'Mara opened his mouth as if to speak, looked at the paper again, back up at Sue, smiling confidently, and then back at the paper. "Yes, of course, now I understand. Well, if that's what John wants to do, I don't have any problem in going that route. Why not start immediately, then—in fact, right now? Make an appointment with me for next week or the week after, and we'll see what changes, if any, crop up."

"Are you sure?" she asked innocently.

"Oh, absolutely. John knows his stuff. God knows—" and here he laughed gruffly, still embarrassed "—the boy's behavior couldn't be much worse."

"Doctor, one other thing: Would you recommend a nutritionist at this time?"

"Well, no," the doctor said. "Let's wait and see if the boy gains weight."

"Thank you."

On the way out the doctor took Sue's arm. "I apologize for the earlier misunderstanding, Mrs. Miniter. This is a wonderful thing you're doing. God bless you."

"That's very kind of you, Doctor."

When she got home, she canceled the appointments with the next two doctors on her list.

If Richard Nixon had had Sue for a chief of staff, he might have served two full terms. Maybe three or four.

A few days after the doctor's appointment, Mike was sitting quietly in the barroom when Sue and I traipsed down to start dinner.

We stood there for a long moment and looked at him. The set of his thin little shoulders was much different—loosened, slack somehow—and his facial tic seemed to be gone. But he looked whipped and tired, defeated.

He saw us there out of the corner of his eye. "Did you ever send any of them back for being bad?" he asked in a low, conversational tone of voice. No anger; no biting, accusatory tone of voice; no cursing. That barbed edge to him had disappeared. But his head was down, and he was fidgeting with his fingers.

Sue answered with a question. "Any of who, Mike?"

You could see he was trying to force his thoughts down a certain path. "Richard, Henry, Frank, Brendan, or Liam."

Sue was genuinely puzzled. "Send them back where?" she asked.

"Back to the foster-children people."

Sue's back got very straight, and she slowly sat down next to him. Her hand reached out to his shoulder, stopped, and then withdrew. "Mike, the boys aren't foster children. You knew that, didn't you?"

A shrug of those tiny, thin shoulders. "No—uh, yes—I guess so."

"Mike."

"Yes."

"Why did you ask that?"

A long pause. Then, "When I first came here, Henry, Frank, and Brendan were here, but then they had to pack their bags and leave."

Sue looked up at me, but I just shrugged. I didn't know what to say.

Finally, Sue did reach out and touch him. "Mike, we'd never send you back. When you're older, you have to go to college. That's where the boys went. They'll be back for Thanksgiving and Christmas." She shook him gently. "Mike, we'd never send you back. We chose you, and you chose us."

Silence.

I said, "Look, Mike, Brendan is at George Mason in Virginia, and Frank and Henry are at Norwich."

More silence.

Sue said, "We weren't going to say anything; we wanted to see how you were acting. But you've really calmed down over the last couple of days, and now we can tell you. Next week you'll come to Vermont with us for a long weekend. You're going to get to see Norwich when the leaves are out."

Mike looked up at her with wary interest, followed suddenly by blooming suspicion. His eyes narrowed, and for the first time since we'd been speaking his head twitched.

"Do they ever keep kids up at Norwich? Kids who've been bad?"

"Mike, this is only a visit. It'll be a minivacation for the three of us. We'll be back here, all of us, three days later."

"They keep kids up there?"

"Men," I said quietly. "No kids, Mike. There are only men at Norwich."

He didn't believe us.

Our son Henry once said about Norwich, "This is my place," and indeed, now that he's graduated, it's hard to think of the school without him there.

In fact, it's hard now to picture the family as it was before its having touched Norwich and come away colored by gold and crimson and cadet gray, autumn leaves, bright October air, company banners, drums and guns, and sons on the old tree-shaded upper parade ground.

There was a time when we thought some of our boys were dropping off life's map. Richard, our eldest, was always an academic. Susanne, as well—she spent her teens, when she wasn't candy-striping at the hospital, in her room studying. But Henry and Frank, the next two along, were a despair during high school. In fact, I think they stayed the course only because they knew Sue and I would poison their morning cereal if they dropped out. Both of them severely abused our hands-off style of parenting by swimming down to the bottom of their class and then staying there, holding their breath, for four years. If sixty-five was passing in a subject, they'd meticulously come in with a sixty-six. If the bottom line was seventy, they'd produce a seventy-one. If their interest in academics was anything above zero, it was so small it required electron microscopy to measure.

Sue and I were so upset by this attitude that we'd violate our own rules and rant and rave when the report cards came in the mail. But it was like shouting down a well. Occasionally you hear a little echo back, but most of the time, whatever you have to say just disappears into a hole in the ground.

What Henry and Frank were interested in was hunting and fishing. When they should have been reading Melville, they were studying the latest edition of *American Hunter* or *Field and Stream*. Instead of practicing math, they were practicing turkey calls or tracking techniques or how to lie still under a pile of wet leaves for four or five hours. As far as I can remember, during their entire career in high school, the only test they ever scored a hundred on was the New York State hunter safety training course exam.

"These guys," I said to Sue on more than one occasion, "are headed for a life of pumping gas and driving blown-out pickup trucks."

But in truth I should have had much more confidence in the two of them than I did. Because when high school was over, one after the other seemed to shrug as if to say, "Okay, that's over," dust themselves off, and decide to get serious about the rest of their lives.

Henry came to me first. It was February 1990. "Dad, I've decided where I want to go to college."

"College?" I wanted to scream. "You just spent four years dragging one wing with your head under the other! How do you expect to handle college?"

But instead I asked, "What do you have in mind?"

Henry looked back at me, deadpan. "I want you to drive me up to Norwich for their open house. I'm ninety percent sure it's where I'll be going."

"Norwich?" I asked. "What's Norwich?"

"I'll show you," he said.

One hundred seventy-five years old, the university looms like a stone-and-brick fortress on a hill ten miles south of Montpelier, Vermont. For most of its history Norwich has sent cavalry and, later, armored officers into the army, but in recent years many graduates have chosen to become marine, navy, and air force officers, as well. A small school with perhaps a thousand cadets, it prides itself on intense undergraduate education. Not particularly difficult academically to get into, it is extremely difficult to stay with. Every student must apply to the self-governing corps of cadets, and although there is a regular army commandant, the cadet officers and NCOs exact a rigorous fee in discipline, training, and submission. The first term is called Rookdom, and in some years, in some companies, a huge percentage of the incoming freshmen give up before Recognition Day, a day never announced in advance, at which the cadet colonel signals the fact that the rest of the corps has finally recognized the freshmen arrivals as members.

By 1993 both Henry, a senior, and Frank, a second-year man, were there, and as always, we were determined to get up for parents' weekend in mid-October.

But this year was low-key. Only Sue, Mike, and I would be making the long drive.

The year before, almost everybody had gone—Richard and his girlfriend came up from Washington, Susanne came, plus Liam, Sue, and I. We rented a nine-passenger van. It was raining, great sheets of cold spray flogging in and out of the valleys, and we were late. But we rushed up the slick granite steps to the upper parade ground just in time to see a shimmering vision out of the last century. The corps of cadets was standing at attention in the sheeting cold rain, rank after rank, company after serried gray company, coming in and out of view as the autumn squall gusted through, a silent sea of wet flags, drawn swords, officers in front, the dressed files of men as motionless as stone, patiently, rigidly soaking in their high-collared gray tunics, waiting for the drums to strike. Then, just as if those thousand men were waiting for us to crouch down into place under our umbrellas, the drums thundered down and they stepped off.

We never could pick our sons out as they swung by. We marked the company flags, but the ranks looked all the same—shaved heads, strict gray uniforms, all the cadets with the crossed cavalry sabers on their collars marching eyes front. The boys materialized later, momentarily strangers; eyes hidden under the brim of their covers, tan and trim and fit, Henry with the broad stripes of a cadet sergeant on his sleeves, Frank slim and smiling in his cocky way.

I was determined that Mike see that—not with the eyes of an overweening parent, of course, but as someone not all that far apart in age from Henry and Frank, who might begin to understand that there is a certain progression in life. That from the house he is living in now, can come boys whom drums can be beaten about.

This year the three of us crossed the Vermont line in the early morning and three hours later checked into our usual B & B in Bethel, Vermont. We had called the owner earlier and explained Mike's problem with bed-wetting. He said not to worry, we were old customers; just bring a rubber mattress cover, and they wouldn't have any problem stripping the bed.

But Mike was nervous about his room assignment. While we

were unpacking, he kept walking from his room through the double connecting doors into our room. The facial tic was back and he was stuttering.

"I can sleep in there."

"Of course you can, Mike. Besides, it's got twin beds, and Frank will be sharing it with you. We're bringing him out for dinner and to spend at least one night away from the school."

Those eyes again. We're lying to him, they're saying. "Can I stay here when you go to Norwich?"

"No, honey. They don't allow children to stay by themselves all day. You have to trust us. Norwich is the boys' school. We are just going to visit."

His face twitched. Now there was anger there, as well as resignation.

Sue bent over and looked him full in the face. "Mike, we never lie to you. We will never lie to you. I don't care what happened in the past. Rich and I will never, ever lie to you about anything. You—" and she poked him in the chest "—are coming back home with us."

He turned his back and walked through the doors.

Sue looked at me helplessly. "He still doesn't believe anything we say."

I shrugged. "Remember what Joanne said."

We were back up on the upper parade ground, and the corps was mustering on the grass.

Mike had gotten out of the car with his head down, but perked up when we started up the endless stone steps. He saw the uniforms, watched the tick, tick, of the drums keeping step as the band took its place.

His first words: "This isn't a school."

"Yes, it is."

"No, it's not. It's an army man place."

"It's that and a school, Mike. We'll see Frank and Henry after the parade."

Silence.

"It's not a children's home, is it, Mike?"

More silence.

"We don't lie to you about anything, Mike."

Silence.

Mike and I walked together up the little grassy knoll by the Band Company, where we had a good view. Sue stayed on the steps in front of Jackman Hall. Close by us was the saluting battery of 76-mm howitzers. Mike kept looking at the guns, and then finally wandered over close to them.

"Mike, come back here. When those guns go off, you'll get knocked over."

Mike looked at me and then back at the guns.

He almost sneered. "They're not real. There's no way they are going to shoot those."

"Mike, I'm not lying to you, and those guns are real. They'll knock you over."

"No."

"Mike, I will never lie to you."

He turned his back and walked closer.

I heard the bass drum out on the parade ground begin to boom and the battery came to attention. The number-one cadet gun captain looked back over his shoulder at Mike and then up at me with a gesture of his chin.

I looked at Mike's thin, defiant little back and all of a sudden felt really sorry for him. Defiance, after all, was the only thing he had. I felt something else, too—something perhaps prompted by the two of us being alone among all these strangers on this sunny day and then added to by the image of other boys out on the parade ground preparing to march off to life. I was starting to care about the skinny little drink of water—I was beginning to feel like a dad.

But parenthood has worn me down. When you're new to being a father, it's easy to wax hard and academic about teaching your children the tough lessons, to sit back and let them take a chance on being hurt. It's easy then, when you haven't seen all that many real tears, to stay convinced that you're doing the right thing by letting them go. Mike needed a lesson, a big lesson. I just wasn't all that certain I had the stomach for it.

I heard Sue calling me; she had seen Mike.

But somehow the decision made itself, and I waved my hand at the gun captain. "Leave him there."

I saw Sue start across to get him, and I tried to will her back into the crowd. "For God's sake, let him see I was telling the truth."

She didn't have enough time.

The battery commander did a right face and saluted. Number-one gun captain barked a command, and the gun went off.

Mike was knocked off his feet and rolled back. He tried to scramble back off when number two went off, then number three.

Then he found his feet and ran back over to me, exuberant, laughing tears down his face. "I can take that."

"Mike, did I tell you the truth?"

"Yes, you did! Yes, you did!" he yelled.

Moonlight in Vermont. Sunday night and we were sweeping through the small, palely lit towns along State Route 12, almost ready to make the sharp turn east, down the mountain on Route 4, to Rutland.

I could still hear the drums and bugles. See Henry with the strut of a senior, see Frank lithe and professional, dressed in the open white shirt and gray trousers of the summer undress uniform, on assignment with the school paper, photographing; dragging us from the soccer game to rugby to football to the Marine Corps Eighth and I drill team. We had dinner in Montpelier, walked the "hill," took a couple dozen pictures of ourselves. Mike got lost in the football stadium. He followed a man with a dog, played on a tank, and then lay down in the grass, watching the ceremonial Civil War battery of brass Napoleon cannon, hoping for a Norwich touchdown so they would go off. Frantic, we found him there, still waiting long after Norwich had lost.

Now he was asleep in the backseat of the car, bundled into an army ranger sweatshirt and nested down into a blanket.

"Well," I continued an argument from the day before, "all the rest of the weekend he didn't tell us we were lying about anything."

"You could have ruptured his eardrums."

"He was well rear of the muzzle blast," I grumbled, "and anyway, they were saluting charges, not a big deal. It wasn't like he was standing atop a one-five-five."

Sue put her seat back and stretched. "Whatever the heck a one-five-five is. Next time, let's discuss it before you stampede off and make a decision on your own."

"Oh, sure," I said with a smile, thinking about Mike's medication.

CHAPTER SEVEN

i don't do work

I quickly sat and smiled across the dinner table, but then was forced into a long look back. Mike's death's-head mask had vanished! No medication, round-the-clock food, and running with the dogs in the crisp air had finally worked their way onto his face. The thin, sallow-white elf of three months ago was now sprouting round, red apple-frosted cheeks, and his eyes rested much more comfortably in his face—they weren't glittery, angrily pasted on any longer.

There were other changes, too. He had started drifting off with the dogs, away from us, away from the grounds for short periods, and had begun using the possessive *our* when speaking of the place. He was even relaxing around me to the point where we could read together at night, the Hardy Boys and Stevenson's *Kidnapped,* and I enjoyed both his marvelous diction and the way he easily accepted direction in pronunciation and usage, often repeating a word or a phrase over and over again, trying to get it right.

Yet over the past few weeks the jagged edges of Mike's personality were also beginning to emerge, like the outline of a strange fish being pulled closer and closer to shore. Mike, we had now begun to understand, was a darkling. First of all, he was relentlessly moody. His attitude and, in our imagination, almost the set of his body or the color of his hair could change, flickering from sunny and smiling into a grainy, angry little gray presence in an instant. When he did that, his language was filthy and unbelievably antagonistic. He also seemed determined to keep wetting his bed and was still absolutely, even morbidly, terrified of the dark.

Although we could live with issues like bed-wetting for the time being and put aside his fear of the dark in the reasonable hope it could be addressed in the future, his thought processes continued to jangle our nerves. Mike was extremely difficult to reason with, often insisting he knew things he didn't, and when he was contradicted, his voice got loud again.

But all that aside, I was really pleased with how he looked now, and so I grinned back over the table. "You look good, you little rodent."

He didn't laugh.

I shrugged, "Ah, be grumpy," then winked at Sue.

It was sunset, the barroom hushed and quiet, and all the guests were away visiting or working. There was nobody else in the place except Sue, Mike, and me. On the table was roast chicken, rice, and peas, of course (Sue has it cast in bronze: if you have rice, you must serve peas).

Then the phone in the kitchen rang, and I got up to answer it. A few minutes later I came back inside and saw that Sue was absorbed in a tax publication open on the table next to her, while Mike was almost finished.

"I want more rice and peas."

"Sure, honey," Sue said without even looking up.

Clatter, clatter, scrape, scrape, as more peas and rice hit his plate and then, before I had even taken two mouthfuls myself, they were gone, too, and Mike had pushed back his chair.

"Mike," Sue smiled at him.

"What?"

"If you're leaving the table, please take your plate, silverware, and glass into the kitchen on the way out."

He sulked. "I have to watch my TV program. You said I could."

"Sure, Mike, but you can take half a minute and clean up your place. And I asked you to bring your sheets down to the laundry room this morning—I don't think you ever did that."

"That was this morning. That's over," Mike pouted.

"Mike, please do what I asked."

Later, I looked up from the *National Geographic* I was reading to listen to Sue express concern about Mike's "regression"—his morning routine had started getting worse, and he got surly when asked to do the slightest thing.

"Rich, think about it," Sue said as she patted the table. "What are we really teaching him about a family? You see how he thinks that issues like his sheets just disappear by themselves. He believes any problem at all is magically solved after thirty minutes have passed, just like a TV sitcom. So we've got to bust up this image and let him put one back together from the real world. Real families work, earn, learn, do together. People have to work for their place in a family, and we have to give him some sense of that."

"Okay, but is there some rush?"

"In a few weeks all the boys will be home for Thanksgiving vacation, and you know how they are. Up till now he's had a nice quiet time of it, with just us and the guests coming and going. But after they arrive, his world's going to turn upside down. The place will be packed and noisy, and he's going to get pushed out of the way."

"It should be good for him."

Sue bobbed her head. "Yes, but he's going to have to compete for our attention, and we're not going to have time to keep following up on him. I'm not sure he can handle all that at once the way he is now, and if he lashes out with some of his institutional language, the boys are going to bounce him off a wall before you can raise a hand."

"They wouldn't do that."

Sue just looked at me out of the corner of her right eye and then continued: "Before he gets threatened by their arrival, I want him to have some sense of the fact that he's earned a secure place here. It's time to get in his face and show him how a real family operates. And besides, I'm getting sick of this little guy not demonstrating any responsibility at all."

"Uh, you lost me."

"Chores."

Mike resists a shower, his underpants are as often as not soiled badly, and he makes an indescribable mess in the bathroom.

"You have to go in there with him when he's doing his business," Sue pointed out. "Treat him like he's two years old."

I tried to dodge. "Uh, you spend most of the time with him. You have the better relationship. I think it would come better from you—and besides, isn't this part of your chore thing?"

"He's male, and he's way, way too old."

"I'll talk to him."

"Rich, you have to go in there and keep going in there until he acts much better. In a couple of weeks we'll have a crowd here, and I will not be embarrassed by this."

That afternoon I followed Mike into the bathroom. How to begin the discussion?

"Mike."

"Yes?"

"This white stuff over here is toilet paper . . ."

"I don't do work."

"Mike," Sue was explaining, "part of being a family is pitching in on what has to be done. You see Rich cleaning and you see me picking up. Now, go carry the garbage up to the Dumpster, please."

Mike's mouth was clenched, and there were stones rubbing together behind his eyes. He stood defiantly still in the middle of the kitchen floor. "I don't do work."

"Mike, here, give me your hand. Carry this bag up to the Dumpster."

"I don't do work."

"Mike. All my boys did chores!"

"I hate those boys. I hate this fucking family. I want to go to a good family."

"Go to your room and think about your language."

Slam, slam, bang, bang, as he kicked his way through all the doors, into his room.

A wet, cold wind was snooping through the orchard blocks, and leaves that had been a sea of gold and orange across the hay meadow two weeks ago were now dun and faded, dropping off to stir into long, brown windrows pointing south.

Deer season and Thanksgiving.

Except for Richard, who was still strafing the West Coast, all the boys were packing up and putting their schedules in order: Frank and Henry would drive down together from Norwich, Brendan alone up from George Mason, Liam and my son-in-law David would block out their time, and just before Thanksgiving holiday my niece Kathryn and her husband Matt would come up. Six of them—seven, counting me, in the days I got moving. They'd be out together every daylight hour, high up on Shawangunk, that miles-long, wild, ancient ridge knuckling up south-southeast out of Ulster County.

Shawangunk in late autumn has a nostalgic and magical attraction for the boys. It is, after all, where they were raised. Morgan

Valley, Turkey Valley, Bonticue Crag, the Bear Cave, abandoned farmsteads high up with tumbledown stone walls snaking through clusters of ancient hemlock walking up out of the hollows, landmarks like the telephone right-of-way, the logging roads, Margaret's Rock, the Hidden Oak. Along the twisting game trails are old deer stands that have names like the Camp, the Tepee, Bill Carroll's Stand, Frank's, the Ambush Ledge, the Owl Rock.

But all of that meant nothing to Mike, and I was afraid Sue was right about how the boys might react if he started one of his scenes.

I mentioned our concern to Joanne.

"Hey," she smiled, "I've met your boys; they're all gentlemen."

"Uhhh," I weaseled, "the way they talk to a lady and the way they can treat each other are two very, very different things."

But she dismissed it. "Brothers are brothers," she said.

In any event, we were stocking the bar, laying in food, and cleaning the rooms. And although in odd moments I was beginning to hear Sue recite her litany of complaints about our sons and their hunting over this holiday—"They better get off that mountain on time for dinner this year or I'll never cook a turkey again," or "God forbid they ever sit down and talk to their mother, always hanging around at night in muddy boots, laughing like idiots," or "If Henry comes in here this year and leans a gun up against my table while he's eating, I'm going to learn to shoot a rifle myself"—she was baking pies, and when she wasn't needling Mike into picking up a broom, she'd turn to me and smile. "My boys are coming home."

A day or two later, just after dinnertime, Sue called me.

"Rich, find Mike. I have something for him to do, and now he's disappeared. In fact, he's been doing that a lot in the last couple of days."

He was not in the house, so I walked out back.

It was late afternoon, the shadows long and lengthening when I saw him moving—stumbling, really—through the sedge far out across the back of the field. The first feeling I had was about how alone and lonely he looked way out there, just him and the dogs. No friends, no brothers around, suddenly fighting with Sue for some reason perhaps beyond his comprehension.

My next thought was that Mike had injured himself, because he was tripping over his feet with his back stiff, his arms down straight at his sides, as the two dogs broke around him in the brush.

When I looked closer yet, I saw that Mike was purposefully walking with his face pointed straight up into the air to watch a red-tailed hawk circling far above the three of them.

I chuckled. Whatever other confusing, sad baggage he carried, right now his thoughts were somewhere far different. I had often asked myself the same question he was perplexed with now. "How does a hawk keep flying without once flapping its wings?" This hawk was slipping through the air in a vast, smooth ellipse and then every so often giving a lazy flip of a wingtip to reverse direction and sail higher into the light.

As I stood there, Mike stumbled across the entire field and into the higher brush around the beaver pond. The two dogs stopped outside the pond area, took a long look at me standing there, hundreds of yards away, and then, when I didn't move, woofed in after him.

Sue called me from the back door. "Rich, did you find him?"

"Sort of."

"I don't do work."

Sue and Mike were in the living room as I walked by.

"Mike, you live here, so get the vacuum cleaner going."

"I don't do work."

I walked in, and Mike looked at me as if I could explain this one simple point to Sue. "Rich," he said, "I don't do work." Then he picked up the remote control and turned the TV back on.

Sue reached down to the set and turned it off.

"Damn." Mike slammed the remote down on the coffee table. "I don't do work."

"You're part of this family; you'll lend a hand. No TV until you get the living room and the hallways vacuumed."

Mike kicked the vacuum cleaner. "I don't do work."

Sue raised her voice. "You kick my vacuum cleaner again and it'll be the whole week without TV."

"I don't do work. I hate this fucking family. I wish they'd put me in a real family."

Sue still had her voice up. "What you see on TV are not real families. Real families have to do something together about keeping the place clean."

"Damn," Mike shouted again, but he picked up the vacuum cleaner hose and turned the machine on.

Later on in our room, I made a crack about how much fun she seemed to be having with Mike's chore program, but she wasn't amused. Instead, she just lay back on the bed and stared at the ceiling. Scattered around her on the covers were Harbour's log sheets and forms to be completed. Things were piling up on her. She was still getting ready for Thanksgiving, her office was a disaster as she prepared to upgrade her computer system for the coming tax season, and the conflict with Mike was eroding whatever bounce there was left. She looked too whipped to sleep. Tomorrow would be Joanne's weekly visit, which meant Sue would have to stop work for an hour or so, and I knew that with her office still torn apart, that would drive her nuts, too.

Sue is a complex person, inclined to burn the candle at both ends, half believing that if she wasn't getting everything done right now she was failing somehow. "I don't have enough time" is a constant complaint, but then she is forever adding something else to her pile, and while she somehow gets it all accomplished, she often exudes tension when we are alone together. But there is another side to her as well, and you see it whenever a client walks into her office. *Here is a close friend of mine who needs my help,* you can see her thinking, and whatever stress she's under vanishes in an instant as she focuses her entire attention on that one person. And it isn't an act. Sue is genuinely interested in people, in the details of their lives, in what their children are doing, in how their parents are or what they have planned for the upcoming year, but most particularly, in what she can do for them.

I was troubled that Mike would be seeing less and less of this right side of her; that instead he was calling up the brusque, dispassionate "get it done now" persona by mindlessly fighting each step of her program. It looked like this saw-toothed half-pint would never understand that he could get anything he wanted, do virtually anything he wanted, if he would just say *yes* and give her a hug once in a great while; if he would just once walk into her office and say, "I have a problem, can you help me?"

I started picking the sheets of paper up off the bed.

"What are you doing, Rich?"

"I'll do the logs from now on, Sue."

"You have to keep up with them every day, or else it gets away from you."

"I know."

Mike never had any friends to the house until the day he announced that Greg in his class had asked to come over.

"Great," Sue said. "It'll be a nice break for both of us. Give me his phone number, and I'll talk to his mother. Maybe he can come over and play with you on Saturday?"

Mike shook his head. "I've already talked to him."

Sue sat down and took his hand. "Mike, before someone comes over for the day, parents should talk. Who is driving who when, is he eating dinner here, what time does he have to be back, things like that."

"His father is bringing him over."

Sue shook her head. "No, Mike, I'm sorry. I have to talk to his parents first, and I'm sure his parents would want to talk to us first, too."

"No," Mike said, answering Sue's last statement.

"Believe me, Mike, Greg's parents will want to talk to us."

"No, Greg always visits friends. His parents never talk to people."

Sue stood and put her hands up. "That's not the way it's done, Mike. I'm sorry, but before he can come over I'll have to talk to his parents."

"Damn, I hate this fucking family." Then slam, slam, bang, bang, as he headed off toward his room.

Sue said to me, "He doesn't understand interaction—that people have to organize things."

A half hour later Mike came up to me as I was painting the foyer and said sweetly, "Rich, Greg's father is on the phone. He wants to talk to you about Greg coming over to play with me."

"Oh, so now you want us to arrange things?"

"You have to! You have to!"

"Okay."

My ears ached after Greg had spent the day with us. The child was bright, but unbelievably hyper. You had to watch him every last minute, or he'd be turning on the gas at the stove, poking one of the dogs until it snarled, running around upstairs where the guests were, and screaming at the top of his lungs.

His father dropped him off with his medication and specific instructions on what worked best in getting it into him.

Medication? If this was what he was like drugged, I didn't want to be in the same county when he sobered up.

The next day I asked Mike, in an offhand kind of way, "Do you have any other friends at your school?"

"No. Greg is my best friend."

The siege had been ongoing—day in, day out, nonstop—for the past two weeks.

"I don't do work."

"Mike, it's your turn to help with the dishes."

"I don't do work."

"Mike: dishes—now."

"I'm a slave in this family. I'm going to call Joanne and tell her to take me away to a good family."

"There's the phone."

"Why are you doing this to me?"

"Because I love you."

"Damn, I hate this family."

"Go to your room and think about your language. I'll get you later to do the dishes."

Slam, slam, bang, bang.

I asked mildly, "Why did you send him to his room?"

"Because he said 'fucking family.' "

"No, he didn't. This time he skipped the F word."

"Are you sure?"

"Absolutely."

"Ah," and she grinned.

Out of such little things one draws hope.

•   •   •

But the next day when Sue called him, he went into his and Liam's room and smashed everything that belonged to him—his clock radio, his lamp, his puzzle, his pictures. He broke nothing of Liam's—only his own possessions.

"Mike," Sue asked him, appalled and almost in tears, "why did you do that?"

"It's mine."

"It's not acceptable in this house to break things, even if they do belong to you."

Mike's face was flushed and his eyebrows seemed to swell and hood his eyes. "What are you going to do about it?"

"I'm going to get you started on your chores."

"Damn, I hate this fucking family."

"Follow me, and we'll find the vacuum cleaner."

Mike stamped his foot and screamed, "I had a bad childhood."

Sue walked over to him, and he flinched back as if he felt he was going to be hit. "Don't you ever, ever," she hissed, "pull a poor-orphan act on me. That was then, this is now, and besides, people have been coddling you, standing up for you, feeding you, clothing you, worrying about you, ever since you were taken out of your home. Now it's time to start walking forward on your own."

"I don't do work."

"Oh, yes you do."

"I did have a bad childhood."

"I couldn't care less."

Sue had started calling the children's home once a week and speaking to Kathy. "It may just be," Kathy had just told her, "that the honeymoon is over and you're getting a new crop up out of those awful roots. So be careful. I know you guys are experienced parents, but you might be confronted with something totally beyond your experience. Still, despite everything, Mike might be open to some sort of responsibility. He's never gained that sort of weight before, and he's never been off meds. The one big thing to remember is that regardless of what he might say, his own image of himself is the most important possession he has. Somehow, not getting involved is tied up in that. Maybe that allows him to feel independent, more in control, less like a castaway, less like a foster child? I don't know."

Later, Sue repeated Kathy's remarks to me. "There's something there," she said, poking her forehead with her index finger. "Something I'm missing."

We were into Stevenson's *Kidnapped* at night, just before bedtime. Mike would read one page, I the next, and so on. Mike was laughing over the old Scottish word *lug,* which meant "ear."

"I really like that," he chuckled, pulling at his own ear.

"Mike," I said, putting the book down for a moment, "what else is it you like?"

"Huh?"

"What sort of things do you like?"

"Nothing."

"You like root beer, don't you?"

"Yes."

"Well, what else do you like?"

"What do *you* like?"

"Mmmm," I thought, "well, I like red dump trucks, old barns, stone walls, a good book. I like baked macaroni with cheddar cheese. I like a lot of things. What do you like?"

His features worked themselves up in a caricature of a thoughtful little woodchuck. "I really don't like anything."

"You play your cards close to the chest, don't you?"

"What does that mean?"

"It means you don't like to tell anybody what you're feeling."
Silence.
"Well, is that true, Mike?"
"Yes."

"Mike, you have to do some vacuuming before dinner."
"Whatever."
"Mike."
"Damn. I'm a slave in this family."
"Mike."
"Whatever."
"Mike, get up."
"You're not my boss."
"Get up, short stuff."
"Damn."
"Don't you dare kick that vacuum cleaner."

The more Sue pushed Mike to lend a hand, the more Mike would retreat into the TV. At first we were ambivalent, and knowing how his TV time was restricted in the children's home, we allowed him free access after dark, before bed. But now we were starting to screw down on it.

"Mike," I said, "you shouldn't just run upstairs after dinner and turn the TV on. You have to help clean up. Now, go see Sue. She's waiting for you."
Silence.
"Mike."
"Damn, I can't even watch my show."
"Mike. Come on, the boys will be home any day, and Sue is trying to get things ready."
"Damn, if those sons come in here, I am going to kill my-

self." And he slammed down the remote control on the coffee table. Pieces of it flew across the room.

For just a fraction of an instant Mike looked frightened. Then he recovered. "I don't care. I don't do work. I want to go to a good family. I'm going to hurt myself."

CHAPTER EIGHT

i can help

Phyllis had left. Lots of smiles and protestations about Mike not bothering her, but we knew.

"We're down to having half the rooms empty," Sue told me, shocked, "and Louis was only going to be here for a couple of months to begin with, so he'll be out in a few weeks."

"Four rooms open," I answered back slowly. "I don't even feel like making coffee and tea any longer. There's just one or two people showing up downstairs."

Sue flopped back on the couch, and for a moment her defenses were down and so was the chain mail armor. I could hear it in the quiet texture of her voice—a relaxed and oddly confused Sue, who seemed to be wondering how things could turn out this way. "We depend on that income."

I shrugged. "This is supposed to be a quiet place, but Mike's screaming or fighting half the time." I was thinking that I had meant it about dropping the coffee and tea in the morning. Up until a few months ago, I had enjoyed the early routine—getting up at five or five-thirty, straightening up the barroom and kitchen, making a couple of pots of fresh coffee, putting hot water on, baking muffins. The guests would start trickling down around six, and within a half hour we'd all be chattering together around the big table in the barroom. A good gang who enjoyed each other—Rick, Phyllis, Ralph, Theresa, and others who came and went for short periods—getting ready for work or school, bantering, watching the news, going outside to warm up the car, and then dashing in for a cup of hot chocolate to go and a shouted good-bye. Sue would usually come downstairs, too, sleepy and tousle-headed, starting her day wanting to touch base, listen to a couple of stories, and joke. But this morning there was only Ralph, reading the paper and rolling his eyes at the ceiling, where somewhere above him Mike was yelling, and Sue had started having her coffee in her room.

Sue shook her head. "How do normal people handle a child like Mike?"

" 'Normal people'?"

She laughed at our old joke. Normal people were people who stayed with the same job for thirty years. They didn't build their own house on top of a mountain or then, in late middle age, buy a monster that had to be completely redone. Instead, they bought a raised ranch in a development and stayed with it until retirement. Normal people had two little pampered children instead of six self-willed little characters. Normal people didn't cut wood; they burned fuel oil. In normal families men watched football on Sundays, while I wasn't even sure how many men were on a football team and usually read or napped or took a walk in the woods after church on Sunday, or perhaps had to pack a bag and drive to the airport to catch a flight somewhere. You know—normal people. They were a strange race, and from our view—outside looking in—seemed to live extraordinarily orderly lives without much upset or angst. Normal people.

Then, from the twinkle in her eyes, I realized Sue had answered her own question. Normal people don't take in a child like Mike.

But she was still shaking her head.

•   •   •

I never thought Mike would actually hurt himself. He had threatened to a number of times, and of course we were familiar with his history in the children's home, but I viewed the possibility as a nonstarter in our home. I hadn't even taken any of the precautions Harbour had suggested (but not required), like locking up the sharp instruments in the kitchen. There were two reasons for this. One was that a trite act like hiding the carving knife would never stop a determined suicide, and the other was that kitchen implements were among the least deadly appliances around the place. Our home was purposely designed for boys to grow up in, and while that meant plenty of books and weight-lifting equipment, camping gear, maps, and dogs, it also meant scores of firearms, bows and arrows, sharp carpentry tools, razors, and hunting knives, most of which by this point didn't belong to me anyway—they belonged to my sons. What could I possibly do? Besides, I thought (perhaps too simply), since the place was an ideal boy's place, why would he ever kill himself?

I never considered the fact that people usually hurt themselves in order to hurt or get back at other people, or to get other people to back off.

Sue had started Mike on vacuuming the downstairs and then left him, and I was upstairs when Liam called out.

"Dad?"

"What?"

"Come downstairs fast."

I rumbled down the barroom stairs. "What?"

"Look." Liam was pointing into the kitchen.

Mike was standing against the ceramic tile wall with his face flushed and his eyes wide open.

I turned to Liam and asked again, "What? Why did you call me?"

Thump.

I looked back over at Mike, who had started rhythmically banging his head into the wall. "I don't do work," he was chanting, and every time he said *work,* he hit his head. It wasn't a joke. I could feel the wall vibrate and the dishes in the cupboard rattle when he hit.

I walked over to stop him, but when I got close he started to hit harder and faster—thump, thump, thump.

My thoughts were shrieking, *Do the right thing!* Mike seemed possessed, the pupils in his eyes tiny black arrowheads, his tongue flicking in and out.

Then, from somewhere, the thought came: Don't give this conduct any respect. Don't act afraid.

So I laughed.

And he stopped immediately.

"You know the best thing about what you're doing, Mike?"

"What?"

"It doesn't hurt me at all."

Angrily he banged his head once more.

I gestured to Liam. "Look at this. Did you ever see anything so ridiculous?"

"I hate this family."

But since he wasn't banging his head, I turned and walked back upstairs.

A minute later I heard the vacuum start up and had to sit down. My legs were weak and rubbery.

Wednesday night the week before Thanksgiving a tall, silent young man materialized in the doorway to our bedroom. Lean, short haircut, dressed in a long gray wool overcoat with a white turtleneck.

Sue smiled. "Hello, Brendan." Then hugs and talk about when the rest of the family was getting in.

"Where's Teddy?"

Sue and I exchanged surprised looks. Teddy Bear was actually Brendan's dog. He had raised him from a pup, and the dog had always slept in his room, sat by his chair while he read. Brendan was probably looking forward to seeing Teddy almost as much as anybody else in the family.

How do you tell a boy that his dog has a new friend?

"He's in the library. Liam and Mike are sharing it."

"I'll get him."

"Brendan."

"Yes?"

"Uh, nothing . . . just make sure you leave Pupsy in there."

"Sure."

Pupsy? No! We hadn't thought this out at all. Just as Teddy was Brendan's buddy, Pupsy was Henry's. In addition to being shoved out of the way over the next two weeks, Mike was about to lose his best friends for a little while.

Sue put her hands out, palms up. "About all we can do is hope for the best and go to bed. They could be in an hour from now; they could be in at dawn. Maybe Henry won't look for Pupsy."

"This is not going to be good, Sue."

Sure enough, about two in the morning we heard Mike crying. When we went inside, he was sitting on his bed bawling, with the sheets over his head.

It was the first time we had seen him cry when he was awake.

Sue went downstairs and then came right back up. "Henry's not downstairs. He must be up in his room with Pupsy. I can't go there and start an argument. I'll wake up the guests."

Sue bent over Mike and rubbed his back. "I tell you what. As a special treat, you can have Jerome. Do you want Jerome?"

Mike nodded, and Sue went and got the cat. Mike clutched it to his chest and then lay back down. But his eyes were staring off somewhere.

"I hate them."

"I know you do, Mike."

Mike avoided the boys in the morning. Then when Brendan, Henry, and Frank had left for the mountain early, Mike got up, reclaimed the dogs, and went out to the stream without a jacket. He stomped up and down through the boggy pools of icy water and followed that up with a long squishy walk through the swamp.

Later he walked back to the house and presented himself in Sue's office, dripping puddles of muddy, filthy water.

"I'm all dirty and I'm freezing. I'll get sick."

Sue looked over. "So take a hot shower and change." Then she turned back to her paperwork.

He stamped his feet. "I'm all dirty."

Sue took her glasses off and peered back around at him. "Look, Mike, the fact that a boy was out with two dogs in the woods and came back wet and dirty isn't the sort of news that ranks up there with the loss of the *Titanic*. Now, run off and let me finish. I'll be free in a half hour or so, and we can get on your chores."

"I don't do work."

"We'll see," Sue said tiredly.

"I didn't have a jacket on."

"Whose fault is that?"

Mike tried once more. "My clothes are all dirty."

"So," Sue said over her shoulder, letting her voice fade off as she got back into her numbers, "the water in the washing machine will be a little darker."

Disgusted with Sue's reaction, Mike stamped inside to where I was working. "Rich, I'm all dirty and I'm cold."

"Yes," I said, "it certainly looks that way."

"I hate this fucking family."

A little while later Sue smelled smoke.

She ran down to the kitchen and found that Mike had lit a stack of wooden matches one by one and thrown them on top of the stove.

"Mike," she shouted furiously, "if you ever touch matches again, you're going to be barred from the kitchen."

"I hate this fucking family."

Sue gritted her teeth. "Okay, I just found some free time, so we can start your chores now. We're having a big dinner tonight, and you are going to field-day this kitchen."

Mike backed up. "I don't do work."

Sue was about to make a savage retort when the look on Mike's face stopped her. He was struggling to say something else.

Fighting each word that was spilling out of his mouth, he stuttered, "I don't do work, please. Please don't do this to me, please."

Sue reached out to touch him, withdrew her hand, and covered her mouth. Then she braced her shoulders and said in a new, softer tone of voice, "Mike, I have a lot of work to do in the kitchen. When I'm doing it, can you help me? That way you and I can spend some time together. You know we have a lot of things to do, but you don't have to do work, just help."

Mike seemed to wilt. "I can help. I'm good at helping."

Sue smiled. "I know you are. Now, go change into dry clothes."

When he ran out of the kitchen, Sue turned toward me and kicked a chair out of the way. "I'm so stupid, stupid, stupid, stupid . . ."

That night Sue got our boys together—Henry, Frank, Brendan, and Liam—without Mike. The four of them— wide-shouldered, lean, defensive—were still in their hunting clothes, dirty, unshaven, knives in their belts, surrounded by the rifles, portable tree stands, and backpacks they had just dropped on the floor. Sue had made them all sit down while she stood up. That way she was taller.

"Look," she said in a sharp bark, "you're just about grown men, and I'm only going to say this once. Mike can't sleep well if he doesn't have a dog on his bed. I know these are your dogs, but he's been with them for months now while you've been gone, and Liam will tell you that ever since he's been able to have a dog, he doesn't cry or moan at night. So here's what's going to happen. Mike will always have a dog, and since I'm not going to get another one to clean up after, it'll have to be one of yours. I don't care which; they can take turns."

"Mom."

"Don't 'Mom' me. This kid has been working all afternoon to make your meal for tonight. So if any of you give me one single little itsy-bitsy word of argument, I'm going to rip your lips off."

"Cinderella."

"What?" I looked up from my book the next morning.

"Cinderella," Sue repeated. "He's a foster child, and he feels it. He's smart, he resents being a foster child, resists it, and he's supersensitive about being labeled one. Any child in his situation would feel the same way. Then it follows that if you hand him chores to do by himself, you're working him like Cinderella was forced to work for her stepmother. To his mind it's as much as hanging a sign on him saying 'foster child,' 'stepchild,' 'I don't fit in.' It's what Kathy meant when she said his own image of himself was the most important possession he has."

"So?"

"So when I asked him to help me, not work for me, he was more than happy to—grateful, even. He stayed with me in the kitchen for over three hours, cleaning, putting the lasagna to-gether, doing pots and dishes, carrying out the garbage."

"It's a subtle distinction—he still worked."

"To us it's subtle. To him there's a world of difference be-tween helping and working. And to tell you the truth, I never saw him enjoy a dinner more, despite the fact that the boys cold-shouldered him. He felt that the lasagna was partially his."

"Hmmm. So it seems both of you got what you wanted. He's not working and you have him pitching in around here."

"Yeah," she said slowly, thinking it out, "although every chore can't be a group effort. So I have to go out of my way to make him think it's inclusive, not isolating. If I manage that, I'm positive he'll look around in a couple of months and feel much more secure and a little bit more responsible. In any event, it's got to be downhill from here."

But instead, it turned into a hard slide up. Acquiring a place in the family requires acceptance, and there was more to this family than just Sue and me.

We had been concerned that the boys' acceptance of Mike would be rough. We should have been concerned about there being any acceptance at all.

Brendan is usually susceptible to a kind impulse, and Liam was doggedly cooperative even as he watched his relationship with us get shortchanged with Mike on the scene, yet both of them also take cues from the older Henry and Frank, and those two were just about unreservedly of one mind about Mike. In the infrequent conversations we'd had since the summer and over parents' weekend, they'd as much as told us straight out that they considered Mike insignificant, a "welfare" child with strange, quirky habits and a bizarre fringe history. Not that they meant him any harm; it was just that they didn't see the neces-sity or the economics in salvaging a grievously wounded animal, and that's how they talked about Mike, as a social cull who had somehow become a fixation of their parents in late middle age.

And besides, he had their dogs.

Not that we were entirely without hope. All the children exhibited a hefty degree of intractability, but Frank and Henry's steel-tendoned and decade-long determination to focus on first the mountain, woodcraft and hunting, and then on academics in college, to the exclusion of normal family amenities; parceling out words as if they were gold coins; staring at you mute when asked to pick up after themselves or perhaps disappearing at odd times; often prompted special worry on our part in the past. In our day-to-day dealings with those two boys it wasn't hard to get the impression that they believed family life, and Sue and I in particular, were just a phase, something to be endured until they were old enough in Henry's case to become a harrier pilot for the Marine Corps or an FBI agent, and in Frank's case a photographer for *National Geographic* or the *Smithsonian Magazine* in some backcountry somewhere. And while we could accept their future vision of themselves as good—goals and striving and concentration were very good, although I did have severe doubts about harriers—what about the first part? What about family? If that's what they believed, would it ever be possible to change their minds, to explain to these two dense guys that family is the only endgame in town? Could they even understand anything like that? In fact, was there any real feeling or attachment on their part at all? Suppose, we sometimes wondered, something really serious happened to us or to the family? Would they even care or respond?

Two incidents went a long way toward our coming to understand that much of Henry and Frank's public facade was just that, a facade. That beneath their distant exterior was some hidden inner ward. That no matter how coldly they came on, something else was there behind a door.

One was Susanne's wedding, when all the boys stood up in a line and spoke in public about their love for their sister. Those five minutes profoundly moved Sue and me. We never thought the boys—Henry and Frank, in particular—would reveal their feelings that way. The other was an accident—one of those bizarre household happenings, usually with fatal result—that one reads about in the paper.

I fell down our well.

The wellhead for our house is located in a large, underground concrete room out back, and one day I was having a heated argument outside with the four of them. I had a heavy item to move, and it was one of those rare occasions when I had four strong bodies right at hand all at the same time. But of course they all had something else to do and couldn't be bothered.

"You are the most selfish, self-centered shits I can imagine," I remember saying to myself.

Then I took a step backward onto the square manhole cover over the underground room. But one of the supports had shifted, and the large sheet of thick steel plate revolved, dropping me eight or nine feet down onto the steel ladder inside. Then the manhole cover rotated ninety degrees and fell in on top of me.

If the edge had come down first, I would have been killed outright, but the large flat top struck me instead, smashing me against the steel ladder and knocking me mostly unconscious.

I couldn't breathe and I couldn't see. But in an instant I could feel the weight of the cover fly off me and then my body floated miraculously up out of the well room.

I came to on the grass with Henry looking me in the face while the other boys were stretching me out and Henry was issuing orders: "Okay, CPR now—I'll administer. Frank, you call Rescue. Liam, get Mom. Brendan, stand by to assist."

"Hey, guys," I managed to gasp and sputter. "I'm okay."

"You sure?" I could feel them searching for broken bones,

poking and prodding at me, their faces furrowed, anxious, all trying to talk to me at once. "Dad, Dad, are you all right?"

Then they lifted me up to my feet and helped me inside, where Sue found me lying on the bed a half hour later.

"What are you doing?"

I was sore all over but able to crack a contented smile and say, "I'm reflecting on what excellent sons we have."

So they aren't all bad.

But they are tough.

And maybe, just maybe, all Sue had done by fighting Mike through to a "helping" position in the family was to set him up for a big fall. Because each night Mike worked in the kitchen with Sue baking cakes, preparing dinner, helping to carry in and then clean up. All night, every night, Mike had some pride of ownership in the meal, in the way the house looked, and all night, every night, the other boys ignored him.

In fact, worse than ignoring him, they openly disdained him. If one of them wanted the potatoes and they were on the table in front of Mike, they'd pointedly ask someone else to pass the dish. They'd never say hello to him when they walked into a room; they never said good-bye. They never once said his name.

It was awful.

Worse than awful, it devolved into one of those pointless contests of will between father and sons. No matter how much I glowered at them, they were determined to ignore my disapproval as much as they ignored Mike. Words didn't do any good, either. I just got the blank-faced look back. Several times I heard Sue arguing with them, but it was like trying to reason with a box of rocks.

For the first couple of nights Mike kept his head up. "I made this pie. I made these vegetables," he'd say to the boys. But they rarely responded, and when they did it was with a sarcastic, *"Really?"*

Every time they did something like that it rocked Mike. I

could feel the stab, and I could see that the next time his head came up it wasn't quite as high as the day before.

But the last and final shot came when, on the day before Thanksgiving, I spotted Brendan and Henry talking with Tony Tantillo and a group of men in front of Tony's sporting goods store.

"Hey, Tony, Brendan, Henry."

Indifferent nods from Henry and Brendan when they saw Mike tagging along behind me; a broad smile and a "Hello, Rich" from Tony.

"Hey, who's this?" Tony asked, looking at Mike. A big man with a beard and a happy, smiling face, Tony was a biologist who used to teach school in Alaska but was from this area, originally, and returned to open Sunset Sporting Goods in New Paltz. He and his wife, Fawn, had long ago become friends. Four of the boys had worked for Tony at one time or another.

Now Tony said, "Is there a Miniter I don't know about?"

"This is Mike."

Tony knew all about Mike, of course, but pretended he didn't. "Well, it's about time your dad brought you over."

Mike smiled back and nodded, but his wary eyes were on Henry and Brendan. They didn't look back.

The circle of men had been discussing the deer take so far this season, and now the conversation started back up again.

"Dave Kirchner shot a six-pointer off the power line opening day."

"Yeah. Well, no big deer anywhere I've seen."

"Fawn and I both got nice racks. Henry here shot a six yesterday. But I know what you mean—most of what I've seen are the size of sick dogs."

"Everybody's switching to .243s."

"They're lengthening Black Powder this year."

"I saw the old ghost in velvet this August, nearly scared the hell out of me."

"Lotsa turkeys in the woods."

"Seven-millimeter Magnum . . ."

Mike's head was swiveling back and forth, fascinated with the conversation but also furtively reading the looks on the boys' faces, waiting for them to say hello to him, even just nod in his direction. Disappointed, I grabbed Mike and wandered off, waving good-bye.

Tony walked after me. "Those guys have a real case about Mike."

"Yeah," I laughed, "it seems it started with the dogs. Now it's some sort of general grievance."

"They'll come around."

"I guess so."

"See ya later, Mike—you're in a good family," and Tony hit Mike in the shoulder.

Mike looked at Tony, his face a steely mixture of anger and hopelessness. "I'm not part of this family. I'm a foster child."

Later on at home I relayed the conversation to Sue.

She shook her head. "I don't know whether to cry or stampede. It makes you wonder why we're doing any of this."

And then Mike wouldn't help anymore.

CHAPTER NINE

the initiation

Early in the morning the house was full of the smell of turkey in the oven and I was sick with a major case of the flu. I hadn't even thought of getting up to go hunting, and when I did come downstairs, it was late in the morning with three or four aspirin in me and a sweatshirt on under a heavy flannel shirt.

In the kitchen, Sue had a mountain of fixings laid out in various stages in the kitchen.

"How're you feeling?"

"Like death."

"Are you going to be able to eat with us?"

"I can always eat."

Then I looked around the kitchen. "Where's your little shadow?"

Sue nodded inside to the barroom. "He came down, got a bowl of cereal, and went inside."

I went in to him.

"Why don't you help Sue?" I asked him.

Head down over his cereal bowl: "I don't help."

"I see."

Then I tried to lower my voice. "Mike, those boys have been together a long time. It's a little bit too much to expect that they would accept you right off. You give them time. They're acting like jerks right now, but that will change."

"Whatever."

"Mike?"

"They think I'm a retard. They don't even talk to me."

"They don't think that. They're just put out."

"I hate this family. I wish they'd put me in a good family."

"David and Susanne will be over."

He shrugged. "I'll talk to David. I hate everybody else. There's nobody else I like in this family."

I went to walk away when the barroom door slammed open.

"Howdy, howdy, howdy." My niece and her husband Matt tromped in, Kathryn smiling shyly and Matt whooping, "Howdy."

"Hi, Uncle Richard," and Kathryn gave me a hug. "Boy, it smells good in here. Where's Aunt Sue?"

I pointed inside, and then Matt came over and took my hand.

Six foot something, tall and spare, with a southern accent, Matt worked a Coast Guard rescue boat out of Fire Island. He had been raised on a farm in the mountains of North Carolina and had met my niece when he was stationed in Florida.

An inveterate deer hunter and woodsman, Matt was ill at ease at first with what he saw of Kathryn's family. He hadn't much in common with her mother, her aunt, and her uncles, all living within the city limits of St. Petersburg. And sight unseen, he transferred that forlorn impression to us. So much so that Kathryn had to drag him up to see us for the first time. "More of this family? Well," gulp, "I'll jest try to be polite."

But when he came up and saw the mountains, saw the deer heads mounted on the walls, and met the boys, he kept repeating over and over, "I didn't know about the Miniters in New York. I just didn't know, golleee!"

And of course he fit right in.

Now Matt peered around me to where Mike was standing. "Who's this?"

Mike hung back and rudely asked, "Who's that person? That's not one of the sons."

"No, Mike, that's the nutcase my niece married. He's up here for four or five days."

Mike stuck out his lower lip and turned away, but was immediately spun around and confronted with an outstretched hand in front of his face. "I guess you're Mike and I guess I'm Matt, so shake."

Reluctantly, Mike took the hand and then had his arm pumped. "Why, you're even uglier than they said. But gosh, I'm new in this family, too, so the two of us have to stick together close, even if you do look like you've been chewing on briars."

Just as a Texan says "tarred" when he means "tired," Matt says "briaaars" when he means "briars."

Matt bent down, looked him in the eye with his head tilted sideways, and smiled.

Against his will Mike smiled back, and then he laughed in shrieks as Matt whipped off his baseball cap, pulled it down over Mike's face, and pummeled him on top of the head.

Sue was watching from the kitchen doorway. "Matt, am I glad to see you."

The boys arrived home and cleaned up, the table was nicely set, and David and Susanne had arrived. It was long after dark—late for Thanksgiving, but we always eat late. The boys want every last moment up on Shawangunk.

Each time Mike came into the barroom he'd walk a big circle around Henry, Frank, Brendan, and Liam, taking a place where he'd be close to Matt or David.

The two turkeys were out of the oven, and Sue had gone upstairs. "Rich, I'm going to change. Don't let the cat into the kitchen."

I walked over to the bar, where David asked me, "Can I mix you another drink?"

"No," I said, "with this flu, everything is tasteless. Besides, if I'm asleep when Sue's dinner is served, I'll never hear the end of it."

David shrugged his shoulders over at the four boys, sitting and listening to a loud story of Matt's. "Maybe you *should* sleep through this one."

"I know what you mean. Sue has been entirely too quiet. Somewhere between turkey and pie there's bound to be an explosion. All I want to do is keep my head down."

David laughed. "Me, too."

Mike popped up next to David with a petulant look on his face. "I'm hungry. When is this family going to eat?"

There was something about the way he said *this family* that touched a nerve, but I let it go. "Mike, the turkeys are out of the oven. I'm going to carve them in a couple of minutes. You can go in there and slice yourself off a little bit."

Then he popped back down and disappeared.

"Maybe I will have that drink."

A couple of minutes later Sue came back downstairs and walked into the kitchen. Then she came storming out in my direction.

"Follow me," she hissed.

I walked behind her into the kitchen, but before I got fully in she turned and poked me in the chest. "What's the one thing we know about Mike?"

"I don't have any idea of what you're talking about."

Her voice was steely. "Haven't we learned if we say he can have one chocolate doughnut and then don't watch, he'll eat the whole box? Don't we know that if we say he can watch an hour of TV, he'll watch all night? Don't we know that if we say he can give the dogs a dog bone, he'll feed them the whole bag?"

I shifted uneasily on my feet. Then she moved out of my way and gestured theatrically with her arm.

Mike was sitting at the kitchen table with a plate in front of him. On the plate was what looked like the complete breast of one of the turkeys, and spread over the meat was an entire bottle of ketchup.

Then I got the finger back in the chest again. "So, knowing all that we know, you send him in the kitchen to slice himself a piece of turkey."

Sue got Mike up and marched him inside with his plate. "You sit right there at the bar, Mike, and eat that whole damned plate."

Then she went inside and started to cry.

I walked back over to David. "David, would you go into the kitchen and carve whatever is left of the turkeys?"

David looked doubtfully in the direction of the kitchen. "Uh, do you mind if I wait a little while?"

"Sure."

The boys seemed to find the whole episode amusing, and a couple of them walked over to the bar, looked at Mike's plate, and laughed. Mike jumped down off the barstool and ran across the barroom and upstairs.

Sue came back in and wordlessly took the plate off the bar.

One of the boys said, "Mom, what do you expect?"

Sue seemed to turn to stone for an instant. Then she slammed Mike's plate down on the table. "What do I expect? What do I *expect*? I expect you all to act with a little charity. That kid has been working all week in the kitchen and trying to make friends with you, and you've been treating him like a leper. He's half your size, for God's sake."

Embarrassed, Matt looked down at his lap, but our sons

glared back, and Frank said, "Mom, he doesn't even know how to eat Thanksgiving dinner."

She picked up the plate and slammed it down again. "You didn't know how either until we wheeled you over to your first Thanksgiving dinner in a high chair to find out. Then, in the following years, we sat you on a telephone book to be with the family at the table to keep learning, and twenty years later you still hold your fork like a shovel. Mike has never ever eaten Thanksgiving dinner with a family. He's only had it served to him in an orphanage or a hospital. He doesn't know. Can't you understand that?" Then she started to cry again.

Major silence and much shuffling of feet under the table from everybody else. I don't think the boys had ever seen their mother so upset or suddenly vulnerable. Susanne was glaring at them now, too, ready to say something they didn't want to hear, and I could sense that they were beginning to realize that this thing had been pushed a shade too far.

Sue got herself under control, walking back and forth to the kitchen and dabbing at her eyes, maybe even angry at herself for losing it. Then we managed to coax Mike back downstairs, David carved the turkey, and we said grace and ate. But it was a very awkward dinner.

After the table was cleared and before dessert, Sue went back upstairs for a moment to use the bathroom and freshen up.

David tried to talk to Mike, but then the boys called him into a corner of the room. I heard a snatch of the conversation as one of them said, "No, bad idea," and another said, "Don't worry, he's really fascinated with animals."

What was that about? I asked myself, but Susanne and Kathryn were talking to me and I was distracted.

David left the group and walked outside.

A minute later I heard Brendan say to Mike, "Mike, there's a deer outside in the back. Would you like to see it?"

All my instincts should have been alive, but instead I thought stupidly, *Well, finally, something kind out of one of them.*

Idly I heard one of the boys coaxing Mike through the kitchen doorway into the dark. I knew he was terrified of the black out there, but I also knew how desperately he was attracted to any sort of animal. *Good,* I thought even more stupidly. Maybe one way to lose a fear of the night is to watch a deer in the moonlight.

Then I heard the worst and most terrified scream of my life.

Mike flashed by up the stairway, still screaming, and his face was entirely white.

David had taken a deer head, put it in front of his own face, and then, dressed in dark clothing and growling, had run out of the blackness of the back lawn toward Mike, who was leaning nervously through the doorway.

I was absolutely stunned by how vicious the whole thing was. I didn't even have the power of speech. It was unbelievably cruel. All I could say as the other boys chuckled was, "David, how could you, above all people, do something like that to him?"

Henry waved it off. "Dad, it was a joke. We thought it would break the ice."

"It's your ice, goddammit. You broke his heart."

"I wasn't afraid."

I turned and looked. Mike was standing at the bottom of the stairs. He was pallid and perspiring, but there was a smile on his face. "I wasn't afraid," he repeated.

"Yes, you were," and Brendan pushed him into a seat over at the table.

A few minutes later Sue came downstairs with a puzzled look on her face at the sight of Mike laughing and joking with the boys.

"I'll serve the pie," she said slowly, still watching, looking a question at me.

"Can I help?" Mike jumped up.

Sue patted him on the shoulder, still looking at me, but in amazement now. "Sure, Mike. You made the pumpkin pies— you can serve them."

A couple of minutes later Henry held up his plate with a half-eaten slice of pumpkin pie on it. "Good pie, Mike."

"Thank *you*." Then everybody started chatting and laughing.

Sue and I shooed Mike into bed about eleven, leaving the boys and girls talking quietly around the barroom table.

"Okay, what happened when I was upstairs? I heard a scream."

I waved the question off. "Some sort of initiation or something. You don't want to know."

"I'm still angry at them," she said.

I just sighed.

Then Sue dropped down on our bed and kicked her shoes off. "Well, it's a start. Mike did get some chores done over the last couple of weeks, and he seems to have earned a little bit of a place for himself after all."

I put my hands up, surrendering to the memory of that scream. "Believe me, he earned more than a little bit of a place tonight."

"I hope his attitude is better after they leave."

"Maybe it will be."

She yawned, rolled over on her side, and said sleepily, "Somehow, this month didn't go precisely the way I thought it should."

I pulled the quilt over her. "Good enough. It went good enough."

On the Monday after Thanksgiving my eyes opened to the dark at 5:00 A.M. and I took inventory of myself. I was magically free of the flu. Then I thought of coffee—cups and cups of hot, fresh coffee—so I slipped out of bed, quickly dressed, and trucked off in the direction of downstairs.

But then, with one hand on the barroom door, some impulse made me turn back and walk in on Mike.

In the tiny glow from the night-light the boy was a jumble of stark white arms and legs tangled up in the shadows of his sheets. I padded over closer and peered down at him, snoring on. He looked like he had just finished fighting his way down into his bedcovers.

What time had he gone to sleep? I asked myself.

A few minutes later I was trying to hurry the coffeemaker along in the barroom when Sue's head peeked around the corner of the stairs.

"Feeling better?" she smiled sleepily.

"Yeah, much better."

We sat together at the big table and Sue, stretching, said, "I love our kids, but once they're gone, I love the peace and quiet, too."

"True."

Then she grinned wryly to herself. "But in less than four weeks they'll be back again."

"True, too."

"Rich," Sue said with her eyes rolling toward Mike's room upstairs, "I want that kid's first Christmas in a family to be a special one. He has that childlike attitude toward Santa Claus, and I don't want him disappointed."

"I peeked in on the way down," I said. "He looks like he's tied up in knots."

"He went into his room okay last night." Sue shrugged. "He's just tired."

"Hmmm."

"Rich, don't worry," Sue said, stretching again. "You relax. I'll get him up. He's had a hard time for the last week or so. I'll try to give him a little extra attention this morning—make him some Belgian waffles, let him watch his cartoons for a while before the bus comes."

"Good." Then I saw the coffee was ready, got up, and poured.

We chatted for a few minutes. Sue finished her coffee and went upstairs. I poured myself another cup and then quietly settled down to watch C-SPAN.

And a half hour later the screaming started.

When Sue went in to Mike he had insisted on staying in his wet sheets, started yelling filthy curses at her, and then, when she again asked him to get up, he started throwing things.

By the time I got involved he was hitting his head against the wall.

Finally, both of us had to put hands on him, and it was all we could do in an hour to get him showered, dressed, bundled up against the cold, and then outside in time for the bus.

Even then he balked about walking over to the little van, and when he did it was to pause half in and half out before running back to where the two of us were watching from the porch.

Still shocked at the horrible morning and much more than half angry ourselves, Sue was huddled down into a thick blue wool sweater, crying behind her eyes, and I was moodily sipping at another cup of coffee. We thought he was running back to say good-bye.

"How nice," Sue said sarcastically. "That's the boy we want to see."

But when he stopped below the porch, knit hat pulled low, white half moons under his eyes, his facial tic flickered back for an instant and what popped out of his mouth sounded something like an accusation: "Karate starts up again this week."

I blinked. "I know how much you like karate, Mike," I said as patiently as I could. "We'll get you there."

But he spit at me, "I hate this goddamn fucking family."

Sue blew her top. "If I have to climb down off this porch, short stuff, you're going to be limping for the rest of your life."

"Fuck you."

Sue started to move, and after one more rushed, angry, frustrated look at both of us, Mike turned and ran back toward the bus.

"Oh, my God," Sue croaked, "what was that about? What was this whole hideous morning about, anyway? I thought we just got past all of that."

Then we stood together on the porch as the bus rattled on down the road, out of sight. Sue, shivering and beating her arms, slowly got herself under control. Taking several deep breaths, she shifted back to the past week. "Sometimes I'm not sure it was right to place Mike in this sort of family. It takes every ounce of energy he has to adapt, and he no sooner gets through that with us than we spring three or four more sons on him."

Sue's lips chattered. "And he still hasn't met Richard, or many of your relatives, or really, too many of our friends and their children. In each of those cases he's going to have to assert himself over and over again with people. It might've been better for Mike to have gone to a couple without any other children."

I shook my head, honestly puzzled. "No, I don't agree. I'm still sick over what the boys did to him on Thanksgiving, but his own attitude later on seemed much, much different. He thought he had won some stripes."

Sue turned and poked me in the chest for emphasis, one little finger sticking out from the sleeve of her sweater. "Anybody who gets flogged has stripes. He needs rest now. He needs peace and quiet. Solitude. So I absolutely don't want him to meet any more new people for a while."

Sue and I didn't understand what had happened the night

before between Mike and Liam, or that in two days I would wind up putting a hundred strangers in Mike's face.

Tuesday morning was a repeat of Monday. Mike wet his bed, screamed and cursed, and had to be manhandled. Then, in the evening, I dropped Liam and Mike off in Highland at the karate school at about seven and went back for them at nine.

Later Mike went upstairs to get ready for bed, and after checking on my hunting gear for the morning, I settled down to read a book. But I had barely turned one page when Liam sat down across from me and asked, "Did you know Mike and I have a karate test right after Christmas?"

"No, I didn't."

Liam put one hand under his chin. "He's really upset about being tested."

I sighed and sat back, thinking. "No, I think you're wrong. He loves karate, and he's always talking about how good he is. If anything, Mike's overconfident."

"No, Dad," Liam said, "he's not. He's given up. He doesn't even want to practice."

"Huh? You two just came back from karate practice."

"Dad, Sunday afternoon I went down to the advanced extra session, and I brought back a flier announcing the test. When I gave it to Mike that night before bed, he read it, then started yelling at me. Yesterday afternoon I asked him to practice and he wouldn't, and tonight he went, but he barely went through the motions for half an hour before he walked out into the hallway to wait for you."

"Liam, all this seems exactly backward. People usually start practicing, not stop, once they find out they have a test coming up."

Liam nodded. "Yeah, well, that might be true, but this is the way it is with him." Then patiently, as if he were talking to a simpleminded, doddering old fool, "So you should figure out what's wrong in his head and fix it."

When he left I tried to go back to my book, but finally put it down and walked into Mike's room.

"Hi, Mike."

He avoided my eyes, just lay back on his bed, listening to his music.

"Mike?"

"What?"

"Do you want to finish the Hardy Boys book?"

"No."

"Okay," I said, not moving.

Eye contact for the first time. "Mike, do you want to talk about karate?"

"No!" he shouted.

I sat down on the edge of his bed. "Let's talk about the karate test."

His face set itself into a frown, and his eyes quartered away from me. "No."

"Are you still interested in karate?"

He shuffled around to get his legs away from me. "I'm good at karate."

"I know you are, Mike. So you shouldn't be afraid of a test."

"I'm *not* afraid."

I should have told Sue what Liam had said, but she was busy in her office and I forgot. Instead I left her working, set the alarm for 4:00 A.M., and just went to bed.

By the time the two of us actually saw each other again, it was late in the afternoon of the next day, long after she had had to wrestle with this new demon in Mike's room all alone, long after I had shot a ghost outside the beaver pond, and long after a hundred or so men had trooped up out of the darkness.

It was as if I had advertised the deer, when in fact I hadn't told anyone—not even my boys. The only announcement I made at all was to hang the deer up under the big hemlock in front, the one you can back a truck up under, the same tree the boys had had four deer hanging from by the end of Thanksgiving weekend.

Every one of the men got out of his car or pickup truck and walked up to look at it, using the exact same words: "Oh, my God, I never saw anything that big. Did you get him, or was it one of your sons?"

I felt a tad guilty about that. The boys were the ones who had really worked for a trophy. The ending days of their hunt together this autumn could have been torn from the pages of *Leatherstocking Tales.* By sunset Saturday they had hiked more than fifty miles around and over those fractured ridges, shot three bucks, and then, despite the fact that dawn Sunday saw the sky choked up with low clouds—cold, sopping-wet cotton pods that drenched the mountain in black, freezing rain—they scrambled back up Shawangunk again and shot one more in the laurel.

Brendan was the last to leave. He came into my room Sunday night. I sat up straighter and put my book down as he said good-bye and asked me if I was going to hunt at all. I said yes, of course. I had blocked out some time and earlier puzzled out the route of a large herd of does that seemed to be visiting various bucks. "Don't worry. I'll be out there," I said.

"Okay, Dad," he said, questioning, concerned about my lying there, and as he walked out added, "I'll call you during the week."

And then on Wednesday afternoon he did call.

"I shot a pretty big deer," I said slowly.

"Really. How big?"

I stumbled over an answer. Rick Stevens, the conservation biologist who is a guest here, had tried to score it by eye. Then he had come into our rooms and told Mike and Liam, "Your dad should be careful with that buck. It might be the biggest one in New York State this year."

But I had a hard time believing it, so I didn't want to repeat what Rick had said. I just said, "Big."

He asked if it was as big as Henry's ten-pointer. Reluctantly I had to say, "Bigger, much bigger."

"*Okay,* Dad," he said, excited. "Way to go!"

When I got off the phone and walked back outside to talk to yet more hunters driving in, I realized that my having trod a sorcerer's line in the woods was profoundly affecting Mike. He was wide-eyed, peering out the windows, walking inside and out, hiding in his room and then coming back out again to find Sue and drift along behind her.

"Who are all these people?" he kept asking. "What do they want? Are they going to go away?"

"They'll leave after they see the deer you helped me with," I said, watching him, thinking of the deer, thinking of the Mike we had seen that afternoon.

A mountain wight, the buck had been glimpsed by other hunters earlier that year and during the year before, but had always vanished like a ghost before anybody got a shot or even a good look at him. Old and wise, he was a master at using the secret, hidden places on the mountain in order to stay alive. And in this, the last year of his life, he had grown into a monster, the best of the gene pool, with enormous dusky shoulders and a huge basket rack of antlers chipped and scarred from subduing other males, stained with the juice of roots. This giant, aged male couldn't, with his molars worn to the gumline, ever feed again; he only cared now for his few short, last weeks of autumn dominance.

I was watching a young male in the stream when he appeared in order to drive the other animal away, and without my seeming to will it, the rifle fired and he vanished.

By noon I had just about given up trying to find him, so I called Susanne's husband, David.

When David arrived, I stood in front of him exhausted, covered with mud, soaking wet, dripping puddles of filthy cold water on the clean kitchen floor. "Dave," I said, "this was the biggest deer I ever saw in my life. This was *the* deer."

David looked at me carefully. "Are you sure you hit?"

"Dave, it was a long, long way to fire, but it was a perfect sight picture. I fired, he was knocked down for an instant, got up, ran ten paces, and then disappeared."

David smiled and put his hand on my shoulder. "Okay, I'll be on it all day if you want. Now, show me where he was when you shot."

I went back to the beaver pond with him, walked him to where the buck was when I shot and said, "I lost sight of him right here."

David looked back to where the buck had been standing, then shaded his eyes and peered off for a long, long minute toward the spot from where I had fired, shaking his head. "That's an impossibly long shot." But when he went to move, he looked down at the ground at his feet and caught his breath.

There he was, dead, facedown in a hole clogged with tiny willow, with just the gray hump of his enormous shoulders pushing up through dead leaves. Right next to him were a dozen sets of tracks from my gum boots. I had been walking past him all morning, looking ahead instead of down.

"Damn," was all I managed to say, almost falling down. "Wait until the boys see this!"

David cracked such a wide grin it looked like the top of his head would fly off. "So much for their theory that Dad can't shoot any longer!"

We could barely wrestle him out of the hole, but it was too wet to get a truck back there, so we tried to drag him.

Eventually, David fell on his back, laughing. "We need help—I feel like I'm pulling a car sideways."

It was getting colder again, with afternoon shadows seeping out into the field. I looked at my watch. "It's well past three. Liam and Mike will be at the house."

"Mike?" said David. "I don't know. Remember Thanksgiving. You know how he is about animals. You'll have to clean it with him watching. Then you'll have to think about what The Harbour Program will say if he's involved."

I shook my head. I was ready to give up on any calculation of Mike's emotional dewpoint, but I did have left a flickering hope that somewhere within Mike's snarly bundle of contradictions was, as in most boys, the one clear thread of an appropriate little savage.

As for The Harbour Program, I knew, of course, that they'd much rather our family didn't hunt, that Mike not be exposed to any aspect of the violence of it. I knew a growing segment of the population shared the same ambivalence, but from my sardonic and irreverent perspective the alternative was blandly despicable. Most children now are far too bleakly segregated from life; they operate in a world of video arcades and television and mind-numbing mall jaunts, isolated schools, and insipid, unmeaningful "meaningful activities." Few of them ever seem to read a book, stake out some territory of interest, or develop any sense of adventure, any sense of future. Hunting, however long it is left to us, is the last activity I can think of that still bridges the gap between what men and children do. And it's all about family. It's not something you send your sons to do while you watch, but rather something they begin to assume responsibility in at an early age, tutored by a grandfather or an uncle or a father, and then involving other uncles and brothers and cousins, and then finally teaching younger cousins, nephews, and children. And all of that is ever so much more than a brief season in the autumn. Hunting extends itself throughout the entire year in preparation and practice, in game meals and in a thousand stories—most particularly in stories. Stories are what you are, were, and will be. And Mike is one of the "will bes" around here now.

So for all of those reasons and because I knew that with Sue gone seeing clients, Mike would be alone in the house, I said to David, "No, we need his help. Leave it up to him. Let him come to us out here in the field if he chooses."

David set off, and five minutes later I heard the distant slam of the kitchen door, then Mike shot out of the house, his blond hair flashing like a mirror under the shadows of the trees as he ran down and down and then out to where I was standing. He still ran with an awkward, toe-in gait, one shoulder stumbling forward and the other lurching for balance. But he ran on and on, laughing when the dogs caught up with him.

As he ran I remembered Joanne reviewing his medical records, picturing the seventy-pound, nervous little waif that he was in the spring and saying, "I don't think he'll ever be able to walk long distances. He may never be strong."

When Mike got there, he danced like a young Iroquois warrior around the buck. "You did it! You did it!" He laughed and laughed. "This is bigger than *Brendan's,* bigger than *Frank's* . . . it's bigger than *Henry's.*"

Impressed and perplexed in spite of my earlier thoughts, I sighed. This was a brighter, shinier piece in the ragged, fractured ten-thousand-piece jigsaw puzzle that was Mike, but I didn't know whether it was a piece of blue sky, a piece of the mountains, or maybe a corner. I didn't know what the picture of Mike was supposed to look like when it was finished.

In a minute or so David and Liam showed up, David shaking his head at the sight of Mike and Liam grinning. Then, with the four of us huffing and puffing, we got the animal back to the house and used a car hitch to pull him up into the hemlock.

An hour later the vehicles started pulling into the drive.

And a couple of hours after that I was standing there in the barroom looking at Mike and remembering the deer, remembering how Mike had acted that afternoon.

"Rich, there are more and more of those people coming," Mike said now.

I groaned. All I wanted was to shower, eat, and lie down. "Mike, you go out and talk to them if you want to."

He took a step forward and then a step back. *"Me?"* He trembled as if with an electric shock.

I hadn't really been serious, but when I saw something work its way into his face I said, groping my way, "Answer their questions, Mike."

"Can I have a flashlight?" he yelled at me.

He looked like a hound chafing at the leash, and I was startled. "Uh, sure—there's one behind the bar."

A short time later I was coming out of the shower in my robe when Sue came in and grabbed my arm. "Do you know what you started?"

"Huh?"

"Don't turn any lights on. Just walk into the office and take a look outside."

I could hear a strange, loud voice before I even put my head close to the window. A dozen men were outlined in the headlights from their cars and trucks, others were pulling in, and Mike was standing in front of them, gesticulating like an impresario as he swung the beam of the flashlight upward, emphasizing various points about the deer. His frosted breath was puffing white in the hazy darkness, and although typically loud, it was a relaxed and totally new voice. No tension, no stress, the words fluid and clear. "My dad shot this. This is the biggest deer in America, even in the whole state. He shot it with one shot even though it was almost a mile away. I helped him bring it home, and David helped, and . . ."

All those fears bundled up inside that strange little person, and yet the commonest of fears, that of getting up in front of a group of new people and talking, wasn't numbered among them.

Then I thought I understood. "Mike's not afraid of or angry with strangers—only with people he has a relationship with."

"*Yeah*," Sue said slowly, "you're right. It's creepy. It's exactly backwards, isn't it?"

Where had I just heard that?

Then I remembered—and also what I had neglected to tell Sue the day before. "I think I might know what's been bothering him."

"I hope so," she said, hunched up and looking through the window. "The little wretch should've been sent to us with an instruction manual."

CHAPTER TEN

the test

We were standing knee-deep in pre-Christmas litter in the barroom. Dusty boxes with newspaper-wrapped Santa Clauses and ornaments, many little decorations various kids had made over the years in grammar school or Boy Scouts. Where to put the large antique crèche scene that Aunt Alice had given us years ago? It takes fifteen or so square feet to set up, and if one of the pieces got smashed, Sue would be heartbroken.

"How's your karate practice going?" I asked her. Her response to my theory that it was the karate test that was bugging Mike had been disbelief, followed by a vow to help him practice, if that really was the issue. ("Hey, I've seen all those Bruce Lee movies. . . .")

Now she was picking the odd piece of last year's tinsel off her sweater. "I haven't done anything. He's been real good in the morning ever since he got involved with you and that deer, so I've just let it go. His problem probably wasn't karate at all. If anything, he acted up because we've been so busy lately and he felt pushed out of the way."

"Sue," I said doubtfully, "I don't think that was it."

"Rich, don't worry. Tomorrow's Tuesday, karate day. I'm sure he'll go."

But Mike didn't go. He found out I was going down to the taxidermist that night and begged and begged until Sue and I agreed he could go along.

The taxidermist was a young guy named Curt Cabrera who had just opened a business called the Wild Art Studio in Highland. Tony Tantillo from Sunset Sporting Goods had recommended him. "This guy just won the nationals," Tony told me. "He does incredible work. Go see him."

So Mike and I trucked on down there, a frosty, clear night with the stars like diamond shards overhead as we quietly swept past the views of the Hudson, the only sound in the truck cab the soft hum of the heater fan.

When we arrived, Mike followed me into the brightly lit studio and then drifted off by himself, quietly walking from mount to mount, studying the displays while Curt and I talked about how he would do the deer.

Later on we stood at the counter while I wrote out a check and Curt looked down at Mike. "Hey," he said, smiling, "your dad tells me you're in karate."

Mike looked back, and the interested, relaxed expression on his face fled.

Back in the truck, I probed. "Mike, you are thinking about quitting karate, aren't you?"

"I'm not a quitter. I'm not quitting!"

"Okay, if you're not quitting, are you still worried about the test?"

"I don't care about the stupid test!"

"Okay," I answered, honestly confused.

Then Thursday night came, and after an early dinner Sue asked me to go find out whether Liam and Mike were ready for karate. Liam was getting his uniform on, but Mike was downstairs in the barroom, watching TV.

"Mike, are you going to get ready for karate?"

A moody, cutting look away. "No. I'm doing hunting now."

"Huh?"

He glared around his shoulder at me. "I'm *hunting*. I talked to all those people. That's what I'm doing new."

"New?"

"I mean now."

"Mike, the other night you said you weren't quitting."

Silence.

"Mike, you shouldn't let a test stop you, and as far as hunting goes, you don't own a gun or any equipment, you're too young, and besides, it's not deer season any longer."

"I hate this whole—"

"Don't you dare say that word!"

"—fucking family!" He jumped down, knocking over the barstool. "I want to go to a *good* family."

I left him there, yelling at my back. Then I went and collected Liam and drove him to karate. But afterward I took a long drive alone, back through New Paltz, down Route 208 through Gardiner, and then down to a white frame house just outside the Shawangunk Prison. I saw the lights were on, got out, and walked up the back path to the kitchen door.

The next day I was home from work and waiting when Mike got off the school bus.

"Mike, I have to talk to you."

"I'm hungry."

"Fine, you can have something to eat after we talk."

He followed me into my room, making exaggerated dragging gestures.

"Mike, I want to talk to you about hunting."

"Boring."

"Mike, you said you wanted to hunt. I have to explain to you what's involved."

"Boring."

I set my teeth. "Mike, we can sit here all afternoon, all evening."

He sat down, cupped his chin in both hands, and stared at the ceiling. "So talk."

I was getting angry, my jaw still clenched and a little muscle working furiously away in my face. But I forced myself to calm down and tried to begin reasonably.

"Mike, what do you think hunting is?"

A long silence. Then he said in the tone one would use to talk to a moron, "You take a gun and go out and catch a deer."

"And then?"

He stamped his foot. "And then people come to the house and talk to you about it. They put your picture in the paper and then you go to the taci, the taxi—"

"The taxidermist."

"Yes, the taxidermist."

"And," I said in an offhand manner, "that's all there is to it?"

He shrugged.

"But you want to do hunting?" I asked.

"I *am* doing it," he answered. "I'm good at it."

"What are you good at?"

"I talked to all those people."

I tried to be as gentle as I could. "Mike, you were great at talking to those people. You did a real good job. But there's something you don't know about that."

"What?"

I stood up and took out a box I had retrieved from the storage area. Inside were hundreds of loose photographs.

"Mike," I said, "these are all the pictures that aren't in the photo album." Then I started to shuffle through them and flip prints out on the bed. "Here, look at these."

Mike got up, slouched over, and angrily picked up the photographs as I tossed them out.

After about five minutes I stopped and walked around behind him. By now he was holding a stack of twenty or thirty photographs. "Here," I said, pointing at the first one. "Do you know who those people are?"

"No."

"Well, Mike, that's me and Bill Allen, a friend I used to hunt with. Bill moved to California in nineteen seventy-two. That picture had to be taken in 'sixty-nine or 'seventy. Now, look at this—it's me standing with Henry next to a deer I shot. Henry is only four or five there, so how old is that photograph?"

"I don't know."

"Henry is twenty-four now, so how much is four subtracted from twenty-four?"

"Twenty?"

"Right," I snapped, "so this photograph is twenty years old. Now, how about this one from nineteen sixty-eight. . . . Here's one from 'eighty-seven with Craig Erhorn. Look, look, this one is from only two years ago."

I went through about half of them, naming the years.

"I don't care about any of this stuff." Mike grated his words.

"How long have I been hunting, Mike?"

"I don't know."

"Look at these photographs and tell me how long."

"A long time," he mumbled.

"Thirty years," I said. "Thirty years. Now, how many times a year do I go out in the woods to hunt or scout?"

"I don't know."

"Mike, maybe forty times during the course of a year. Not forty full days, but at least thirty scouting walks and ten times hunting, even just for an hour or so. So how much is forty times thirty years?"

"I dunno."

"Yes, you do. How much is forty times thirty? You can do that in your head."

Grudgingly, "Forty times thirty is one thousand two hundred."

"Right," I said. I sat down on the bed and pulled him over to me so that I could look into his eyes. "I went out one thousand two hundred times over the course of thirty years. Now, Mike, I want you to listen very, very carefully to what I'm going to say next."

"What?" he said, dropping the photographs on the bed and struggling out from under my arm.

"Mike, in all those times out, in all those thirty years, this is the first time any people have ever come to my house to look at the deer I've shot."

Silence.

"Mike, did you understand that?"

"Why?" Now he didn't seem so angry. "Why didn't the people come?"

"Because, Mike, that deer was a once-in-a-lifetime deer. People can hunt every day of their lives and maybe only once, if then, get a chance to take a deer like that."

He shrugged.

"So, Mike, talking to people has very little to do with hunting. Being able to is great—you have a great command of yourself in front of a crowd and you can use that well later on in life—but that's not what hunting is about."

He shrugged again a little bit more helplessly. Was I making my point?

"Another thing," I said, standing up and walking over to my desk. "Last night after I dropped Liam off I went over to a farmhouse by the prison where the local firearms safety instructor lives, and I picked this up for you." Then I handed him a legal-sized piece of paper covered with type.

"What's this?"

I put my hand on his shoulder. "That, Mike, is the fifty-question test you have to pass to get your hunting license."

Mike held the page in one hand, staring at it, and his hand, his arm started to tremble. He got a helpless, lost look, which turned to anger, little red splotches on his face, and his eyes closed.

"I can't do hunting." It wasn't a question; it was a raspy statement.

"No, Mike, not now."

"I want to go to another family."

"Mike."

I saw movement and turned around. Sue was in the room. I didn't know how long she had been there or how much she had heard. But she didn't look very pleased.

The next morning was Saturday, two weeks till Christmas, and Mike's behavior when we woke him was more disturbing than it had been at the beginning of the month. He wasn't screaming or cursing, he didn't fight; he just refused to react. He got out of bed, took a shower, dressed, and went back into his room. He wouldn't talk, nod his head, or look anyone in the eye.

And it was the same again the next day.

After dinner that Sunday evening Sue was reading the paper and drumming her fingertips on the table at the same time. "Rich," she said without looking up, "there had to be a gentler way to make your point about hunting than shoving that written test in his face . . . and anyway, he's an emotionally disturbed boy. You could have let him pretend a while longer, at least until we were past Christmas. Now it looks like we're either going to have Mike the monster or Mike the zombie in that room in the morning—all morning, every morning—for a long time."

"Sue," I protested, "he was off on a tangent, and I wanted to bring him back to his problem with the karate test. That's what's been causing this behavior; that's what he has to come to terms with."

"No," she said quietly, "no. I've spoken to him endlessly today and yesterday about that, and I'm still not convinced karate's the problem. Mike is afraid of that test, but when I offer to talk to Bob and let him skip it or take the test another time, he's just as upset. So there's something else there—something deeper, that I can't understand."

Then she did look up. "So he needs some professional help. It's gone beyond the anger and depression or whatever is going on in his head emotionally. He's not sleeping anymore, he staggers through each day burned-out and groggy—he might even be losing some of the weight he gained."

I didn't know what to say.

Sue put one hand to the side of her head and looked back down at the paper. "But that's not something we can get done by tomorrow, or even in the next week or so." Then she was silent a long time before saying in a low voice, "Before all this started I had a heart-to-heart talk with Mike about Christmas."

"And?"

"Well, I almost had to cry. One thing he mentioned several times was that he had never given anyone any real Christmas presents, that more than anything else he wanted to buy some Christmas presents for the brothers, as he calls them, and for us, and for his sister and brother, and so on."

"We can handle that, Sue," I said quietly.

"Yeah, well, I don't think it's going to happen now. I think he's going to slide right on by us on Christmas."

Sometimes the hand of providence becomes discernible, like a wisp of pale smoke caught in a sudden beam of sunlight. This was the case when a pile of unforeseen work sailed into Sue's office the following week and she said, "Rich, you do the cluster meeting tonight. I can't get away."

"Ugh." Once a month Harbour sponsors an evening get-together for the parents of the program. Sometimes there's a class on paperwork or medical aspects; sometimes it's just a relaxed forum for exchanging notes.

But there are far too many females there.

"Listen," I said, "when General Douglas MacArthur was running Japan just after the second world war, he changed the Japanese constitution to allow women the vote. His reasoning was that women were more inclined than men to address social concerns."

"So?" and her foot was tapping.

"So," I said plaintively, "that's exactly the problem: they address them and address them and address them and address them . . ."

"Rich, just shut up and go."

So I went, and after half an hour I was bored and hadn't much to do but listen when two women next to me began a private conversation.

"We've involved John in a half dozen different activities," said the first woman, "Boy Scouts, 4-H, the after-school book club, horseback riding, and none of them have worked out. Each time he comes to the point where he has to go it on his own or turn in a project, he just automatically drops out, and if we try to encourage him, he gets unbelievably angry and starts to act out his fears. We keep praising him, we keep trying to build up his self-esteem, but he just doesn't have the basic confidence . . ."

"Yes," said the other parent, "Joey's exactly the same way in school. We do everything we can to build up his self-esteem, but it's awfully slow going. I don't know why—the children's home told us he participated in many different activities—but now that he's with us, we just can't get him to stay with one."

Off on a train of furious thought, I spoke to some other people there—a *lot* of the other people there. It was after midnight when I walked into Sue's office.

"Sue, I know it's not early, but can we talk?"

"Okay. I'm through, anyway." Click, snap, click; she shut the computer down and killed the power. "What?"

I hesitated. I knew she was still angry with me for the way I had talked to Mike about hunting. And that crack about women hadn't helped.

"Sue, I learned something tonight."

"See," she said with sweet, sticky sarcasm, "I knew all those nasty, nasty ladies wouldn't hurt mummy's little boy."

"I learned that they're all the same way."

"Who's all the same way?"

"The Harbour children," I said. "Most of 'em, it seems. Mike's not really all that much of an exception. They all pretty much overreact when their parents involve them in long-term activities."

Sue groaned, flipped her pen over her shoulder, and began to look around the office for something else to do. Then she said something else under her breath I couldn't quite make out—something about not letting "him" out again.

Finally she looked up at me, biting her words. "You sound like you were hatched out of an egg a couple of hours ago. I mean, where have you *been* for the last eight months? Of course all the children are the same, you idiot. That's what The Harbour Program is, a refuge for the same type of children—emotionally disturbed children."

"But Sue, I'm not sure being emotionally disturbed has anything to do with it. Suppose those children overreact because we don't handle their activities the way they think we should?"

She heard the question in the midst of another gathering snarl, stopped, and then asked with a puzzled expression on her face, "What? What does that mean?"

"Sue," I said, "I admit it was pretty brutal when I rubbed his face in the firearms safety training course test. But I didn't understand what was going on. I thought he was being flippant about something important to me, something that requires a lot of honest skill and experience. Now I realize he was just doing for himself what in his mind he had every right to expect us to do for him."

Sue gave me a tired, guarded look, but she was listening, so I took a breath and plunged in. "I think there are two factors unique to these children—one very emotional, to be sure, but the other simply an expectation that comes from a long period of training. Further, that the effect of the one reinforcing the other results in a very special sort of handicap."

"And what does that gobbledygook mean?"

"Remember back in the beginning of the month, on the first morning when Mike went nuts, we were standing on the porch watching the school bus leave, and you said we had to remember how he has such a frightful lack of pride of place?"

"Yes. Yes, of course I do."

"Well, I think that's factor number one in this handicap. Mike is special. *All* these children are special. For his whole life Mike's been outside looking in at real families, at people with real lives doing real things, and I think to a considerable degree he still feels that way. He knows, for example, that he's not irrevocably bound to us for life. He knows that with one brief phone call he's bundled back into a car and off somewhere else. So his time with us still has some quality of make-believe about it, and that must transfer over to everything he does and has. His own room, the dogs, getting on the school bus, karate—it's all not quite real to him, not yet, not by a long shot."

When I looked at Sue expectantly, she nodded, so I continued. "And when I tried to think of how I would feel in that position, an awful simile came to mind. Mike is like the poor relation invited to the ball. A poor relation who's dressed up as best he can and, while outwardly self-assured, barely has enough inner self-confidence to look on. To Mike, the handsome, well-dressed people confidently sweeping each other around the dance floor aren't him, have never been him, may well never be him. So he can't participate, really participate, he can't ask someone to dance, he can't take a chance, he can't ever test his position in that way because he might stumble, make a mistake, step on his partner's foot, and in his mind, that would instantly translate into people finding out about him, finding out who he is, finding out that he doesn't belong, and, Sue, that's got to be why Mike's so relaxed among strangers, among people who will never ever really know him or anything about him."

"Like all those hunters who came to look at your deer?" she said.

"Like all those hunters," I agreed.

Then I continued, "Feelings like that are enough to cripple anybody, and it must be one big part of his problem. But perhaps even more of a factor in how he feels about being tested is the way in which he's been trained to engage in activities."

I was tired myself, pacing as the words came on with a rush. "It all came together for me tonight when I heard a puzzled woman at the cluster meeting complain that in the children's home, her Harbour child participated in many activities, but that in their home, they couldn't get him to stick with one. When I thought about what she had said, I realized she had unknowingly identified the one factor confusing her. The problem wasn't at all that the child was incapable of sticking with one activity, but rather that he expected many."

"So?" Sue asked. "Expectations change."

"Yes, I guess they do, Sue, but slowly, over long periods of time. And the fact is that nobody's ever thought out how the endless round-robin of activities in the system that everybody's so proud of actually contributes to a child's inability to get beyond the simplest beginning stages of anything in particular."

"Huh?" Sue shifted in her seat.

"Sue, you remember all those 'activity resources' the children's home was so proud of? They had a pool for the children, crafts, art class, puzzles, games, TV time, baseball, basketball, a little natural history museum, a library; they took them fishing, tubing, hiking, had a computer room with games. They even had an activities coordinator who set up weekly trips, and a dozen other resources I can't remember."

"Yeah?"

"Well, I remember being terribly impressed, even overawed. But when you think about it, you have to concede that few families on earth can come close to that ideal. In a real family there's one or two or three things, and a kid spends most of his time on one of them. When I was growing up, the introverts among us had a stamp collection and the extroverts played baseball after school. Oh, we all had bikes and went to movies, and some of us read books and some of us daydreamed a lot, but basically we concentrated on one or two activities."

Sue nodded. "With me it was Girl Scouts."

"But not Mike. Not only was he shifted from placement to placement over the years; he was also ceaselessly shifted from one activity to another. Year after year, new staff members, new teachers, new placements, and new activities. I feel awfully, helplessly sorry for him. Mike has never, not once in his life, had to do something like he's being asked to do now—to stay, to just settle down and work with something. Then, when you couple that demand with a test, with an attempt to push him out onto the dance floor, where a single misstep might whip away his disguise and reveal him for what he is, an already difficult transition becomes exponentially more terrifying."

"So?"

"So after Thanksgiving, after that gut-wrenching emotional experience of dealing with our sons, he was smacked in the face by Liam waving this test around, and who knows how Liam handled it? Maybe there was some of a child's nah-nah-nah-nah-nah in the way he put it to him. But in any event, Mike's initial feeling must have been abject fear—fear at taking that first step out onto the dance floor with the real people, fear of being found out. Then he must have been angry and confused—

why hadn't we presented him with something else? Why? No wonder he went over the edge; no wonder he then clutched at hunting. He probably even thought or hoped I had purposely engineered that deer for him. That's why he was so happy and excited, so enthusiastic with those people who showed up, so immediately good in the morning again."

"Okay," Sue said weakly, stunned by the blur of words, "if you're right or even half right, how do you want to deal with Mike and this test and his feelings? How do we get this kid back?"

I tried to think through the options as I spoke. "We can't make the mistake of just letting him switch off onto something else—that just continues the routine and makes him even more vulnerable. At some point in his life, pride and self-confidence have to come to him, and they must come from his own lonely effort in some activity. So I think we must get him to take the test. Let him drop out if he wants to after that, but he should take the test."

"No," Sue said. "Again, assuming you're right in all this, if you tell him to take the test, he'll be upset and crazy for the next two weeks. I won't have that. I won't have him miss Christmas."

"Then," I said, "we have to find a way to get him to take the test without upsetting him."

"How?"

"I don't know," I said weakly.

There was the flash of a sudden thought in Sue's eyes. "I do," she said slowly. "You're not going to like it."

"How?"

"Well," she said, "perhaps we can get him to the test by announcing we've decided to start him in something else. Maybe Cub Scouts—he has spoken about that before. You could even go out and buy him the *Cub Scout Handbook*."

"You want to lie to him? Think back to Norwich and my promise never to lie to him."

"And then," she said dryly, "the day of the test we tell him he'll have to come with us because we have to take Liam and don't have anyone to babysit. That way Mike'll have a good Christmas under his belt when he's confronted with a choice— the possible humiliation involved in getting up and taking the test or the guaranteed humiliation in sitting there for three hours in front of his entire class."

I was dumbstruck. "Sue, you were angry at me for what I did to him with hunting. But this is even lower. We wouldn't be telling him the whole truth when we say he doesn't have to take the test."

She shrugged. "He doesn't . . . and we *will* start him in Cub Scouts if he wants."

"But . . ."

Sue stared at me for a long, long time, then she said, "Rich, sometimes you scare me. What did we do with our other kids besides feed the little ignorant jackals the facts of life one tiny chunk at a time? They're children, for God's sake. There's a limit to what they can digest. If you knew a child was going to have a tooth pulled in a month, would you tell him right away and let him worry about it every day for four weeks?"

"Well," I said doubtfully, "no."

"Point made."

I sat there silent for a moment or two, mentally wrestling with Sue's approach to this thing, when she walked around and punched my shoulder.

"Hey, Rich."

"What?"

"Good job tonight."

Christmas was a happy, busy twenty-four hours.

We had told Mike he was free of the test and off on Cub Scouts if that's what he wanted to do next. Once we repeated it seven or eight times, he had about a solid two days of sleep and started eating like a horse again. (And yes, I felt guilty about the deception involved.) Finally, we took him shopping and tagged along as he bought little presents for everybody—a paperback book for me (unfortunately Danielle Steel), a paperback for Sue (a rock guide; I guess we'll switch), little outdoors items for the boys—a fishhook sharpener, a lure, a rubber worm, a tiny compass—a key chain for Susanne, and his big purchase, a screwdriver set for David.

On Christmas Eve all the boys were back (except Richard, still out west and doing who-knew-what), and Susanne came over to wrap presents. We piled into three separate cars to drive to midnight mass, everyone in suits except Henry and Frank, who wore Norwich cadet gray dress for the long mass. Then it was back to the house at 2:00 A.M., where Sue had a turkey and a ham and lasagna laid out. We ate, opened one present (Mike the Sega Genesis he had lusted after), and then we went to bed.

"Mike," I said aloud just before I went to sleep.

Sue answered drowsily, "I let him stay up on his own. He'll go to bed when he's ready. I'm sure he wants to get up early and open the rest of his presents."

"Did anyone get him wrapping paper for the presents he bought?"

Sue had her face in her pillow. "I'm sure Susanne or somebody took care of him."

I was first up in the morning and found Mike asleep, still with the Sega control in his hand in front of the TV. Then I walked over to the tree. There was something oddly different there. Each pile under the tree was topped with a tiny new present wrapped in yellow legal paper, carefully folded and fastened with Scotch tape. On each was written the person's name in pencil, and each had a little Christmas figure—a tree, a reindeer, a little Santa Claus—drawn on it.

I got a pretty big lump in my throat.

• • •

"I'm not going back there. I'm not going to watch Liam take that stupid test."

"Well, you're going to have to, Mike. We don't have anybody to watch you, and it will be three hours long this Sunday."

"No."

"Sorry. But listen, Mike, if you decided to take that test, you'd be as proud of yourself as I am of myself and that deer."

"Goddammit, I hate this fucking family."

"Mike, we've told you a thousand times about that language. You keep it up and you'll have to spend every hour until the karate test in your room. Now go there and think about that for a while."

He turned back on his way to his room. "Yeah, you're trying to make me look like a fool. I want to leave this family. I'm going to call Joanne."

"Mike, nobody but you can make you look like a fool."

"I don't like karate."

"Fine. Just go up there and tell Bob in front of everybody."

Slam, bang, bang. "Fuck you, fuck you, fuck you," I could hear him chanting through three closed doors.

On Sunday afternoon, Sue, Liam, and I waited out in the snow-filled parking lot. Liam was in his jacket over his karate uniform, Sue in her long leather coat with her back to the wind, and I stood there head-on, flinching at the gusts of icy flakes whipping through, watching the porch door.

Liam chattered, "Mike said he was coming."

I turned away and Sue said, "He should have his jacket on."

I turned back and looked. Mike was running toward the car without his jacket, hat, or gloves, his karate uniform flapping open against his bare chest.

"I have to take him back and get him dressed," Sue snapped.

"No," I said. "It looks like it was a last-minute decision. Let him warm up in the car."

Four hours later it was dark out and Mike had a sweatshirt we had found in the trunk of the car stretched over his uniform. We were eating pizza in a restaurant in Highland just down the street from the karate studio, the only customers having a Sunday dinner, sitting on cold Formica seats in the little storefront shop.

"Maybe I passed," Mike said hopefully.

"Ahhh," Liam said, tapping him on the shoulder, "you didn't win the yellow belt, but Bob said you'd be awarded a yellow stripe for your white belt because you knew a lot of the moves."

"Then I passed the test?"

"It looks like it."

CHAPTER ELEVEN

snow and conflict

We were into January and piled up with snow everywhere. We were down to two guests and the general activity around the place settled into the morning routine of finding out if Mike's school bus made it through, then getting the walks shoveled and cleaning up inside. Sue spent most of these days in front of the fireplace, reading. The sand was running out on her quiet time, with tax season just a week or so away.

The big change was Henry being home. His academics were finished, and he'd return to Norwich in May for graduation, but meanwhile, he was refocusing. His goal had been a flight commission in the Marine Corps, but a high octave of hearing turned out to be missing in one ear. Despite a retest, and despite our getting him to a civilian specialist, there wasn't anything to be done. He joked about it—maybe not being able to hear a dog whistle would entitle him to a handicapped sticker for his car—but I could see he was rocked. The Marine Corps did offer him a commission as an infantry lieutenant, but he would have to wait a long time for that; the military was shrinking.

So Henry was reverting to Plan B: get appointed to a state police department, earn a law degree, enter the FBI. Meanwhile, Lake Mohonk, the vast preserve and old hotel property from the last century, perched high atop Shawangunk, had hired him as a hunter culling individual deer under state permit. It was brutal work—waist-high snow, dead cold, inching his way with his rifle hard among the cliffs where hikers had been killed during summer months.

He loved it.

"Henry," I said seriously, "you're one of the few people left in the world who can add the words *professional hunter* to their résumé." He gave me one of those reserved smiles.

For the first time, this most mystifying son of ours and I were able to talk quietly at night—no girlfriends, no brothers or holidays interfering. It wasn't only the fact that we had the time and opportunity, but that for the first time in a long time, if ever, he'd found himself willing to talk.

The time had blurred by a little bit too fast for me lately. The years seemed to shade, with the images of boys flickering in and out at random. Yet sometimes, not often, it all seemed to slow and pause and I could study one single reflection for a brief moment. It was that way with Henry on those snowed-in winter evenings. He reminded me of other men—boys, really—who had once worn Marine green. But most of all I realized now, with intense shock, that most of all he reminded me of my father.

Henry even looked like my father. He had the same soft, extra-polite, measured manners, and the same cocky stance, with laughter trickling through a wry smile as if he knew how much all of this was a joke and how much you didn't. My father was a fighter, a seaman, an inventor, and then he became a fireman in the City of New York. It was Depression days, and he just made the height requirement by having himself driven downtown for the physical lying stretched out on the backseat of a car until minutes before they measured him. Then, when he passed out of training, he started a career that seemed bent on proving he was bigger than any fire. Before he was through, twenty-odd years later, he had fallen ten stories in an elevator shaft, broken both arms a few times, broken his back, been blown off the stern of an exploding ship, and then, as a lieutenant, calmly waited until every one of his men had been evacuated from a tunnel beneath President Street in Brooklyn before even thinking about starting out himself. He had almost made it when the leaking gas main they were fleeing exploded behind him. Although he stood up afterward for a few moments, the muscles had been torn apart in his legs, in his back, in his heart.

A battalion fire chief's car came to school for me and drove me downtown, bell clanging, siren screaming, weaving in and out of the city traffic at seventy, eighty miles per hour to have me see him before he died. Although he didn't die, not then. He was retired and only later, still what I'd now consider a young man, passed away from those injuries. Afterward there was a ceremony at Grant's Tomb on Riverside Drive, words from the mayor, a medal, and the life of this wonderful man whom his children loved unreservedly, whom his wife loved out of mind and forever, was over.

Tough guy.

Why he did what he did was always a mystery to me. I was never a tough guy, not really tough. Something about my father's life and the way he loved life had held me back. Something that, when thinking of him, told me no, not this way, this didn't work.

And suddenly here he was again, drinking a cup of coffee and laughing gently with me at night, planning his life, reassuring me.

Mike's attitude toward Henry was a farrago of feelings. Remembering the first disdainful distance over Thanksgiving, he was leery of Henry and also resentful of the time I was spending with him. Yet still Mike followed him around like a worshipful little acolyte whenever he had the chance.

"I don't like Henry. I don't like him living here all the time. He should go back to Norwich."

"So, you want him to leave?"

Little knots of confusion ran across his face. "No, but why does he have to go to work and not come back until it's real late?"

I walked into Sue's office to find her on the phone, speaking very softly. I didn't want to interrupt, so I picked up a magazine.

A couple of minutes later she hung up, and when the phone immediately rang again she didn't put her hand out for it. Instead she sat there until it had rung three or four times, then reached over and turned her answering machine on.

"Sue, can we talk for a minute?"

"Huh?" she asked, slowly shaking her head.

"Can we talk?"

She looked over at me blank-faced and said, "Rich, my mother has cancer."

"What? When?"

She shrugged lightly, then shivered. "Her doctor upstate diagnosed her, and she's going to Boston General for a second opinion. Then, if it's confirmed, they'll operate right away and she'll do chemo and radiation treatment for six weeks in Dutchess County."

"New York?"

"Yeah," she said. "That was Eileen on the phone. We agreed that she'll stay here for those six weeks, not at Eileen's. Even if Eileen's place is closer, there are just too many steps down and back up from her house."

I nodded. Sue's older sister, Eileen, lived in a development built above a lake on the other side of the river. Her house was out of sight of the road, forty or fifty feet down the face of the hill, with a very long set of concrete stairs.

"How will we avoid steps here?" I asked.

Sue raised her eyebrows. "We'll have to put her on the first floor, in the room Mike is sleeping in. It's a tremendously big room—much too big since Liam moved upstairs."

"Okay," I said. "Number three is open. We'll redo it for Mike. How long do we have?"

"Only about a week, maybe two."

Then I forced myself to look back into her eyes. "The prognosis?"

There were tears in there, and her voice was brittle. "Not good."

In contrast to the depression everyone else was feeling, Mike seemed excited, even ebullient, about the move. In fact, he was so bubbly and happy that it grated on our nerves and we got a little snappy around him. But he ignored that and worked with us getting both rooms ready. He talked and talked about nothing else for the next week—how he liked the view, liked being up on the same floor as Liam, liked the long shelf running along one side of the room.

I quickly repainted number three, hung up Mike's pictures, mounted his big stuffed bear up high in one corner where it would look down on his bed, and then, on Friday night, we spent an hour or so getting everything else of his up. He had accumulated quite a bit over the past few months—clothes, models, games, books.

Then he got under the covers and we read together for half an hour.

"Good night," he said with a lilt in his voice.

"I'm glad Mike rose to the occasion and settled in upstairs," Sue said a couple of days later.

"I don't know how settled in he is," I said. "He's still jumping up and down about how much he likes it. In fact, he's running out of adjectives. Each night he spends more and more time telling me what a great room it is. He's so excited he doesn't even seem to be sleeping all that well."

Sue looked thoughtful for a moment or two, then she shook her head and said, "Well, it's new. I'm sure he'll be okay."

I nodded.

"The underwear?" she asked.

I sighed. I usually got up first and made coffee, so I usually dealt with Mike in the morning. "He'll still hide it if you give him half a chance, and when you question him he gets defensive and starts yelling."

"Then he's wetting every night?"

"Yeah," I said, "it seems so."

"Odd," Sue said, slowly shaking her head again. "When he was downstairs, he was starting to have dry nights a couple of times a week."

I shrugged.

Sue stood up and stretched. "We should pick a fight with him over hiding the underwear. But not now. We've got too much on our plate. Too much to work out."

When Sue's mother Lee was driven down from Boston by Eileen she looked wan and weak and had lost a lot of weight. We set up a double bed in the old library room, a hospital table, a good light so she could read, and a stack of books she had asked for. It was a good arrangement. Lee could work her way out the few paces through the connecting French doors into the living room and take her meals in front of the fireplace.

"Hello, Mike," Lee said in almost a whisper, smiling. "I'm glad I'm getting to meet you again."

But Mike looked down at her sitting in one of the wing chairs in the living room and asked in a loud voice, "When are you leaving?"

"Mike!" Sue protested.

• • •

We had followed through and started Mike in the local Cub Scout pack. His weekly den meetings were only a mile down the road in the Quaker church, the Friends Meeting House in Clintondale, built in 1810.

The den leader was a pleasant, patient man named John Thomas who did his best to fit Mike in. Mike was on the older side for Cub Scouts. Most of the boys had been there two or three years and were getting ready to move on to Boy Scouts in the late spring. But the den meetings themselves were artsy-craftsy sorts of sessions, just the sort of managed activity Mike was used to, and he seemed to fit right in.

"Maybe Cub Scouts is more Mike's kind of thing right now," Sue said. "At least it's exposing him to normal children. More than that, the kids are local, so he might make some friends."

"So?" I asked.

"So don't prod him into going to karate on Thursday nights if he wants to take a pass."

I looked the question at her.

Sue arched her back. "I think the socialization shock treatment has had its effect and he's proud of himself for it. Right now I think he should concentrate on friends and parties and get-togethers."

"Why?"

"I don't know why. There's something there. He's swimming out of focus, acting weird. You heard how he talked to my mother. I think he's getting ready to turn sideways again."

The next morning, half asleep myself, I padded into Mike's room at six-thirty, shook him awake, and got punched in the jaw.

"Mike, time to get up."

"No!" he screamed, then jumped to his knees on the bed, pulled back his left hand in a fist, and swung a long haymaker.

I saw it coming, but just couldn't believe it. I even had a hard time believing it when his fist connected with my chin.

Then Mike threw himself back down on the bed and wrapped himself up in his quilt. "Fuck you" came up at me.

I reacted out of reflex—or rather, I overreacted. I reached down, grabbed one side of the mattress, and flipped. He spun off and hit the floor. I had logrolled him.

He lay there for a moment before starting to make hurt sounds. "Oh, oh, oh, oh."

I got him up on his feet, and he wasn't injured. He had, after all, landed on the floor still wrapped in his quilt. But I was deeply ashamed of myself. Angry, too. How could he do that? *Why* did he do that?

That afternoon he slammed into the house after school.

"Mike, you have to lower your voice. Sue's mother is trying to get some rest."

"When is she leaving?" he yelled back.

Finally, Sue decided she would take over getting Mike up in the morning. "I'm going to have to make the time. You're far too abrupt," she said to me that night. "With my mother here, he's getting pushed out of the way a little bit, and you treat him like he's in the Marine Corps."

But when she went up in the morning, Mike smashed the window next to his bed. His fist went through the inside pane and then the storm window.

Sue just stood there for a few moments, the wind swirling through the window, and watched the snow dust his little figure. Then she reached under the quilt, grabbed his pajamas, and hoisted him bodily half upside down over the broken glass.

"March," she hissed.

"No."

"March."

•   •   •

As January snowed and snowed on, the morning confrontations escalated. Each night we'd put him to bed, read to him, tuck him in, and give him a hug, he'd tell us what a great room he had and how happy he was, and then, in the morning, there'd be open warfare.

An endless series of discussions went like this:

"Mike, it's terribly inappropriate to hit people or break windows."

"I don't care."

"Mike, why are you so angry?"

"Everybody really pisses me off."

"You're frightening the dogs. They don't want to come in the room with you anymore."

"I don't care."

"You're forfeiting your allowance to pay for this glass."

"Whatever."

"Can you tell us what's bothering you?"

"You. *You* bother me."

"How?"

"You really piss me off."

"Mike, how do we make you angry?"

"Everybody really pisses me off."

Sue was inwardly cringing, not only because we were down to two guests and they were getting ready to move, what with Mike's yelling or breaking things in the morning, but also because her mother was in the house.

One morning, while slowly sipping a cup of coffee in front of the fire, Lee rolled her eyes at the loud scene unfolding upstairs yet again and then looked shrewdly sideways at me. "Sometimes I feel like hobbling up those stairs with my walker in one hand and a belt in the other."

I laughed ruefully. "That's not part of his treatment plan, Lee."

Then she lit one of her unfiltered cigarettes with a wooden

match, took a sip of the coffee, exhaled, flicked the match into the fireplace, and said, "Have you considered getting him out of that room?"

"He loves that room, Lee."

That crafty sideways look again. "*Really,* now."

January ended, and Sue finally did have to give up almost all involvement with Mike as tax season opened and the long parade of clients began trooping in. Lee gradually seemed to improve, and her appetite quickened. We started making her some decent meals—London broil with new potatoes, baked chicken, good strong soups with dark bread and butter. She had the strength now to get up and watch TV for a couple of hours and, finally, to come downstairs for coffee in the morning, where she'd chat with the guests about her home in the Adirondacks.

But Mike wasn't any better. With the unending sequence of storms blasting through, school was closed as often as open, and on many mornings we'd defer the morning fight until after the guests had left. There always was a fight. And there always was breakage: lamps, his alarm clock again, the desk, his toys, and more and more windows.

After school and on weekends we could avoid further conflict by letting him park himself in front of the TV. But TV was a baleful influence. More so than anyone else we ever saw, TV drew Mike in.

So, thinking it must have something to do with his morning behavior, early in February we terminated his TV. The first day this happened, out of boredom Mike spent the afternoon at the winter barbecue in the St. Charles Church Hall. He went down early and helped set up (for which Deacon Carroll slipped him a twenty-dollar bill), and then he cooked hot dogs all afternoon.

"Okay," Sue said, "he's accepting it."

But he was actually striking back. A few days after TV

termination, things started to arrive in the mail that he had ordered over the phone.

"Mike," I said, holding a hefty package of custom-printed stationery in my hand, "you can't do this."

"I didn't order anything," he said with his big blue eyes wide.

I opened the covering letter and started to read, "Dear Michael, thank you for your telephone call . . ."

Then the range of conflict narrowed, as if Mike had decided that random surgical strikes were more effective than this "fight 'em every step of the way" morning routine. We didn't understand what was happening, at first—only that the mornings got suddenly better.

When they did, we foolishly felt a little guilty over some of our reactions to his behavior over the past few weeks, and we surprised him with boots, cross-country skis, and poles.

They seemed to be a big hit. Mike was outside all day long that first day. He even went out at sunset and tried to ski down the lane to the orchards, but as soon as he started into the dark under the trees an owl hooted in a branch just over his head and he set a land speed record coming back.

Then he put on a charming little pretense at indignation over Teddy, who was with him and had ignored the owl.

"You can't trust Teddy," Mike said, laughing.

"Well," I said in a happy, bantering tone, glad to see him in such a good mood, "you can't expect a dog to climb a tree in the dark and chase an owl. Besides, owls are good luck."

"Yep," he said, laughing again, and then he walked into the kitchen to get a snack.

"Whose dinner is this on the table?" I heard him shout in to me.

"It's Sue's Mom's," I shouted back. "Be careful. I'm just waiting for her to get out of the bath before I bring it up to her."

Smash!

I walked into the kitchen, and the tray and the dishes I had left on the table were broken on the kitchen floor.

"Mike, what happened?"

Those big blue eyes again. "I don't know. It just fell off."

"Mike, you had to have moved it. I left it in the center of the table."

"Whatever."

"Sue, he smashed that dinner tray on purpose."

It was late at night, Sue had finished with her last client, and we were having a quiet drink downstairs.

"Why?"

"Why?" I said. "I don't know. But he did it."

Sue just looked at me, exhausted, trying to force herself to think. "But why?"

Then he flashed again two days later on the next Cub Scout meeting night. Mike was picked up by the scoutmaster and his son, and then, at about eight, Henry and I went over to get him in Henry's truck.

When he ran out the door, Mike seemed very happy. He had made place mats for the blue-and-gold dinner and was chattering on about the upcoming event.

But thirty seconds after he got into the narrow cab of the truck, crowded in the middle over the gearshift, he started to call Henry names, then filthy names.

Then filthier names.

Every time I told him to stop this bizarre behavior he'd say, "Whatever," or "You're not my boss," or "You piss me off."

I was dumbfounded, but Henry stayed silent until we pulled into the parking lot and then said to me quietly, "I'll take care of this, Dad."

Mike was walking toward the house when Henry attacked him from behind. He picked him up and threw him into a snowbank, let him struggle up, then chased him. Mike started screaming, "Help, help, help me, Rich," but Henry shouted back the same snide little phrases Mike had used on me in the truck: "You're not my boss." "Whatever." "You piss me off." Then he caught him again and threw him into another snowbank.

I walked into the house, and Sue stormed into the living room from her office and shouted, "What's Henry doing to Mike outside?"

I shrugged.

Lee was sitting by the fire, quietly reading with a pot of fresh coffee next to her. She looked up and out the front window as a screaming Mike was making another circuit of the snowdrifts. "Sit down, Sue," she said pleasantly. "Have a cup of hot coffee and relax for a couple of minutes. Mike must have started it."

"No," Sue said, "the point is that you don't let him provoke you."

A few minutes later Mike came in red-faced, tears streaming down his face, soaking wet and shivering, but with an enormously satisfied smile on his face.

"What's this all about, Mike?" I asked.

He wouldn't answer. Instead he ran upstairs, changed into nightclothes, and then for the first time ever, came back down and said that even if it wasn't his bedtime, he was tired and wanted to go to sleep.

"What?"

"I have to," Mike said, grinning. "Henry said he's going to come upstairs and watch me."

"Huh?"

But he scampered off without answering.

"Okay," Sue said, flustered. "Okay. I give up."

The next week was the Cub Scout blue-and-gold dinner. I was tired and didn't want to go. But Mike was baking brownies, we had promised, and, of course, Sue wasn't available.

I washed and ironed his uniform—shirt, pants, neckerchief—

and he looked very sharp at first. Unfortunately, he then put something in his trouser pockets that spread out in a red stain.

It was like a barely controlled riot—seventy-five scouts, a hundred or so parents, and a million younger children. When the gym doors opened, the sound hit you like a sonic wave from a squadron of jets. I stood there, appalled, but Mike happily ran in with his brownies.

Somehow, the scoutmasters got it organized, all the tables were set with tablecloths, place mats, and a blue-and-gold bouquet of flowers, and the food was actually very good. There was an enormous buffet—meatballs, lasagna, baked ziti, beans, salad, chicken, rice, etc. Mike ate three hot dogs at home before the dinner under the theory that "you never know if there's going to be enough food." But on the serving line he loaded down anyway, a heaping plate of meatballs, chicken, and sausage. Then, when they set the dessert line, he came back with four or five types of dessert, grumbling that his brownies were all gone before he got there.

He now weighed one hundred seven. Maybe we should start cutting back.

The awards. Mike was the first up. He was getting his bobcat badge and his "mother" pin. I was nervous because I had to go up with him and put my arm on his shoulder while he recited the Cub Scout promise in front of the whole crowd. When he hesitated, I thought, *Oh, no, he's going to be embarrassed. Why didn't somebody warn me? I could have practiced with him!*

But he recited it flawlessly.

Then, after we came home, and almost as an afterthought, Mike ran back downstairs and started a fire in the kitchen.

The Harbour Program does not place or continue to place children with a history of fire-starting.

Joanne was the first to speak. "I'm going to lay it out to him:

he starts fires, he has to leave. And it won't be back to the children's home. He's almost too old now."

Sue nodded tiredly. She seemed suddenly beaten, unable to cope with Mike, with her mother, with tax season. It was all piling up too high. "I can barely go to sleep in this house, worrying about him finding some matches or going back down to the stove in the middle of the night."

Joanne looked at her. "Are you asking for a withdrawal?"

A long, long moment passed while Sue looked around as if she wanted to get up and run off somewhere. Then she said in a low voice: "Let's have him in here."

After Joanne said her piece and Sue and I followed up a concurrence, Mike gave us an appraising, deep look and then slowly nodded. "I'll never, ever do that again."

Sue was crying behind her eyes. "Okay."

Joanne reached over and touched her hand. "You do realize, Sue, that it's not entirely your decision or Harbour's decision? We are going to have to report this to Social Services."

Sue sat up straight, finally summoning some sort of energy. "Perhaps he's been alone with us too much—all this snow and these school cancellations. Maybe . . ."

CHAPTER TWELVE

i never went to a real school

Mike had another friend over for the day, a Joey from down the road, also a foster child. Sue knows the family and arranged it. We gave special dispensation, and they played Sega Genesis all afternoon. Mike made Joey lunch—hot dogs, of course.

No fights that day or the next, but the day after, he smashed the glass in the French doors. Sue's mother watched him do it. In fact, it looked as if Mike had waited for her to come inside.

"Get him out of that room, Sue."

"No, Mom, that has nothing to do with it. He loves that room upstairs. It's something else."

But the confirmation of Lee's deduction began to come our way several days later, when Liam told us that Mike got up at about four in the morning to go to the bathroom and then wouldn't because he couldn't get Teddy Bear to go out into the dark of the upstairs foyer with him. Liam had awakened when he heard Mike cajoling the dog, but was groggy and went back to sleep.

How many other times had that happened up there? I asked myself.

The next night I set my alarm for 4:00 A.M. and went upstairs.

When I opened Mike's door, he was sitting half asleep in his desk chair, holding Teddy around the neck.

"Mike, what are you doing?"

"Nothing."

"Mike, are you waiting for it to get light outside?"

Silence. .

"Where else would we put him?" Sue asked.

"Sue," I said, "I don't think he's slept at all in that room. He's absolutely terrified of the dark. The dark outside the windows, the dark in that foyer."

"Let's test it out," Sue said. "Call him in here."

When Mike walked in, Sue had him sit down. "Mike, we're going to offer you a choice. You can sleep in your room or take a sleeping bag and sleep downstairs outside our bedroom door on the floor. Which would you like to do?"

Shuffling feet, then he said, "I don't mind sleeping in a sleeping bag."

"Thanks, Mike. Now let us alone to talk for a little while."

When the door closed, Sue shrugged. "Well, you're right, but what do we do, and why didn't the room downstairs bother him like this?"

"It's a change," I opined, answering the second part of her question first. "He shared the room down here with Liam for a few months, so he was used to feeling safe in it. He could always hear some activity going on, and there usually was a light on in the living room or out in the downstairs foyer. Besides, we were just a door away. Up there he's isolated in the corner of the house in a strange room, nobody next to him, no sounds, no light coming in under the door. Everything you or I would view as a benefit is to him a danger."

Sue shook her head. "My mother is talking about going to

Eileen's for the last two weeks of her radiation. She's much stronger now and would like to get away from the long car ride. But that's a couple of days or so away and the basic fact about that big old room remains. There's just too much noise coming through. With my mother here we've been staying out of the living room, but when she leaves we'll go back to normal."

I made a proposal. "We could rebuild, remove the French doors, put a hallway down one side, then build two smaller bedrooms—one for Brendan, who's now sharing a room with Frank and hating it, and another small room for Mike, with just one window and a glass door facing a permanent night-light mounted out in the new hallway. That way he'll have quiet, a light outside, and still be close to us."

"Rich, are you nuts?"

"No."

Then she laughed. "So you've thought all this out?"

"Yeah." I got up and opened my dresser. "Here," I said, taking out a roll of paper. "Here's a floor plan I drew up."

"And for the next couple of weeks, until you get all this done?"

"Put the roll-away bed we have upstairs in the downstairs foyer, and when your mom moves out, roll it into the construction site."

The first night on the roll-away bed Mike slept like a dead man. When we woke him, he got up without a word, walked the few steps to the bathroom, and started his shower.

Sue's mother did move out the next week, and we started rebuilding in earnest—two small bedrooms opening on a new, short hallway, which then opened on the downstairs foyer. There was one window in Mike's room and a fixed night-light on the wall outside his room, shining through a glass-paned door.

Mike helped at every step of the way, loading in the material from where the flatbed truck stacked it in the snow, cutting the framing, studding it up, hanging the doors, Sheetrocking and painting.

Two weeks of peace in the morning. I asked Sue if the banging was disturbing her clients.

"No," she said, "those are happy noises."

Once the rooms were finished and Mike moved in, Sue took a walk through, sniffing the fresh white paint. "You know," she said, "he would never have told us he was frightened or upset. He would have kept up his act and his behavior until, in desperation, we moved him out of his home here and back into the system."

I sighed. "We've seen that phenomenon before, Sue. He believes he just has to deal with things as they happen to him. He reacts to circumstances, but he just won't ever act to change them. His mind-set says he can't."

She grimaced. Then she looked again at the freshly painted new walls. "I wonder if he understands how much we care about him."

For days Mike just slept and slept when he wasn't in school. We tried to be as understanding as we could to compensate for the very bad time he had had upstairs. We tiptoed around him, gave him lots of hugs, told him how great he was.

But then, once he was rested, and despite how understanding we were trying to be, the east wind blew again. It almost seemed we were back in mid-January. If it wasn't for how terrified we finally realized he was up in that room, we would have regretted going to the effort and expense of the construction downstairs.

It began again innocently enough, mindlessly enough. Sue complimented Mike on the dessert he had made for dinner, and he started rumbling and grumbling, got louder, louder yet, and then went into his tantrum act. "This family sucks. I want to go back to the children's home." And so on.

Suddenly blindingly angry, Sue called his bluff. She put the phone in his hand and told him to call. Then, when he hesitated, she got him the phone number and demanded he call. But he wouldn't do it. Sue then said she never wanted to hear that out of his mouth again.

Head down, Mike just looked up at Sue, sour and glowering.

"Well, Mike?" she asked. "Well?"

He screamed back at her, "I won't do that fucking homework."

"What?" Sue said, puzzled and taken aback. "What does homework have to do with anything?" Then she walked over and tried to give him a hug. "Mike, we don't want anything but good for you. Either Rich or I will help you with the homework."

On her weekly visit Joanne and I shared a pot of tea in the barroom.

"It's mid-February already," she said brightly. "You're making it through winter."

"Maybe."

"Rich," she said, sipping at her tea and not liking the look on my face, "the room issue has been resolved, hasn't it?"

I put my hands out in sort of a helpless gesture. "But now that we're past that, he wants to fight about homework. He wants to fight all the time."

It was true, and as far as I could understand Mike's tortured reasoning, if he didn't have homework, he'd have a chance at regaining unlimited access to the TV. Then he believed (I think, although I still can't understand it) that the way to get us to throw in the towel on homework was to fight with us over other issues in the afternoon and evening when he should be doing the homework.

But we didn't want to fight anymore. Both Sue and I were sick over the thought of more confrontation. Compounding the issue was the snow. It seemed day after day we were trapped in the house with him. The snow was so deep we weren't having the parking lot plowed any longer. Instead, we'd hired a man with a payloader and a backhoe. Even getting to the supermarket was a chore. We couldn't take a walk, send him outside, drop him off at a friend's house. It was always us and that voice, and he seemed to display an infinite degree of reserve strength. He could fight, argue, ridicule, insult nonstop from dawn to bedtime.

As Sue said, "There's a downside to Mike getting a good night's sleep."

But we couldn't let the homework go. First of all, the only reason the school was assigning him any work was that we'd complained about the lack of academics and asked for homework. Second, the effect of TV was like a drug to this child. If he watched it for half an hour, there was a mild confrontation when we asked him to eat dinner or go to bed or do his chores. But if he watched it for an hour, there was a major fight. Anything over an hour meant open warfare, the worst sort of language, unimaginable tantrums.

I explained all this to my son-in-law David when he, Sue, Henry, and I were eating a late dinner together. Being an orphan himself, I thought he might have some insight I lacked.

But what he said was confusing.

"Look," David said, "I think homework is a big symbol to him. It's something normal kids in normal schools do, and the fact you're insisting he do it means you care about him. The combination is deadly."

I looked at David, feeling stupid. "That can't be right."

David shrugged. "I think it's even worse than that. I think

you're facing this sort of issue right now because you went to all the trouble and expense of building him a new room."

"Okay," I said. "Now I'm thoroughly confused."

David grinned and settled down into the discussion. "Mike is starting to care, and he doesn't ever want to think about that. But showing *you* really care forces him to confront the beginning of his own feelings, and that makes him very angry. What he wants to do is have you back off. Then he's relieved of any obligation to care in return."

"Are you sure, David?"

"Well," he said, "I can only tell you how I felt. I was so angry, so bitter over what had happened to me that when I was placed with my adoptive parents I resented every nice thing they did for me. I wanted to stay bitter and angry."

"What happened?" I asked.

David made a dismissive gesture with his head. "I finally understood that my adoptive parents were just two people doing their best."

"How long did that take?"

He laughed. "About ten years."

"So then none of this is really about TV or homework?"

"Sure it is."

"Huh?"

David tapped one finger on the table. "If he can get back to the TV, he can avoid you and Mom, avoid what he's feeling, avoid this whole little world here that you're trying to move him into."

March had arrived. We were looking forward to some blue sky, a thaw, any sort of change in the weather.

Mike got up all right on the first day of March, but then didn't do what he had to do (take his sheets down to the washer, etc.). When I asked him to put a belt on, I got the same old "I don't have to." When he got home this afternoon, was uncooperative, and said he wanted dinner early, we set a time and gently explained to him how important his health and regular habits were to us. Then, when we left the kitchen, he came back in and cooked himself four hot dogs. We took them away and made him wait the half hour for dinner. He ate dinner with David. Then, when David left, he refused to do his homework again and wound up sitting at the table until bedtime, when he tore up his assignment and said, "I'll just lie about it." Then he went upstairs and smashed the glass in his door. Again.

Sue and I were beyond anger.

But it got worse.

The second week of the month I walked into a strangely quiet house. Stepping through Sue's empty office, I called her name—no answer.

When I walked down the hall toward our bedroom, I passed the downstairs foyer where the two doors were open leading into the hallway outside Mike's room. I saw him look out, then silently withdraw his head. There were shards of glass everywhere.

I pushed the bedroom door open, and Sue was lying facedown on the bed, her head in a pillow.

"Sue." When I shook her shoulder, she rolled over and sat up, her eyes red and bleary, her face puffed. She put her head on my shoulder and started to cry. "Rich, he broke the glass in his door again, then Brendan's glass, then he smashed the clock in my office and said he was going to wreck my computer."

"Sue, let's talk."

"No!" she screamed and pushed me away. "I don't give a damn. He has to get out of here. He has to leave."

"What set it off?"

Sue stood up and started pacing, sobbing, wiping her face

with the arm of her sweater. "Set it off? I just asked him to help me carry in the groceries, and when he did I gave him a little hug and a kiss."

"Mom?"

I turned around. Henry was in the doorway, his eyes flicking back and forth between our bedroom and the glass in the foyer, seeing his mother cry. Then he headed in the direction of Mike's room.

"Henry," I called after him, but Sue grabbed my arm.

"Let him go, Rich."

Henry didn't beat Mike up, but he did scare the bejesus out of him. Then he had Mike sweep up the glass, vacuum, and mop. Then Henry put him to bed.

After Sue's last client that night, we sat down in the barroom and shared a pot of very strong tea.

"Rich," Sue said, trembling, "there's not a nerve that hasn't been stripped right out of my body. He *will* smash my computer; he *will* set fire to the house. This place and our kids are what we've worked for all our lives. I won't give it up. I *won't.*"

I was a choppy mix of emotion myself, wanting to just walk away from everything and have our life back the way it was.

And then Henry came into the room, walked behind the bar, opened the refrigerator, twisted the top off a bottle of Sam Adams, and thirstily downed half the bottle.

"I'm beat," he said. "I was up and down Bonticue Crag today and then up on the cliffs on the east face—ten miles in the snow. I'm drinking this beer and then hitting the sack for about twelve hours."

"Henry," Sue said quietly, getting down off her barstool, "I'm thinking about sending Mike back."

Henry shrugged. "Well, that's your decision. Good night." Then he started to walk off.

Sue stopped him. "But do you think that's right or wrong?"

Henry looked at her, deadpan. He just stood there for a few moments, broad shoulders, head turned, hands on hips, in a thick green flannel shirt with the collar turned up.

Then he said, "It doesn't matter what I think."

Sue blew out her breath, exasperated, then said, chopping each word into an individual statement, "Henry, darling, if you were us, would you send him back?"

There was the hint of a grin on Henry's lips. "No, I would treat him a lot differently."

"*How* differently?" I asked.

"Look, Dad," Henry said patiently, "I heard what David had to say, and I know if you think it through, you'd agree with him and Mom would, too. The fact is, though, whenever you deal with Mike, you're one hundred eighty degrees off in the other direction. You know the kid has a problem with your caring for him, you know it's going to take a long time for him to come to terms with that, but whenever you deal with him you don't do anything except pile on more caring and understanding than he can digest."

"Henry," I said, protesting, "we *do* care, and we're just trying to treat him like a reasonable human being."

"But, Dad," Henry said, "this isn't a reasonable, a reasoning situation. It's all emotion, all feeling. Mike doesn't understand reason or reasonableness in his current state of mind."

"Doesn't understand?" Sue asked. "Piling on more caring than he can digest?"

"Mom," said Henry, "would you put fifty pounds of steak down in front of a dog and expect him to just eat what he's comfortable with? Well, Mike is just like that dog. Day after day he's eating it all and then getting sick all over the carpet."

"So then, how he's acting now is our fault?" she asked.

Henry nodded. "Yep. If you want him to stay here, back off. Remember what David really said. Stop acting like brand-new parents."

Then he walked out and upstairs.

Sue put her head down on her arms for a few moments and then sat up straight and pushed the pot of tea away. "Rich, I want you to make me a real drink."

Sitting at the bar, she quickly downed a stiff vodka and orange juice and asked for another.

She drank the second one just as quickly, then rapped her knuckles on the bar for a third.

"Whoa," I said.

"Whoa, yourself," and she took a big sip from the third.

She sat there silent for a long ten minutes or so before her body began to shake and quiver. Then she had an attack of the giggles.

I let her run on and on until she was laughing out loud to herself before I said glumly, "Okay, are you going to let me in on the joke or what?"

She struggled for breath and gasped out, "Yes. Yes. Rich, think about this. Here we are, two experienced parents, having raised six children, almost at the point where we want to start putting together our retirement, and we decide to take in a child who drives out most of the guest income we depend on, eats up all of our time, breaks forty or fifty windows, defecates in his pants, wets the bed, makes it difficult for us to leave and see our friends, steals, lies, has us do reams of paperwork for Harbour, and the best suggestion we can get out of anybody, the *best* suggestion, is to ignore him."

I had to laugh, too.

"Well," Sue said, struggling off the barstool, "I certainly wouldn't have any problem at all acting distant and unemotional."

• • •

Late March, and it was forty degrees and raining. You couldn't see Shawangunk across the valley. It was hidden in thick, woolly blankets of wet cloud. The snow was melting, running away in silver, ropy streams off the roof, exposing the stone walls and then draining off into large black, icy pools on the walks, on the lawn, down in the hay meadow.

One more week until trout season, and it had been almost three since Mike settled down and stopped fighting with us.

I was standing outside, dressed in knee-high gum boots and a slicker, sipping at my coffee, gulping down great drafts of the wet, warmer air, when he walked up to me. Mike had on rubber boots with laces, his yellow rain jacket, and a sodden-wet knit cap. The two of us had been searching the property. The oddest things turn up when the snow melts.

"I'm all finished," he said.

I tried not to smile, forcing myself to develop an indifferent expression. It was getting easier after two or three weeks of practice. "Okay," I said blankly, but wanting to hug him, punch him lightly in the shoulder, tousle his hair.

"What about you?" Mike said. "Are you going back inside?"

I knew I was going to smile then, maybe even start laughing, so I turned my back to him and walked off. "Yeah, in a few minutes."

Sue and I had replenished much of our strength as March melted away into April and the middle of the month—the end of Sue's tax season—approached. Mike was still quiet, and suddenly we could think about spring. There were house repairs, we had to buy a new car, we had ads to put up so we could start filling the guest rooms again—things to do, positive things.

But then Mike escalated the homework issue to a new and higher level.

It was sunset and we were at dinner in the barroom. Sue was studying another tax publication open on the table next to her, while Mike was quietly looking down at his plate and not eating, just listlessly stirring his food together.

I nudged Sue, and she peered over the top of her glasses. "Mike, aren't you hungry?"

Mike hesitated for a moment and then lurched his head up. "When Liam was twelve, did he go to a normal school?"

Sue swallowed hard and then put a heaping forkful into her mouth. Her eyes said, "Rich, your turn."

The school? I didn't want to talk about the school!

I had settled into a certain accommodation with the special program Mike was attending, but at most it was a live-and-let-live-at-dagger-points arrangement. For months now there had been no further "restraining" incidents, and I was more than willing to concede that they had a daunting range of conduct to contend with, but overall, they spoke too much of a murky, wordy jargon I didn't understand. What are social peer interactions? Dysfunctional groupings? What is transitioning or aging out? I had been getting in there and trying to talk to them for a few minutes now and again, but it was difficult to keep a pleased, plastic smile on my face when I felt like I was being bumfoozled.

And it was particularly difficult to be pleasant when I knew what Mike really thought about it.

Not that he'd ever told us. Mike didn't talk about his likes or dislikes, except in the most trivial way. He was really vocal about what breakfast cereal he liked or what TV show he wanted to watch, but that was about the depth of it. If you wanted to know what he was really thinking, you had to trail along behind him and snag any clues that happened to drop.

If we'd learned anything at all about the kid, we'd learned that.

But regardless, we'd still managed to assemble a crystal-clear picture of what he thought about school.

He hated it! He didn't hate the idea of going to school or the concept of academics itself, but what he'd come to see as the exacting, day-in day-out humiliation of a "special needs" program.

It started with the "special" van that picked him up. Not only was there a bus driver, but there was an assistant bus driver who strapped the kids in as they boarded. Adding to Mike's discomfort was the fact that he could not wait by himself outside like the other children up and down the road—the rattling little bus would not load or discharge a child unless the parent was standing outside observing, and as a result, you could actually see Mike cringe and set his shoulders before he'd walk over to it.

Then, once there, he had to contend with the shoulder-sagging focus of the "special needs" program itself, a program that he viewed not as compassionate or helpful, but rather as a fairly nasty brand of differentiation in its emphasis on "socialization" and peer-group behavior interspersed with "reward play-time" or "quiet-room time," instead of the "normal" classwork he could see going on through glass walls in other classrooms with other children—"normal children."

And regardless of what we saw as real intelligence and ability in Mike, we couldn't nudge the program into doing anything else with him.

The dictionary incident was a good case in point.

Mike questioned a word, so we handed him a *Webster's Dictionary* and walked away.

An hour later: "Mike, are you having a problem finding that word?"

"No."

Of course not. His room could be on fire, with lightning

crashing in the window on the heels of a burglar following a charging water buffalo, and when we called in to ask him if he needed any help, he'd just as calmly answer no.

"Here, let me see what you're doing."

It seems he knew enough to go after the correct starting letter, but beyond that was lost. In searching for a word beginning with *s*, he would turn to the beginning of the *s* section and then proceed to examine each and every entry that followed. So half amused and half angry, I workshopped with him until he thoroughly understood the organization of the dictionary and could find any word he chose.

Later I wrote a complaint letter to the school, saying in essence that we should have a little forward motion on academics here, that "being eleven years old, almost twelve, and not knowing how to use a dictionary" was unacceptable.

When a few days passed without an answer, I followed the letter with a telephone call and was promptly dismissed with a short, condescending lecture. They knew Mike had big "gaps" in his learning, but in their professional judgment it was much more important to focus on his behavior—particularly his behavior in group settings.

That got my fur up. Behavior in group settings? What in God's name did they think we were doing? Ahhh! Why couldn't they just teach him to read and do sums?

In fairness, my paranoia could have been working overtime again. What I took as an all-too-typical reaction to foster parents—that we can be blithed off as a temporary "residential resource," untrained, uneducated, perhaps taking in children for "sniff" money—might in fact really just represent a sincere desire to be left alone to do what they had to do. Yet on the other hand, the school system—the BOCES system, rather—when not amused by our prodding, invariably seemed to whet its response with a suspicious degree of indignation.

So I tried to avoid it, and I tried to avoid discussing it. There was just nothing I could do about it then, no matter how hard it was to watch Mike trudge over to that "special" bus each morning.

Harbour felt more or less the same way. Whenever we tossed these issues at Joanne, she bounced them right back with a grimace and a standard comment. "When the CSE meeting rolls around, we'll get our chance to vote on what they're about. Meanwhile, you guys have enough to do focusing on family issues and, hey, Mike looks great. Whatever you're doing, keep it up."

The last time she said that I waited until we were alone and then asked Sue, "I forget. What does CSE stand for?"

"Committee on Special Education."

"How many people are on this committee?"

"I dunno, five or six—his special education teacher, maybe one of his assistants, the BOCES therapist, the social worker, a couple of people from the special education department of the school district, maybe the nurse."

"Well," I rumbled back, thinking it through, "I don't even need to take my shoes off to add that one up."

Despite my belief that Mike's school should be helping him use the intelligence he obviously had to catch up on academics, deep down I felt that in the most perfect of worlds Mike wouldn't be going anywhere outside this house for a long, long time—not even to a "regular" school. I remember when Henry first began classes. The kid had a lot of problems. When we finally sat down with the principal and pressed her on what was wrong, she said, "Look, there's nothing wrong with Henry. What's wrong is his being here in the first place. We should go in there right now, pick him up, and put him back in the sandbox for a year."

And that's sort of the way I feel about Mike. This was too

much on him. If he had to be educated at all this year, it should have been in front of the fireplace reading *The Wind in the Willows* with the two dogs snoring next to him. Let him read, learn on his own; let him nap, eat, get up and talk when he's moved to. Leave him alone!

So I didn't know how to answer Mike's question. If I gave him the extended answer and said what I really thought, I'd be parting company with Sue because she had an entirely different viewpoint. Never one for sloppy gradations, her attitude was, "You're a child? Then go to school. Stay home and get yourself together? Complain because you don't like your particular school? *Are you out of your mind?*"

But on the other hand, if I gave Mike the short answer and just said, "Yes, Liam went to a normal school," I'd be as much as smacking him in the face.

So I produced the trite "party line" answer: "Mike, you'll be going to a normal school one of these days. What you have to do is concentrate on what you're doing right now."

Mike didn't answer, so Sue prompted him. "Mike, what Rich means is that you have to work hard and improve your behavior, and then you'll be moved out of that school, into the same type of school as everybody else. You understand that, don't you, Mike?"

"No," he answered. "I'm in a family, so I should be in a normal school right now."

"That isn't always possible, honey."

"I want to! I'm in a family!"

"I'm sorry, Mike."

Then he bored back with the original question. "Did Liam go to a normal school?"

I sighed and gave up. "Yes."

No movement, no response. The fork stopped stirring.

"I'm not really a member of this family, am I?"

Whew! But then Sue spoke up. "Mike, we couldn't love you more if you were our own child. You have to remember that you chose us and we chose you. That makes us even more special as a family."

"I'm not special," he screamed.

Sue got flustered and backed up. "Hey, I didn't mean special in that way."

Mike relentlessly pushed the point. "Did Brendan go to a normal school?"

"Yes," and I winced.

"Susanne?"

"Yes."

"Henry, Frank, and Richard?"

"Yes, yes, and yes."

"Are you sure?"

I could only slouch and answer, "Yes, I'm sure."

He put his head down, shouting, "I don't want to see them. If any of those sons come near me again, I'm going to stab them with a knife."

"Mike," Sue said, shocked, "what an awful thing to say."

I had a brilliant thought. "David, Susanne's husband, didn't go to a normal school, either. He was in an orphanage in Vietnam a long, long time ago. Then he had to fly out of there on a plane, and it was very dangerous. In fact, he took off right after a plane with other orphans was shot down, and then, when he got here, they didn't put him in a normal school. He had to work and learn the language and learn how to behave."

The food stirring started again as Mike thought about that, but after maybe thirty seconds or so he dropped the fork. "I'm not an orphan, I'm a foster child. I have a mother and father. I'm just not living with them."

• • •

I walked into our bedroom and dropped the morning *New York Times* on the bed.

"Mike's on the bus and you've been down to town already?" Sue asked.

"Yeah, I had to get milk."

"So," Sue said, taking a cursory look at the paper, "what are your plans today?"

I yawned and stretched. "I'm sanding the floor in number five."

"And?"

"And what?" I asked.

"And," Sue said sweetly, "you're going to go out and pick up Mike's birthday present."

"Oh, I forgot," I said. "It's this Friday?"

"No," Sue said patiently, "it's the day after tomorrow. His brother and sister will be here, some friends from school, and maybe Joanne will come down. I'll be here, too, of course, but I have to see clients in Middletown all the early afternoon, so you'll have to decorate the barroom before he gets home from school."

"How should I decorate the barroom?"

"Oh," said Sue distractedly, "just a couple of balloons. Remember, we're still keeping our distance."

Balloons, balloons, balloons. I spent the entire afternoon putting up a mile of streamers and a big "Happy Birthday" banner. Then I put balloons on the mailbox, on Sue's sign, on the door to the barroom, over all the lights, the mirror, even on the deer head hanging off in the corner.

Liam came in an hour before Mike was expected. "Dad, are you out of your mind? Mom told you to keep this thing relaxed and low-key."

"The hell with that. I've been a good boy for weeks now, and I'm sick of being low-key and detached. Today I'm going to overload every circuit in Mike's feeble little emotional brain path."

Sue walked in from the parking lot then, an attaché case in one hand and a box of accounting records under the other arm. She just stood there with her mouth hanging open.

"Mom," Liam said, "I think Dad has been drinking or something."

Then she started laughing. "Oh, my God."

The party was in full swing, but Mike was tense and edgy, quietly watching.

His half sister, a short, quiet girl about thirteen, and a much taller but just as quiet half brother a year or so older, had arrived with their adoptive parents, the Johnsons, and I thought their presence might have been difficult for Mike. Was he embarrassed over them? Or feeling awkward at having wound up with a different family?

There wasn't any chemistry at all between Sue and me and the Johnsons, despite having spoken on the phone any number of times, and there was always that mystery hanging fire in any appreciation of them by us—the whys of their failed adoption attempt in regard to Mike. But their behavior at the party seemed downright strange.

When we offered to lend their children a couple dozen videotapes, the Johnsons picked through the tapes in front of us and the children, rejecting Walt Disney movies like *Parent Trap* as "garbage" and "immoral," movies that "exalted" divorce and violence. Yet both of them were divorced. And almost the first words out of their mouths when they walked in had been that he was an alcoholic and could shoot somebody (he actually worked for the post office), and she explained to us that she had a medical condition that caused her to faint every half hour or so, but she could be revived with cigarette smoke. Throughout the party they discussed their children in a derogatory way right in front of them, consistently calling their youngest adopted child "the crack baby."

Despite what we viewed as hurtful behavior, the two older children seemed pleasant, although extraordinarily reserved. Mike's sister looked away whenever she smiled. Oddly, there had been no hugs and kisses between the children when they arrived.

Sue, however, was ignoring any straight faces and trying to whoop it up, popping balloons and making a big show. She had the children from Mike's class at school laughing and even nudged Mike's brother into half a grin.

Then I realized what was going on. Mike was wondering what he would get for a present from us. He had been talking about little else for the past few days. He had tried the toe-in-the-water technique in regard to TV time by asking for another Sega game cartridge, knowing that we would let him play it. But pathetically, he also asked for a new tire for his bike. Liam had given him an old BMX and helped him get it going, but it was in bad shape, with parts always falling off and the rear wheel wobbly and out of round.

Finally, Sue dashed into the kitchen for the cake and candles, and I ducked into the cellar to get his present, too big to wrap but as safe from being found by him far back there in the dark as it would be in Fort Knox.

A brand-new, adult-size, metallic-blue, eighteen-speed mountain bike, an air pump, a water bottle, and a helmet.

I watched his face as I wheeled it out into the barroom. He wouldn't look at it directly at first, just stared out of the corner of his eye. But with everybody prodding him, he finally got up and put hands on it, then gave a big, big grin.

Sue whispered to me, "I hope this doesn't get him angry enough to take out four or five windows."

"Later," I said sarcastically, "later. Right now, he's actually happy."

Then, an hour or so afterward, Mike and I were outside in the parking lot and he was shouting at me. "I know how to ride this bike. Leave me alone."

"Fine," I said. "Fine," and just backed away with my hands up.

A few minutes later I was checking one of the truck tires, bent down on my knees at the bottom of the parking lot, when I saw him start into the drive up above.

Seconds later he hit me. He hit me so hard I thought my legs were broken and I actually blacked out for a few seconds.

When I came to, Mike was looking down at me, spinning the pedals backward on his bike. "I'm sorry," he said. "We have to get some brakes on this thing."

"Hand brakes," I managed to grunt out. "Those things on the handlebars are hand brakes."

"If there's one thing I'm certain of, Rich, it's that Mike desperately requires the services available in the special educational program."

I tried to be patient. Sue had made the appointment with this school psychologist and at the last minute couldn't go. She wanted to explore the possibility of shifting Mike over into at least a few real classes. But the chemistry between us was bad from the get-go.

"But *Tom*—" I insisted on calling him Tom because he had insisted on calling me Rich "—this is a fundamentally bright kid. He's made enormous progress at home socially, and he wants to try mainstream classes."

"I don't know what we can do. Mike has a long history of emotional disturbance. He's been duly diagnosed."

"Well, then," I said, "suppose we get him to another psychiatrist and have him duly undiagnosed?"

"Hah," he said with a self-deprecating little smile, "even under those circumstances, BOCES will insist upon special resources being made available. There's an immense amount of prior documentation, there's the federally mandated IEP, the Individual Educational Plan—too much to ignore, even if it wasn't legally required."

"So he's trapped."

The psychologist sat up somewhat indignantly. "This is one of the best programs in the state. There's even a waiting list. Mike was very fortunate to get in here."

"Tom," I protested, waving my hand at the modern offices and complex of rooms, "Mike doesn't consider all this a resource for himself; he considers this a stigma. He wants to be a normal kid."

"But he's not a normal child."

I got my back up. "I don't know what's normal, what an average kid is. If we were all average, every one of us would have one testicle and one breast."

The psychologist gave that remark a perfunctory, flat smile and then said, "Mike's severely emotionally disturbed—just look at his handwriting. After months of coaching, he still writes a scrawl. It's not possible for him to keep written words between the lines on a sheet of paper despite fairly good small-motor development. There are emotional issues there, deep emotional issues."

At seven-thirty that evening Mike was doing his homework on the coffee table in front of the fireplace. I picked up his homework paper and saw that his penciled answers were scrawled all over the page. So I tore it up.

"Hey!" he yelled.

But I sat down and pulled a fresh piece of paper over in front of him. "What's the answer to the first question?"

He looked at me sullenly. "Apple."

"Fine. Write the letter *a* and keep it between those blue lines."

"Why?"

"Just do it."

Scrawl.

"Okay, erase it and do it over, and this time keep it between the lines."

He erased it and wrote again.

Scrawl.

"You didn't keep it between the lines, so erase it again."

Rub, rub, rub, and then he picked up the pencil again.

Scrawl.

"Erase it."

In a couple more tries he had worn a hole through the paper and I put a new sheet in front of him.

It was about nine o'clock when he angrily wrote it between the lines. "There."

"Good," I said. "That's a perfect *a*. Now write *p,p,l,e,* keeping the letters between the lines."

When Mike finished his assignment, I stood up and over him.

"Mike, why don't you keep the words between the lines on all your schoolwork?"

He glared up at me. "I hate that fucking school."

"Don't use that word."

"I hate that fucking classroom."

I leaned over to give him a punch in the shoulder, but he ducked away laughing, pleased at his wit.

Then I went into Sue's office, made a copy of his homework, and attached it to a very angry letter.

Later I tried to put this dispute into context. I knew why the school backed away from pushing Mike onward—they had looked at his file and didn't really think he belonged in their relatively open setting in the first place. A fact which ties into the mystery of why we were ever introduced to Mike, because we've come to understand in a backhanded sort of way that he should never have been selected for The Harbour Program.

It wasn't anything said directly, but rather what was hinted at—that Harbour is a therapeutic foster-care program designed for children who stand a reasonable chance of benefiting, and that Mike's file was much too daunting for any of that.

So, then, why was he here?

Somehow he sailed through the first independent selection committee, through Harbour's own screening, and then was handed to Sue and me as our first and only file. I suspect the hidden hand of personal interest. I think somebody felt really sorry for Mike and took a long, long chance.

Which goes a long way toward explaining why Joanne and Paula, the director of The Harbour Program, trundled on down here this afternoon, the day after Joanne's latest visit with Mike, primed with a "stop pushing Mike, keep a low profile, don't rock the boat" lecture.

After a preface, what we got was a blunt caution against any further unilateral action, and then an even blunter reminder about who should be calling the plays. In fact, Paula told us that we were to regard Harbour, in the matter of Mike, as "our employer."

I suppose this conversation had to happen. When you sum up Mike's peculiar status, along with our behavior, it must have equaled extreme organizational discomfort. At our weekly meetings we always told Joanne exactly what had happened, but rarely what we were planning. Not necessarily because we didn't want her to know (although, to be honest, that was sometimes the case); it was just that we ourselves often hadn't the foggiest idea of what we were going to do. Yet I could see how that would appear from the other side of the fence: getting the medication dropped, taking him to the Adirondacks, taking him to Vermont and what happened there—"I got blown over by a cannon. Wow!"—Joanne's initial anxiety over the karate school, putting dogs on his bed, household chores, Sue's smugness about shutting him up by yelling back (what she calls "tantrum therapy"), the fact that Mike must have told Joanne that we took him "hunting" and that we had physically dragged him out of bed morning after morning. All in all, a picture of a self-willed couple more than a tad out of control.

But somehow, I thought today's meeting would have more to do with the school than any other one issue.

I looked over at Sue. Under most circumstances Paula's remarks would have had the effect of a lit match connecting with an open pan of gasoline. But today she was just radiating sunshine. So I made a self-justifying stab on my own. "You know, Paula, Mike has gained thirty pounds since he's been with us."

Paula looked at me, startled, and said, "No, I didn't know that." Then she turned to Joanne. "You should put that in the report."

Sue said lightly, starting to get interested for the first time, "A report? Is somebody, somewhere up the food chain, interested in Mike?"

Paula waved the question away. "It's just what we do from time to time."

Sue made a low sound in her throat, and I topped off with another comment. "He's getting up in the morning. He wouldn't do that at the children's home."

"I remember reading that in his file," Paula said. Then she looked at Joanne again and Joanne scribbled.

Sue finally kicked in behind me, "And he's had a friend—friends, in fact—over for the day. We had been told he couldn't handle that sort of one-to-one relationship."

"I see."

"He had been diagnosed with Tourette's syndrome, but his facial tic has disappeared."

"Really?"

I snapped my fingers. "He's helping with family meals."

"And doing chores."

"His night crying has stopped."

"He's writing between the lines."

"He learned how to play chess."

"He's taking long walks with the dogs and not hounding us for attention any longer."

I looked at Sue and smirked. "And don't forget, he's wiping his ass now."

"Yes, there's that," Sue said, smiling sweetly at Paula, then carefully punctuated every syllable with her voice like a rasp on slate. "He is wiping his ass."

Both of us stared across the table at Paula with the unspoken question on our lips: After that shot about an employer-employee relationship, what are you prepared to do?

A long, long eye contact, and then Paula put up her hands and smiled. "Okay. Now look, folks, I'm on your side, because I know you're on Mike's. Please don't take anything I said personally. But Mike is severely disturbed, and in many ways, you folks are still in the honeymoon stage with him. So we have to understand a couple of things. First, how important it is to maintain the proper services . . ."

Aha, I thought. It *is* about the school.

"And," Paula continued, "maybe, just maybe, we don't have to shove Mike along quite so vigorously."

"Yes," Sue said, smiling again, "of course."

We had missed having a big dinner on Easter because Susanne and David were away and so Sue decided to hold it later in the month. Mike pitched in and peeled potatoes. Then, since we were all still very busy, he decided that he would take a walk. He and the dogs loped up and down the mountain for almost two hours, and he came back tired, relaxed, with red cheeks and windblown hair, and very hungry. He slid into the kitchen and started lifting pot covers. "Ah, excellent," he'd say with one—*clang.* "My favorite," with another—*clang.*

Sue bumped into him with a heavy, hot pot in her hands. "Mike, get the blazes out of here and go wash up," she said and he ran out.

Roast lamb, potatoes whipped with sour cream, gravy, lots of vegetables, salad, two types of pie, brownies, and rocky road ice cream. Mike was the subject of a lot of well-thought-out ribbing from David, Liam, and Henry (he had started it by remarking in a hurt tone of voice that last Saturday he had had only one-and-a-half hours of TV). But Mike seemed to revel in the joshing. He asked for a beer and I said no, then asked for wine and I gave him cranberry juice in a stemmed glass. Later Liam asked him if he was drinking wine, and Mike said aggrievedly, "No, Rich did the cranberry switch on me again."

Mike ate both brownies and lemon pie for dessert, then quietly played Scrabble with David with the table light turned low and everybody else silently reading next to them or chatting, whispering together in the still shadows of the room. Then, at bedtime, he went off happy and sleepy and holding a kitten named Calico that Theresa, one of our guests, had given him.

Wow, that was almost civilized.

A sunny day. You could stand on the back lawn and see the Catskills forty miles off or a hawk start from a tree a mile distant.

I restrung Mike's fishing pole with Stren fishing line, fixed the ferrule, and we practiced casting on the grass. Mike was fascinated with the way Stren fishing line fluoresces purple in the sunlight but goes clear when it hits the water (so am I, for that matter). He went back to the lakes to fish and stayed there with the dogs almost until dark. I checked on him once with the binoculars and could clearly pick out his figure casting into the big lake, with the two black blobs of Teddy Bear and Pupsy next to him on the grass.

Later he ate dinner at the bar—hamburgers, french fries, salad—and we actually allowed him to watch TV until bedtime, which he did relaxed and sleepy on the couch with a quilt over him. The kid was actually tired, not keyed up or hyper.

On his way to bed he asked me if he could grow a ponytail. I said, "Not while I'm drawing a breath."

Late in the afternoon several days later, Mike headed up to the mountain with his bike, and when he didn't return I followed him on Brendan's bike. No matter what you do, you think the worst. Maybe he ran down the road out of control and crashed into one of the lakes and drowned? Maybe he took a spill and hit his head?

I found him talking to Gene Coy about a mile or two back. Gene is the farmer next door. Gene was in his truck with his black Lab, Cinder, sitting next to him on the seat. Mike was telling Gene his life story and asking a thousand questions about the dog. "Does he help around the house? Is he a good guard dog? Does he swim? Does he poop on the walk? Does he get carsick? Does he . . ."

Gene sat in his truck, lean, tanned, saturnine, with graying hair, carefully smoking a cigarette while trying to nod as fast as the questions ran by. Finally, he blurted out, "Nice to meet ya, gotta spread calcium, so long," and got out of there with his tires spinning gravel and the dog looking back vaguely out of the passenger window, no doubt wondering what all that noise was about.

The next day, Mike upped the ante on the school issue—or at least, that's what we thought it was about.

I had to meet someone at 7:00 A.M. in Kingston, which is about thirty miles north of our place. It was a recreation day for me, shooting skeet farther up the river at Germantown, so I was long gone from the house when Sue shuffled into Mike's room, still half asleep, dressed in slippers and a robe and sipping her first cup of coffee.

The awful way in which Mike's eruptions could astonish us is something we had never gotten used to, particularly since we were forever thinking he'd grow beyond these things. But they were his weapon of choice when he was dissatisfied about something, and the hard fact was that on any night at all Mike could go to sleep happy and exhausted and then rear up out of his sheets in the morning like some demon from the pit. Often we couldn't help thinking that something this awful couldn't be emotional, that it was organic brain damage, perhaps from when he was so young and beaten so severely. But we also knew that he'd been examined and CAT-scanned and X-rayed and tested time and time again. And the targeted nature of these fights told us that there was a strong element of control involved, that he was actually making decisions. For instance, when he smashed something, ninety percent of the time it was something of his own or a window in his room. And while his behaviors used to be distributed over any and all social settings, they had now narrowed their focus to Sue and me or the school, to people acting in a parental role.

Knowing that we'd become the sole target was little consolation, and perhaps most unnerving was the fact that these explosions usually occurred when we were most vulnerable or least expectant.

And apparently Sue got it with both barrels this morning. Then, later in the day, she got a call from school. It wasn't over by a long shot—big trouble on the school bus, big trouble in class, lying, shouting, and so on.

On my unsuspecting way home I stopped in town and picked up his bike from the repair shop and the new Boy Scout equipment he required. Then, when I walked in after four in the afternoon relaxed and smiling, laden down with his parcels, a repetition of the morning began—screaming, smashing more windows—and it went on until late in the evening, with Mike having to be restrained any number of times. It ended only when he had depleted every ounce of energy he had and dropped, sobbing, into a corner of his room.

Not for the first time, we wondered if it was right to get in his face and stay in his face, driving him through these cycles. There just didn't seem to be any option, and we told him that over and over again, trying to put as impersonal a face on it as we possibly could: "Mike, it's our job as parents to get you up for school, or to see that you do your homework, or that you're dressed and clean and fed, and no matter what you do, no matter what anyone else does, that's what we're going to do. We will never, ever stop."

Late that night, with Mike washed up and changed and slumping on his bed, I tried to think of another way to get through to him and said, "We don't want to fight anymore over getting up in the mornings, but we will. Wouldn't it be better if you got us up, instead? Can you come up with a plan?" Interestingly, he did come up with a plan, mumbling something about alarm clocks being set for certain times, a better attitude on his part, and so on.

But I didn't have all that much confidence he'd follow through. He still hadn't gotten what he wanted.

●　　●　　●

Liam got his braces off this afternoon, after two years in them. He asked me if he could have some "real food."

"What does that mean?"

"McDonald's."

So Mike, Liam, and I went to McDonald's for dinner. Mike was upbeat from time to time, saw a kid ride by on a bike and said with a grin, "I have a better bike than that one!" He chattered away over the food, but there was something to his attitude, like a dark mirror flashing through his eyes from time to time. It was making me edgy and nervous. I felt like a twitchy dog who can sense a thunderstorm working up close by. Then I remembered that Mike had talked to his sister several times over the phone during the last few days. That was unusual— they usually spoke only once a month or so. Did that have any bearing on his behavior?

When I mentioned this to Sue, she recalled that Joanne had taken Mike to visit his brother and sister at the Johnsons' a short time before, and we decided to ask her about Mike and his sister's relationship.

What Joanne reluctantly described to us was a very sad situation. Although schooling was something of an issue, Mike's sister constantly complained about the broader position of herself and her older brother in the Johnson family. Apparently they were enrolled in a small, restrictive Christian academy, had to come home immediately after school, and then were rarely allowed out unsupervised. Where Mike's brother seemed withdrawn and uncommunicative, his sister was rebelling and fantasizing about getting out on her own. Joanne thought it possible that the sister might be passing on this vision to Mike in a manner that suggested that, despite being only thirteen, she might escape from the Johnsons and come for him.

The three of us tried to sort this out. There was a special relationship between Mike and his sister—not overtly affectionate, but rather, based on shared secrets. In a very counterproductive way, the sister might only be trying to perpetuate a role she had assumed many years ago, and although it was very difficult to ferret out the details of what actually had occurred in their biological home, it seemed that Mike as an infant got something to eat only when his sister stole it for him, and the same seemed to be the case for any other sort of care or attention he received.

How could adults deal with that relationship? His sister might be the only person in the universe Mike really trusted, and we certainly didn't want to touch that. But we couldn't reason with her, either: apparently she was just too angry about her own predicament.

Did Mike sense that he had pushed things far enough, for now, or did he know something we didn't? Apparently one or the other, because the next day he surprised us by coming home from school and getting his homework done all by himself. Then he ate a good dinner and went outside around dark to play with the dogs on the back lawn in a warm misty rain, tumbling, slipping, sliding, laughing for an hour or more. Later he worked out with Henry in the basement. Henry had set up a new bench press with butterfly-type workout bars and was spending an hour or so every night in there. This evening Mike was allowed to join in. Later Mike came in and told me he could now do a pull-up and was trying to do more. Good. The kid needed some sort of fitness goal.

But where had the anger gone?

It hadn't returned by morning, either, because in a complete surprise, he woke me up with a cup of coffee at 6:15. A number of days had passed since we had worked out that morning plan, and I was certain he'd let it go.

I was grateful—pathetically grateful.

• • •

April was almost over when Henry came back from a trip to Connecticut to take Mike up to Shawangunk, where they cycled the woods roads together until dark on their mountain bikes. All in all they covered four or five miles, and it was Mike's first introduction to the wild, high little world where the five older boys grew up. Pretty rough country, the woods roads overgrown and brambly, the forest mostly second-growth hardwood—oak, maple, and ash, with scattered clusters of virgin hemlock castling up like the forbidding old trees of Mirkwood. Lots of rock and high little bogs where the seeps work their way through the terraces. Far back in there are the foundations of farms abandoned a hundred years ago. It's spooky and dark in some places where the canopy is high and all very wild. But very pretty, too, if you enjoy deep woods. They saw deer.

When they didn't turn up by nine I called Susanne's house, and sure enough, they had stopped there on the way back. Susanne was baking cookies, and David let Mike play with his samurai swords. Another thing not to tell Harbour. I asked Susanne to get them on their way so Mike didn't get to bed real late—he was tough enough in the morning. They showed up at home about nine-thirty, ate dinner, and Mike went to bed exhausted, muddy, and sunburned, around ten. Henry said Mike's physical stamina was still deplorable, but that he was showing improvement.

"What did you two talk about?" I asked Henry.

He shrugged. "About the only thing he *would* talk about—how much he hates his school."

I walked in the door, and Sue was sitting at the barroom table having a glass of wine.

"Is that an adult beverage I spy there? Before dinner and not on a weekend and all alone?"

"Yes," she said, smiling. "This is a special occasion."

"What?"

"Joanne called. She said their report had an effect, as did apparently all of your bitching. Mike is being moved to a transitional classroom, a full day of schoolwork, grade-level subjects, and it looks like a normal classroom."

I sat down with a thump. "Did she ever tell you who their report was being made to?"

"No, she didn't, and I didn't ask, either, but I guess they have lawyers as well as therapists and social workers."

"So they were on our side, after all?"

"Well," Sue smiled, "on Mike's side. Harbour is all about being on Mike's side."

"And next year?"

Sue turned her hands up. "He'll be moving into the school district dragging that file of his behind, so I guess we'll have to fight this thing all over again."

"Yeah, I guess so," I said doubtfully.

"But Rich . . ."

"What?"

"I want to say something." There was a dead, brittle seriousness in her eyes. "If we didn't get this break and he started up again, he would have had to go somewhere else. I was at the end of my rope. I just couldn't take living in a war zone any longer and was looking for a way to tell you. I've given one hundred ten percent of what I have in me. I don't think I have anything left, and there's no payback with this kid. In many ways—in most ways, in his mind—I don't think I'm any closer to being his mom than I was last summer. He's still calling us Rich and Sue, he's still just thinking of this as another placement."

"That will change, Sue."

"Maybe."

A long silence, and then I looked up. "Where is he now?"

Sue pointed out the window. "I told him, he started crying, and then ran off toward the beaver pond."

I looked out toward the beaver pond area. "It's still flooded over back there."

"Oh, Rich, don't worry. The dogs are with him."

CHAPTER THIRTEEN

broken glass, broken-paw, medicine man

A week or so of work, morning walks up the mountain, a quiet Mike, and endlessly relaxed dinners. So relaxed, in fact, that Sue took off for a few days to visit her mother. I was alone on that first sunny Wednesday in May when Joanne picked Mike up from school, stopped at McDonald's, and then brought him home at about five-thirty.

Mike made his usual gracious entrance, banging in through the upstairs doors, but when Joanne accepted a cup of tea I could sense something was wrong—something out of sorts.

She was fussing.

"He's upset with his new class," she said finally. "It's steady work from 9:00 A.M. to 2:15, with only lunch and one fifteen-minute recess."

"So?"

"So." She grimaced lightly and then continued with that circumspect speech of hers, the words measured, thought out, and soft, "Mike didn't fully understand what he was asking for when he said he wanted to go to a regular class. He's never had to sit that long in one place, and so now when he keeps asking to go out and play, the other kids pick up on that and make fun of him. Then he responds with inappropriate language, the teacher intervenes, and there's a scene."

"We haven't heard any of that. It's been very quiet here."

Joanne shrugged. "Well, that's what I got by putting together the little bits and pieces of what he told me this afternoon."

"Making fun of him?"

"Every day. Apparently it's been going on every day, Rich. Every day since he began."

I stood up and paced. "That's horrible."

Joanne stretched and then sipped at her tea, but she was watching me carefully. "Rich, just how emotionally vulnerable are you two?"

Puzzled by this tack in her conversation, I could only state the obvious. "Mike's been a child in this house for eight months."

"Well, be careful," she said, nodding. "I don't think you can avoid becoming close, but you must remember that he can, and when he does things, it's not meant to hurt you or Sue; it's just how he deals with issues that aren't going well."

Still puzzled and now a little bit put off, I said back slowly, "Well, yes, you've said all of that before."

Then, starting to understand what she was saying, I sat down. "Joanne, are you telling me that Mike's going to start fighting with Sue and me again?"

She shrugged one shoulder and made a hapless face. "We may have made a big mistake in getting him out of that special-needs program, because sooner or later he's going to act out here in response to what's happening to him there."

I looked down. This was all too sad. I thought the school issue had settled something in his life, in our life.

Why didn't he talk to us? Why didn't he just keep his mouth shut in class? And how would Sue react if he did start acting out again?

Joanne was reading my mind. "What about Sue?"

I blew out my breath and tried to think the issue through out loud. "A month or so ago I came home and found Sue crying facedown into her pillows. She won't go back to that. She'll never go back to that."

"Too much pain," Joanne said.

"Yeah, way too much pain or rejection or disappointment. Push comes to shove, Sue wants to mother Mike and was ready to give up when she couldn't."

"But she didn't give up," Joanne said quietly.

"No," I said, "she didn't, we didn't, but without some sort of gesture from Mike, I'm afraid she will pack it in if he starts smashing things again."

"What sort of gesture does she want?"

"Anything—a word, a hug, any sort of gesture. Some one little act that acknowledges her role in his life."

Joanne made a bleak gesture with her hands. "But again, that's the way these kids are."

I shook my head helplessly. "And that's the way Sue is."

Then, like dark little shreds of cloud that run before a storm, ominous changes began to occur in Mike's behavior. The first was the day after my conversation with Joanne when, with Sue still away, I cooked hamburgers for Liam, Mike, and me. When I walked out of the kitchen to call Liam, Mike walked in and fed Liam's dinner to the cat.

Difficult call. Was he wanting to pick a fight with Liam? With me? He'll often portion out some of his own dinner for the animals, hiding it in a napkin if we let him and then delivering it upstairs. There's no control on his part when it comes to the animals and I just gently said, "Wrong thing to do, Mike. Liam will be hungry." Then I tried to lead into the subject of school. "How's your new class going?"

"Okay."

"The teacher?"

"I like Mrs. Vandenburg," he said slowly.

"The other children in your class?"

He almost spit the words. "The kids are stupid."

The next day Mike wet his bed and was just a tad more difficult getting up in the morning. Then, early that afternoon, Sue arrived home. I briefed her on what Joanne had said, and both of us watched him get off the school bus.

"He *looks* okay."

But a half hour or so later, when we had a talk with him about his schedule that night—he had to get his homework done before dinner because of a Boy Scout meeting—his response was all out of proportion: "I'm not going to that fucking Boy Scout meeting."

Shortly after that little scene, Mike was blasting the TV in the living room when Henry had an incoming phone call. When Sue asked him to turn the TV off, a really tremendous scene ensued—screaming, kicking, "This is a free country; I can do what I want." When Sue tried to get him out of the room, there was more kicking and screaming and, "You fucking asshole, you fucking bitch." Outside he picked up a piece of cedar shingle and jabbed himself twice in the face by his left eye, yelling, screaming, threatening to run out on the road and throw himself in front of a car.

Later, he tried to act like nothing had happened and did his homework on his own after dinner.

Yet no Boy Scouts.

And Sue was awfully quiet.

Two days later he wet his bed and was very difficult to get up and into the shower. He raised his voice. "I'm tired. Why are you always getting me up?" Then he added something new: "I don't want to go to school."

I told Sue, "I have to get him up earlier. He uses up so much time, the bus comes before he's eaten anything."

"Sure," she said, then just walked away.

The next day he was very difficult in the afternoon. He kicked a hole in the living room wall when neither of us was around, and when Sue asked him why, he screamed at her, "I hate you, you fucking bitch. I *hate* you. I hate *all* of you."

But the day after was Saturday, and Mike went with me for a long ride, performing errands in the pickup truck. Along the way we got his favorite doughnuts and then several hours later stopped again, this time at Burger King for lunch. He appeared tired and listless, exhausted after his week, although later on that afternoon he perked up and helped me clear brush.

Sue and I tried to have a serious talk with Mike.

"Mike," Sue said, her hands flat on the table, "you can't behave like this. It's entirely unacceptable. I know you're having problems at school, but there's little I or Rich or Mrs. Vandenburg can do about the other kids liking you or not liking you. This is something that only you control. You have to act pleasant and friendly, and if they make fun of you, then you have to just let it go, shrug it off, and not let it make you sick."

"I'm not sick," he screamed.

"Okay, okay."

Later, he smashed one of the big windows in the living room and the following days continued his downward spiral. On the next Monday Mike wet his bed and gave us a fractious, roiling twenty-four hours. He took my utility knife from my toolbox, feigned innocence, and effectively stopped me from hanging Sheetrock. Hours of discussion with him did no good. He pretended to look for it, told us he had put it in four or five different places. But by bedtime he still hadn't produced it.

Then on that Tuesday, almost mid-May now, Sue went to BOCES to have a talk with Mike's teacher. Later at night, with Mike sound asleep and the house darkened and quiet, she led me out to the screened-in porch to talk.

"He *is* sick, Rich."

I looked away, out over the starlit orchards, and felt like slipping far off into the glimmering dark like a shadow on the night wind. Events were out of my control, and Sue was speaking like a robot, in a flat, unemotional, metallic monotone.

She shook her head slowly back and forth as if dumbly searching for something. "According to Mrs. Vandenburg, Mike wasn't being picked on any more or any less than anyone else who comes into the class, and many of the children even made an extra effort to be friendly. But he's still making really childish remarks, and he's not settling down. In fact, he's getting worse—using filthy language, stealing things. The school has even had complaints from the bus driver that Mike is threatening the other children—a handicapped girl in a wheelchair, for one—threatening that he's going to cut her up with a knife!"

She raised her eyes, looking for mine in the half-light. "Rich, this kid runs in cycles. He's childlike and charming, then he's vicious, mindless, and mean. His emotions are on a roller coaster. I've tried, both of us have tried, to sort him out, solve one problem after another for him, and in the process we've both become emotionally attached. But you get little of that back—*none* of that back. If we keep him, we'll probably see another good few months come about after yet another struggle, but I'm convinced that inevitably we will down-cycle again. Meanwhile, the house is back to being a war zone. Since he came here you've replaced maybe thirty or forty windows, I don't know how many holes you've fixed in the walls, we've seen dishes go—lamps, toys, alarm clocks by the score. He's started fires, and we've had to put up with screaming and the foulest language imaginable. He's still wetting the bed, he lies, and he's getting stronger, a lot stronger."

"Sue, I don't think he's mean."

She raised her voice. "Breaking windows in my house is

mean. Calling me a fucking bitch is mean. Threatening to stab a handicapped little girl in a wheelchair is mean."

I sighed. She was right. "And?"

"And I've talked to Joanne. We've set a tentative extraction date for the twenty-second of next month, June. That's about the length of time Harbour needs to get him placed into a teenage group residence."

"And that's it?"

"As far as I'm concerned, unless there's some sort of miracle, that's it."

I should have seen it coming, but I was still stunned.

Sue softened and reached out her hand. "Rich, I know you care a lot. So do I. But he doesn't care for us. He doesn't think of us as parents. He never will."

Samuel Johnson said, "When a man is to be hanged in a fortnight, it concentrateth his attention wonderfully."

That's the way I felt. Suddenly, everything I did or didn't do was somehow related to a particular box on the calendar. It was difficult to imagine walking past his room without him in it.

I tried to put the thought of Mike away from me for a day, and early in a red dawn shoved off to pick Frank up from Norwich. The day rose into a gloriously sunny morning as I drove over the state line into Bennington, then north on Route 7, stopping for breakfast at a little restaurant in a tiny town ten miles or so south of Rutland. Starched white tablecloths, fine china plates, delicious blueberry waffles with real maple syrup, and three cups of coffee. Four dollars twenty-five cents and a "come again."

I rolled through the back gate of Norwich at about ten-thirty. The upper parade ground seemed forlorn and scruffy with thousands of boxes, stereos, computers, and piles of clothing being loaded into cars from Massachusetts, New Jersey, Pennsylvania. Most of the cadets were in camouflage field uniforms, swarming in and out of buildings, checking out. I managed to park in front of Bravo Company and went up to Frank's room. Not there, his roommate shrugged, so I walked down the "hill" and spotted him a couple of hundred yards away, walking up. I'd recognize that deliberate, shoulder-forward walk anywhere. He had a big smile on his face when he reached me.

"You're early, Dad. I haven't finished."

"Take your time. I'm going to take a nap in the sun."

And I did, with Frank shaking me awake at about twelve. "I'm all loaded. Let's go home."

Then down Route 12, through Randolf, Bethel, and a dozen other small towns, until sixty miles later we popped up onto Route 4 for the long, sweeping downhill run into Rutland. As we made the turn I looked up on Pico. A thousand feet above us there were still broad fields of snow.

"We're letting Mike go," I said to Frank.

Frank shrugged his shoulders, but he must have been thinking about it, because after we got gas in Rutland he asked me, blank-faced, "Have you ever told Mike a Broken-Paw story, Dad?"

Mike knew. I don't know how. I'm certain nobody had told him. Joanne, in particular, stressed keeping our own counsel until the day was close at hand, and to be honest, she was hoping for that miracle, too. But somehow, Mike knew or at least suspected. I suppose he could sense a certain withdrawal, the detached looks. He had, after all, been through this twelve times before.

But he was still nervous and frightened, suddenly walking on eggshells.

And he was very, very quiet.

The thing that bothered me most was not knowing what would happen to him. Would he be all right? Would somebody even know or care what he liked to eat? Would he ever have a dog around him? I will think of him for the rest of my life with the dogs. The dogs in his room at night, nuzzling him while he slept, loping around him in the hay meadow, slipping around his feet in the living room.

I met Sue in the hallway. "Sue," I said, choked up, "I don't care about the windows."

Sue started crying and pushed past me.

Back up to Vermont, this time with Sue, to attend Henry's formal graduation from Norwich. We left Mike at home, watched by Frank.

Another beautiful day, the graduating cadets in their dress-blue uniforms, a speech from the chief of staff of the army: "Just get up in the morning and make one good thing happen that day." Henry received high honors for his marks. Then cannons firing, the cadets' covers in the air.

Afterward we had lunch with Henry and his fiancée Peggy in the dining hall, all cadet blue and gold with the senior officers walking from table to table.

"Almost five years, Henry, but it seems like six months ago that you, Brendan, and I made the drive up in February to take a first look at this place. It was winter carnival time, with the huge snow sculptures on the upper parade ground. You watched the companies falling in to march to noon meal, and you said then that this would always be your place."

"It *will* always be my place," he grinned back.

"Are things shaping up for you?" Sue asked.

Henry raised his eyebrows. "Yes, I'm on the list for the

Vermont state police. There's only two hundred seventy troopers in the entire state, and they had a couple of thousand applicants for the ten openings. But I made the list."

"When?"

"Don't know. Sometime in the next few months I have to report up here for a physical, then orals, then there's a couple of months of background investigation. They'll be sending an investigator down to the house, too, in a month or two."

Peggy laughed. "I hope Mike isn't cursing and smashing windows when the trooper pulls into the parking lot."

"Little chance of that," Sue said tersely.

When we made the turn onto Route 4, I looked up at Pico and the snow was gone. We were driving into June.

The day after we got home from Henry's graduation I found the old leather box high up in my closet. I took it down, opened it on the bed, and spent half an hour or so sorting out the thick stacks of yellow papers, lost in the memory of the boys, younger, listening at night to the Broken-Paw stories. Sometimes I wrote them down and then read the stories. Sometimes I made them up, told them, and then wrote them down. Sometimes I just wrote them and tucked them away in the box.

Richard was blasé, a little bit too old when I started, Henry and Frank interested, Brendan and Liam most interested. Until he was eleven or twelve, Liam would often jump on my bed at night and ask, "How about another Broken-Paw story, Dad?"

It was something I had never started with Mike. Somehow it was too personal, too intertwined with the image of the five small boys on the mountain and, to be honest, very much out of mind these past few years.

But now that Frank had mentioned them, I seemed compelled in a mawkish, morose way to tell Mike at least one of the Broken-Paw stories. It was as if I felt I could press a little bit more of us into him before he left.

"Mike."

"Yes."

"How would you like me to tell you a story?"

Later he sat on the bed for a long time and then asked, "I don't understand why Uncle Nigel didn't shoot Broken-Paw or why Broken-Paw didn't eat Uncle Nigel up."

"Well," I said, "Uncle Nigel couldn't shoot Broken-Paw anyway. He's a magic bear, very strong medicine, and he was almost two hundred years old at that point. Besides, once Nigel understood what Broken-Paw was doing—once he understood that the only reason there were any wild spots left in the mountains at all was because Broken-Paw was guarding the Painted Mask Caves—the last thing Nigel would have done was shoot Broken-Paw. Nigel loved the mountains, loved the wild spots. And as far as Broken-Paw went, once he realized Nigel wanted to protect the caves as much as he did, the last thing he'd ever do is harm him."

"But who were these two medicine men, Widdersop and Obedience, who fought over the caves?"

"Ah, and that's another story—the story of how Broken-Paw was born and orphaned on the Coxinkill in seventeen fifty-seven."

"Orphaned?"

"Yes."

"And why does Broken-Paw always help members of this family?"

"Well, we're related to Uncle Nigel, and we think the same way he does about things."

"Is Broken-Paw real?"

"What do you think, Mike?"

He furrowed up his forehead and put his lower lip over his top one, thinking. "You wouldn't have told me this story if it wasn't real, would you?"

I just looked at him.

"Since I'm with this family, could I call Broken-Paw to help me if I was in trouble?"

"Mike, if you climb up past the lakes to the top of the mountain where the cherry trees are and look north, what do you see?"

"I see the Catskills."

"Right, you see the whole range—you see Blue Mountain and Panther and Slide, you see Platte Cove and North Mountain and South Mountain, you see Wittenberg and Terrace and dozens of others. Your thoughts would travel right in a straight line to wherever he is."

"I'd be too afraid," he said quietly, "to ask him to help me."

Joanne picked Mike up from school today to see Betty Smith, a therapist in New Paltz. Later, he did his homework on his own.

The next morning he cleaned out my wallet. Sue called the school and got the money back. Luckily I didn't have much cash, just twenty-one dollars. Mike went and got the money from his jacket when asked, and then said he thought it was two dollars, not twenty-one. I recalled that Mike was standing next to me when I opened my wallet at about seven in the morning and gave Liam two dollars for lunch money. Then I put my wallet on my dresser and went downstairs. Mike then must have gone to the wallet and taken the two bills out. It's rather sad. I think he just wanted to imitate Liam.

But am I just making more excuses?

He burned a hole in his mattress cover, too. Where had he gotten the matches or the lighter? I searched thoroughly but couldn't find anything. He was uncommunicative, and I gave up. Since today is Saturday, I tried to make it a pleasant day for him—TV, video games—and he acted happy, ate well, and went to bed okay.

The next day started out well when Mike went to church and behaved okay, then played on the computer, spent a short time on the bike, watched some movies that Sue got out, and had a good supper hour when we all ate together, chatting away. But at bedtime there was an explosion of the first magnitude. The trivial cause was Sue carrying his cat into his room at bedtime when he wanted to. Toys broken, a window smashed with his fist, cat litter thrown all around his room, screaming, curses, threats of suicide, trying to punch Sue, his books thrown through his bedroom window. This went on for almost two hours. When restraining him didn't work, the two of us put him in the shower. That was a tremendous struggle all its own, but finally we could leave him alone in there, and he stayed under the running water for twenty minutes talking to himself (although he did proceed to empty all of the shampoo and conditioner down the drain in a final gesture of protest). When he came out, he was calm. No significant injuries. His hand was not cut from putting it through the glass, but he'd lost a piece of skin on the inside of his arm about the size of a silver dollar. I think I did that when I was holding him. Sue ducked all of the punches, but I got a piece of glass driven into the sole of my foot, which I extracted with a razor blade and tweezers.

Sue cried again and started counting off the days until the twenty-second of next month. I was sick at heart, agreeing with her now—he was getting stronger and there was a lot of breakable stuff around. It would have been different if we could have seen these hurricanes coming, but we couldn't. On the upside, I had my emotions in check. I was becoming more detached, I guess, but also because Mike looked like a completely different individual by the end of the fight. His entire body was wealed red with hives and his eyes were swollen closed.

The next day he wet his bed, I replaced the glass, Sue field-dayed his room, found several sheets and pairs of badly soiled underpants in a toy box, and moved his bed around. But he seemed to like the attention, was happy at dinner, did his home-work on his own, and went to bed okay.

The day after that he went with Sue to Kingston for one of a series of educational evaluations. Later, I picked him up at school for his session with the therapist. We had a few minutes before the appointment, so we walked down to the bridge over the Wallkill River in New Paltz to the site of the old Indian village. Then we stopped at the library on the way home, and Mike checked out the *Aladdin* tape. That night he went with Sue to the mission at our church, the first of five evening masses in a row, each with a different theme.

The next day he was very easy to get up and actually tried to be pleasant, even going off to school in a positive mood. Every-one else was out at dinnertime, so I made him French toast and he ate at the bar, apparently without a care in the world, just chatting away.

The next morning he did wet his bed but still got up okay and even ventured a conversational remark: "I don't like to talk in the morning." Even after he tried to dodge the shower and I turned him around, he didn't make a scene. Later, he was pleas-ant with Sue.

Then that night he went again to the mission with Sue, a healing mass this time, where with Sue he was anointed and the congregation sang to him. Then he had his picture taken with the visiting priest and other children.

"Why did you have that done?" I asked her.

"Don't know," she said abruptly.

"Sue?"

"No, nothing has changed."

On Friday he was up okay and off to school. He had a fight with Liam that night—minor stuff, but it was Brendan's twentieth birthday and there was a party in the barroom. Susanne and David came over and Mike later happily participated.

When David was alone with Sue and me having coffee, he sat hunched over with his back stiff, reaching forward with his face, searching for the right words.

I saw him struggling and asked, "What's wrong, David?"

"Don't do it."

Sue answered him long before I could have gotten any words into motion. "You're a different person, David, a better person. We don't really mean anything to Mike, not really, and we never will. We're not his parents and he doesn't ever want us to be his parents. If I hear him call me Sue once more I'm going to throw up." Then she dropped her coffee cup and almost ran upstairs to be alone.

Joanne called and said Mike would be placed at St. Finbar's. She described the facility as a collection of residential cottages set in spacious grounds. There was staff on duty in all the residences, and they had their own school. We could visit him there if we chose, probably even take him home for a weekend now and then.

Sue got me off the computer at about ten that night.

"I called Steve Lender. He does a lot of work for the state." I recognized the name. Steve was a psychologist and a tax client of Sue's. "I asked him about St. Finbar's."

"Yes."

"Well," she said, stroking her chin, "he knows Mike, too. His advice was to keep him out of there. Most of the boys are a lot older, and psychologically even older yet. Many even come

232 / Richard F. Miniter

there out of alternative sentencing programs after committing serious crimes."

"And?"

"And there's been drugs, violence, homosexual rape. Steve even said the staff has been assaulted on occasion."

"Are you changing your mind?"

"No," she said, tracing patterns in the tabletop with one finger and not looking at me. "No, Rich, I've had enough."

"Then it's not our call, Sue."

It was Saturday and he wanted to sleep until he got up on his own. We said okay, but then finally woke him at two in the afternoon. Interestingly, his behavior was not unlike when awakened on a school morning. We'd seen this before. Being tired had little or nothing to do with his getting out of bed. He always clings to sleep, resents being pulled out of it.

Later in the day we went to the library, then Mike took a long walk with Sue and me over the mountain at dark, talking a mile a minute. He carried a book to identify wildflowers but kept looking at us strangely, as if seeing us for the first time.

Or maybe the last.

Then it was Memorial Day, and because he seemed particularly open, with no attitude, Sue had a long, serious conversation with Mike. She told him what he so evidently suspected—that his stay here was being evaluated with a probable removal in the cards at the end of school. This was because of his behavior—that it did not appear we could help him further. He started to tremble but was articulate and thoughtful in response, saying that what he wanted to do was to go live with his sister and brother and the Johnsons. Sue told him that if he did manage to dampen his behavior here over the next couple of weeks, she would fight for his goal.

In the afternoon Mike asked to go food shopping with me,

and in the few minutes before we left he pored over his fancy cake cookbook. On the way to town he announced he wanted to make a Black Forest cake and produced a list of ingredients. After we returned he spent a couple of hours making the cake and served it with great fanfare after dinner. Then silently and until sunset he kicked around a soccer ball with Liam.

And after dark he was ready for magic.

I was standing on the back lawn, smoking a cigarette and drinking a cup of coffee, when Mike walked out of the lighted barroom.

His face was a white blur in the darkness. "Do you think Broken-Paw would really help me?" And for the first time ever, perhaps because he could let some defenses down when I couldn't see his face, he sounded desperate.

"Help you with what, Mike?"

"Just help me?"

I put my arm out and gathered him in. He was trembling. "Mike, who did you make that cake for tonight?"

The words were muffled. "For Sue."

I held him a while longer. "You're all screwed up, kid. But you can figure some things out, can't you?"

We stood there a while longer, with Mike softly breathing against my chest. Then he asked again, "What about Broken-Paw?"

"Well," I said, trying to get my throat unstuck, "we've tried everything else."

A half hour later we were in the thickets just off the country lane, hundreds of yards away from and hidden from the house. I had built a small fire and had Mike strip off his shirt.

"If wishing him to help you doesn't work, Mike, then we can call him with this ceremony."

"Will we see him?" Mike asked.

"No," I said, "he doesn't know you all that well. But you can tell he's here when you feel a cooler wind moving around. First you have to blacken your face to show him you're sorry and you need help."

I smeared some soot over his face.

"Then we need smoke." I covered the tiny fire with wet leaves and Mike's face disappeared in the soft, luminescent blue cloud. We were all alone in the dark, hidden from each other, unable to see even the blackness around us.

"Mike."

"Yes." He was stammering.

"Call him."

Silence.

"Mike."

"I'm here."

"Call him."

A low voice. "Broken-Paw."

"Again."

"Broken-Paw."

"Now, wait."

We waited for a long while until it must have been an hour, an hour and a half after sunset, and I could hear the night breeze moving up the hillside, drifting through the thicket.

"I feel it," Mike said in the barest whisper.

"Feel what?"

His voice was breathless. "I feel the breeze. Is he here?"

"Ask him."

A long silence from the other side of the drifting pale smoke, and then I heard the faintest whisper. "Help me stay home."

The wind grew stronger, and the smoke whisked itself off and away. I could see Mike again in the moonlight, the embers of the fire reflecting in a soft, pale green glow on his chin, his cheeks, deepening the dark of his eyes.

"How do I know he heard me?"

I couldn't control myself well enough to speak at first, but finally, long, long minutes later, I said, "You'll meet something wild, an animal or something, that will help you do what you have to do." That sounded safe. Two days didn't go by that Mike didn't come up with a toad or a lizard or a chipmunk. But I also said a long prayer that this bizarre therapy would help him find the strength to get a little bit better, or at least stronger, if he was to go.

And sensing that Sue was balanced on a knife edge, I was also hoping against hope that Mike could do the one little thing that would topple her back over in his direction.

But it was only the next afternoon when I heard Mike start one of his awful, horrible scenes again.

I was upstairs, working at my computer, reformatting a prospect list Sue had come up with, when things started getting knocked over downstairs and there was screaming, more screaming, and then more screaming yet. I couldn't make out the words, but I knew Mike's voice, and I knew Sue was down in the barroom, trying to eat an early dinner before a client arrived.

And then the screaming stopped.

I was almost ill, hunched over the keyboard, sorry—so very, very sorry. Yet finally, unable to just sit there, I forced myself to get up and go downstairs.

When I walked into the barroom, nobody was angry or upset. Instead, Liam was off in one corner watching Sue as she held a softly sobbing Mike in her arms and stroked his hair, kissed the top of his head, and murmured over and over again, "Everything will be all right, honey, everything will be all right."

Stunned, I could only prod at Liam sideways with an elbow and ask, "What's going on?"

Liam gave me a disgusted look back. "I don't know, Dad. We were outside on the lawn kicking the soccer ball, and a bee landed on Mike's hand. He tried to flick it off, but his hand went into his eye and the bee stung him. Then he ran in here like a little baby, screaming, 'Mommy, Mommy, help me,' and ever since then she's just been holding him."

Sue found me in the kitchen the next day. "Joanne called, and I told her St. Finbar's is out. So she told me the only alternative for Mike is a temporary placement in Rockland State Psychiatric Hospital until something else opens up."

"Yes? And . . . ?" I said slowly, watching her eyes, knowing what was coming and afraid I'd smile.

"And," she snapped, "I'm not going to accept that."

Frank walked through just then. "I heard Mike calling you two Mom and Dad. What's up?"

"Nothing," I said. "It's only a gesture."

The next afternoon, when David had his head under the hood of my truck working on the engine, he quizzed me. "I understand Mike is sticking around?"

"Yeah," I joked, "we can't let him leave until he works off the glass bill he owes us."

"No, seriously," David asked, "what happened?"

I put my hands out helplessly. "Quite a number of things happened. First, he went to a mass for the sick, was anointed, and the parish prayed for him to get well."

"Yeah . . ."

"And then he woke up and realized he was on the way out of here."

"Okay . . ."

"And then a bee stung him and he forgot for a moment that he wasn't allowed to show how much he's come to need Mom. But . . ." I stopped.

"But what?" David asked, sliding down off the fender, grabbing a rag, and starting to wipe at his hands. "But what?"

"But what I like to think really happened was that in the

year seventeen fifty-seven an evil Indian shaman and a good Indian shaman fought each other for the hearts of their people. The evil one poisoned the good man, but before the good man died he cast his power into a badly injured bear cub, whom he named Broken-Paw . . ."

"Okay, okay, forget about it," David said, laughing. "I'll ask Susanne."

CHAPTER FOURTEEN

truth, goals, and an anniversary

"Wow! This has been some week for you guys."

Joanne was bright and bouncy, but it was hard for us to smile back. The close involvement of Harbour in our lives had the ability to annoy us infinitely from time to time. Joanne was a friend and tremendously supportive, but as experienced parents, it was sometimes wearing to have a third party forever popping up. And it was not simply these weekly sessions; it was the detailed daily logs that had to be kept, the records of counseling sessions and the review of the treatment plan. It was the cluster meetings, the organized outings, the coordination of school and pickup. It was making sure the house was deadly clean on Wednesday afternoons, and above all, it was the fact that sometimes we just didn't want to relive and rehash our struggles with Mike constantly.

Sometimes we wanted to put it behind us, sometimes we wanted a little space, sometimes we just wanted to be left alone.

Like today.

Still, both of us kept a good face on until Joanne raised an old issue, a program requirement we thought we'd long since circumvented. "Sue, Rich," she said quietly, "please take this the right way—you've done marvelously, better than anyone would have thought . . ."

"*But?*" I asked, wondering what was coming.

Joanne sort of slid her head sideways and said with a rush, "But, now that we're past this crisis, we have to insist on respite."

I stared stupidly at Joanne for a moment or two, then lamely joked, "Good! Send us to the Bahamas for a week or two."

Joanne smiled back, but it was perfunctory, dismissive, and flat. "Rich, it is part of the program, and it's time."

I looked over at Sue. She was coiling and uncoiling in her seat.

Harbour had twisted our arms with respite before, but we'd always managed to wiggle out of it. Respites are weekends, even weeks away for the child that The Harbour Program organizes to give the child and parents a break from the routine. Although we'd acted as respite parents ourselves, in almost a year we'd never had to send Mike away.

"Don't worry about Mike," Joanne said defensively. "These kids almost always enjoy a respite as much as the parents do."

"Joanne," Sue answered back at last, her words clipped and brittle, "our relationship has changed over the past week or so, really changed. I don't think he's the same Mike. I think he'll take this the wrong way. I think he's pretty vulnerable right now, so let it go. Maybe later, maybe during the summer."

But Joanne was determined to put our objections aside. "I know he's calling you Mom and Dad, I know you're closer, I know you feel we've passed a big milestone, but he's been through a rough time and needs a break. Besides, this is still just a placement for him. He knows it; all our kids know it. They're used to being shuffled around."

Inwardly I was grinding my teeth over the words "just a placement," "our kids," and then, irrationally and emotionally, I thought, *What's this* we *stuff? Where were you when he was shitting on the toilet seat cover and smashing windows?* Afraid I would actually say something out loud, I looked away.

Sue could hear me mumbling, and she kept looking back and forth between Joanne and me as Joanne hunched forward in her seat, pressing the issue. "Sue, respite was explained in your training sessions. It's something you two agreed to, something that's as much for your benefit as his, and it's long past due. You guys need a break, too. Past needing a break, in fact. Both of you are too wrung out—far too wrung out."

Sue opened her mouth again, but closed it when Joanne put her hand down firmly on the table. "Sue, this is a program, and I know that some parts of it are more comfortable than others, but all the parts are there for a reason, and that is what makes the program work."

When Sue sighed and sat back, stymied, not knowing what else to say, I got up and walked out.

Mike wet his bed again, and we've decided that it's time for a reversal of policy here. There were just too many corners to Mike's behavior, and we were slowly being taught the futility of trying to catalog them all.

Mike had been wetting his bed on and off for almost ten months, and we'd been consistently supportive and understanding on the issue. But now we wondered if it was to some degree deliberate, an old and odd implement of control for Mike that he couldn't quite let go. On more than one occasion we'd observed Mike forcing himself to drink large amounts of water just before bedtime, or even getting up at night to do so, and we're not going to be terribly understanding much longer.

Whenever Mike had acted up over this past year, various social workers and therapists seemed compelled to spend a lot of time theorizing with us. We'd been told, for example, that Mike was demonstrating repressed anger over his childhood; insecurity with a new school, with new friends, with a guest moving out whom he'd become attached to; or that he was responding to the aftershocks of no medication, of puberty, of changing diet, of rivalry with our sons or of overlarge expectations, limited expectations, fear of failure, fear of success, low self-esteem, unrealistic self-esteem, and so on.

But while all this may have been true, psychiatrists Mike had to see from time to time usually took a much broader view. I suppose because they're medical doctors they tended to focus not on specific behaviors, but rather on broad changes in his overall condition. Was he gaining weight? Was he growing? Was the pattern of his behavior generally better or worse? Was he doing better in school, in social settings, at home? Was he dangerous? Then, if the answer to most of these questions was positive, they tended to snap their notebooks shut, pat us on the back, say, "Don't worry," and walk out of the room.

I saw this phenomenon again when Mike had to make a periodic visit to one of these doctors. After the psychiatrist examined Mike, he called me in and asked if I had any questions. I said yes and then recited the latest list of issues and incidents that we were discussing with Harbour and the therapist, and asked if he could help us with them.

But the doctor just sat back and grinned. "What," he asked, chuckling, "makes you think that you can develop a rational response to each and every irrational act?"

"Huh?"

"Mr. Miniter," the doctor said, leaning forward, "is Mike healthier than he was a few months ago? *You* tell *me*."

I thought about it. "Yeah, I guess so."

The doctor nodded. "I guess so, too. In fact, I know he's a lot healthier, and I know he's going to get healthier yet. But that doesn't mean I can tell you how to respond to every bit of stupidity, temper, or anger he's going to display from this point on."

"I guess I see what you're saying," I said slowly, but really not seeing it.

"Look," the doctor said, chuckling again, "you and I, I will assume, are healthy, normal people, but both of us still do dumb things from time to time. Much less so than Mike, of course, but we still do things we have trouble explaining."

"You're not saying we should forget about therapy and just accept Mike's behavior?"

"No," he said deliberately. "Therapy calls Mike on his behavior. It checks him and makes him think about what he's doing and wants to do. But don't get lost in the minutiae. Just keep doing whatever it is you are doing, and if you're going to worry about anything at all, simply worry about whether or not you're producing a child who as an adult can function within the range of normal human confusion."

I grinned back. "Like I am now?"

The doctor laughed. "Like you are now."

From time to time a lone beaver will stroll out onto the old country lane and spend half an hour or so studying the back-yard, looking for a way around.

The lane is really an old wagon road leading off the moun-tain. How old, I don't know. It was overgrown and choked with trees when we moved here, and in putting in the parking lot I had the heavy equipment operator run his machine along it for a thousand feet or so until the road disappeared into the swamp.

Later we cut the grass that sprang up, and Brendan and I built a small bridge off it, over the tiny stream that ran down one side. The lane then became our foot route to the orchard and the mountain.

But we hadn't given the history of this old road much thought until one spring I discovered that the route had stone culverts draining the water from the west side east into a drainage ditch around the hay meadow and then, in exploring further, that it emerges again on the other side of the swamp, where it crosses the larger stream on the north side of our little valley with a fieldstone bridge—in particular, two huge slabs of rough, hand-quarried granite.

When I studied a topographic map I discovered a little more. What remains of this old road follows the natural contour of the mountain as the newer, shorter roads, cut into and through the hills, do not. So, in the days before earth-moving equipment, the old road must have been a route, maybe the first route, across and down the mountain. Another fact that leaped out at me from the map is that in shadowing the contour, the ancient path crosses and crisscrosses, follows downhill the network of rivulets, streams, and ferny seeps that become the Black Creek, opening on the Hudson River, fifteen miles away.

It's natural, therefore, for the beavers to try to pass the house because it appears they've followed this old abandoned road all the way up from the mouth of the creek. In speaking to neighbors farther downhill I could trace their progress. In the 1960s there were no beaver anywhere along the waterway. Then, in the '70s, a few appeared ten miles down along the state route, a few years later higher, then in the late '80s, they were making trouble in the orchard ponds two-thirds of the way up the mountain. Finally we, almost at the top and almost at the end of the water, noticed them felling trees in 1990, one less than four hundred yards from where we had built the footbridge.

But I didn't understand who else they were bringing with them until Mike took me to see a lunatic show at dusk.

I watched Mike start walking down the country lane and called out to him.

"Mike, where are you going?"

He turned around, exasperated. "Nowhere."

"Are you going into the orchards?"

"No. I'm going to watch the ducks land."

"What?"

"I'm going to see the ducks land." Then he turned his back and started walking away again.

"Mike."

"What?"

"I think I'll come with you."

Mike slouched like he was being put upon, but waited for me to catch up and then impatiently led the way down the lane, over the small footbridge, into the orchard, along the east edge of the apple trees, and inside the brush by the big old oak that nestled an ancient deer stand high up in its huge, spreading branches.

This is the back way to the beaver pond, I thought to myself. *You're not going to see any ducks back here, kid. It's way too thick.*

Then I asked, "Where are the dogs?"

"The dogs don't like the ducks," he said tersely, trying to cut off further conversation.

Even more puzzled, I followed along behind Mike, step by step, as he picked his way through the thorns until we came to the long, snaking dam and within it, the weed-choked pond. The water had the husks of a hundred, two hundred trees rising up out of it. Trees killed by the rising water, leafless, the maze of their dry dead branches reaching up into the darkening sky like the supplicating arms of sinners lost.

An eerie place when night is creeping out of the shadows.

But Mike soundlessly squatted down now, and I joined him.

A few minutes later a beaver silently streamed by fifty feet out in the pond, just its heavy head above the mirrored black water. Then another.

Okay, I said to myself, *we're watching beaver. What was this about ducks? There aren't any ducks here.*

Then they came crashing in.

I heard them before I saw anything. Their high-pitched quack-quack distant at first, and then right overhead. How many, I don't know—there were lots. I could hear them circling above the wood, gathering, calling to each other.

"What are they going to do?" I asked Mike.

But he hissed at me to be quiet and looked up with a smile as the first few ducks started down.

There was no way for a wood duck to stretch its wings and sail down through that tangle of dead branches high up in the air without breaking bones, so they simply folded their wings and dropped like stones, crashing through, breaking off dead twigs and tree limbs, and in the process tumbling upside down, backward, and sideways through the trees and into the water, where they hit in great splashes. Then, once the first few were down, they called back up into the sky above the dead trees, as if encouraging others in that insane drop out of the night sky.

It was an uproarious, mad two minutes. Ducks everywhere crashing, spinning, bouncing through, shrieking quacks back, splashing in, and then indignantly trying to avoid the next wave of bodies and broken-off branches hurtling down.

Mike laughed.

He stood and laughed and laughed. His arms up high, he stepped forward and slipped into the mucky water but still stood laughing, twigs showering down, ducks falling every-where now, quacking, popping back up out of the water shak-ing their heads, swimming off.

And then it stopped. Silence again in the now-dark pond, just the odd subdued quack of ruffled ducks far off, paddling through the brushy water in the gloom.

Mike was leaning against the dam, holding his sides, with tears streaming down his face.

"Mike, does this happen every night?"

"Every night," he said, shaking his head. "Those crazy ducks do this every night."

I suppose I looked concerned, or at least reluctant to speak, when I had to remind Mike about respite, because he gave me a deep, searching look back and said, "It's all right, I don't mind going."

In the morning his sheets were dry, but Sue washed them out of force of habit, and he got really upset when he found out! Later, Sue had him clean up his room and remake his bed. He did a neat job. I got home from work about four and lay down on his bed. Then I pretended I was him. "I hate this family. I'm a slave around here. I do all the work in this house. I'm not getting up. I'm tired, I want to leave, I've only had ten hours' sleep."

Mike's face turned red, very angry, but then he laughed and came over and punched me in the belly. Hard!

Another issue that we'd been hard put to address with Mike was petty theft. Coins, a tool, a poster from one of the other boys' rooms, Liam's watch—the list went on and on. An odd collection of missing personal miscellany that, for the most part, turned up in Mike's room or schoolbag.

We'd spoken to him about it many times, and he'd continually apologized, but we'd never made it the issue of the moment. But now events had forced our hand, or rather his. Because this time he had stolen exactly the wrong thing from exactly the wrong person.

Frank had taken Mike fishing, and Mike had admired Frank's knife—the same fishing knife he's had since he was ten years old. After they returned home, Mike had slipped into Frank's closet and taken the knife. Several hours later Frank found out, got very upset, and tore Mike's room apart.

Mike admitted taking it, said he was sorry, but wouldn't tell Frank where it was. I don't think he could—I think that he had dropped it down the well or otherwise put it out of reach. So now Mike had an immense problem because he couldn't return it, Frank wouldn't let it go, and we wouldn't interfere in what was going on between them.

Now whenever Frank came home, the first thing he did was loom over Mike and demand the knife back.

"Dad, Frank is very mad at me."

"Well, you stole his knife and won't tell him where it is."

"You should make him stop. I'm afraid. He's mean."

"Mean enough to take you fishing and have his fishing knife stolen?"

"I told him I'm sorry, but he won't stop. He's mean."

I'm not big on biblical references, but I remembered one that was used on someone else under identical circumstances and, anticipating this conversation, spent the time to find it. I was determined to do a very hard thing.

"Mike, get the Bible down."

He walked over to my bookshelf and took down the old Pilgrim Edition of King James.

"Mike, there's something in Jeremiah."

" '. . . thou art gone backward: therefore I will stretch out my hand against thee and destroy thee; I am weary with repenting.' "

"Mike, do you know what that means?"

"It means Frank is going to destroy me?"

"It means that even God loses patience with people who would do wrong and think they can make things right by apologizing."

Mike wet his bed again, and we called him on it.

"Mike, this is getting old. Your room smells like the elephant house at the zoo. I think we're going to get you up in the middle of the night to go, and we want you to stop drinking water before you go to bed."

Hooded eyes and a set face. "I have to have a drink before I go to bed."

"No, you don't. Now get in the shower."

But while he was in there he put a toothbrush down the sink drain, then wadded up toilet paper and forced it down on top of it. I had to disassemble the drain, take the sink away from the wall.

When he got off the school bus, I had him bow down and apologize to the sink.

"Dad, this is really stupid," he said.

"Not as stupid," I said gratingly, "as stopping up the drain."

Sue and I packed Mike up for respite with some very mixed feelings. We still had a hard time believing that sending a child away so the parents could have free time was the right thing to do.

In fact, we were on the point of calling Harbour and pleading a sickness or an emergency or something when Mike's attitude stopped us. He was indifferent and matter-of-fact about the weekend. Not a big deal, he seemed to be saying.

He didn't say good-bye to Sue or even pet one of the dogs on the way out.

The respite couple's home was about five miles from our place. Mike wouldn't look back as he slowly walked away with the husband. I kept watching, hoping he'd turn around and wave, but he never did.

When I got home, Sue was waiting for me. "How did he act?"

I shrugged. "He couldn't have cared less."

"Well," she said, slowly shaking her head, "I just don't understand."

"You can't be on target one hundred percent of the time, Sue."

"What are we going to do this weekend?"

"I don't know."

Sue got up, walked into her office, and slammed the door.

And suddenly it was awfully quiet in the house.

Then, at about 7:30, the phone rang in Sue's office and she picked it up. There was a tremulous, stuttering voice at the other end, then tears. "This is Mike. Are you doing anything special? Can I come home?"

"What's wrong?"

"I want to come home." More tears, lots of tears.

Sue stuttered herself. "Ten minutes, Mike. We'll be there."

We jumped in the truck and scooted down to the village. Mike was waiting in the kitchen with his bag between his legs, ignoring everybody else while he waited for us.

In speaking to the wife, we found out there wasn't any particular problem. She thought perhaps he was bored. She didn't even know he had called until we showed up.

Mike didn't have anything specific to say either except, "I just want to go home."

So we went home.

Later, Sue looked at me with tears in her eyes. "He got us again, didn't he?"

I thought out loud, "What's Harbour going to say?"

Sue grimaced. "What I care about is not pushing the fact that he's a foster child into his face ever again."

It was mid-June now, and Henry got Mike up early with the dogs. We got the first bad report we'd had recently from school:

apparently Mike had said no when he was told to put something away. But he did his homework on his own. We had more or less a potluck dinner, and he went to bed without a lot of grousing.

Then Henry got him back up at 11:00 P.M. to see an enormous bullfrog he found outside the back door. Mike caught it and put it in his room in a bucket with some water, then went back to sleep.

I found out about it when at two o'clock I heard the strangest sounds coming out of Mike's room.

"Mike, my God, that's the biggest frog I ever saw. Where did you get it?"

"Henry found it for me."

"Yes," I said, groggy and still amazed at the size of the thing. "How nice of him to find one that can sing."

Mike and Sue had been very close ever since the attempted respite—heads together, whispering, talking, quietly laughing—but this morning we saw something else. When Sue gently reminded Mike of the time, the stultifying blank face came back, and with it, the same old poisonous words.

We never seem to lose our vulnerability. No matter how many times Mike demonstrates his ability to switch instantly from sunshine and light into a pocked and vicious persona, we're always and every time surprised.

But being surprised doesn't mean we always react the same way, and this morning Sue responded like a cobra touched with a lit cigarette. She didn't act patient, hurt, shocked, or reasoning. Instead, she instantly went ballistic and wall-eyed, chased him down and cornered him in his room, then, shaking him, screamed, "You will not call me those filthy names any longer, ever again. If you do, that disgusting mouth is getting washed out with soap."

Then Mike switched back, the look on his face saying he'd been bushwhacked. ("Hey, you're not supposed to get that mad that fast.")

"Calm down, please calm down," he said, obviously worried.

I watched the entire show, and when she stalked back out of his room asked, "What happened with you?"

"I dunno," she snapped. "It hit a nerve this time."

"Well," and it was a compliment, although a very wary one, "at least you didn't play the game."

"Huh?" she said indignantly, straightening her skirt.

Although these scenes with Mike were getting much more infrequent, they still followed the same rigid routine, like a dance he took us through. There were facial expressions, then words—lots of words—then kicking and hitting odd things, then screaming. It was a set, scripted procedure that took an hour or more, a perfidious pirouette. But Sue short-circuited him this time, and you could see confusion written all over his face.

"You didn't let him work you. After you exploded, Mike looked like a matador who waved his cape, but the bull went straight for his legs instead."

"Mom, I'm sorry," Mike said, peeking out of his room.

But Sue continued to seethe, refusing to talk to him in the car and making him sit three or four pews in front of her in church. Yet she was watching him and noticed that when the collection came he reached into his pocket, pulled out one grimy, wadded-up dollar of his allowance, and put it in the basket.

"Damn," she spit later, not knowing whether to keep her mad on or not.

But then she said something very interesting. "He goes nuts when we push him into some forward movement, whether it's a schedule he has to keep or organizing his own time to achieve some goal. He hates plans that he has to follow. He doesn't like to deal with the future—it's as if he's afraid of the future, any sort of future."

In the afternoon we all went over to Susanne's for dinner. Susanne and David, Sue and I, Mike, Liam, Frank, and Brendan. Lovely dinner, very nice table set.

During coffee and after Mike walked outside to play, David sat back and looked at me. "What a difference," he said, chuckling. "I remember last fall. Trying to eat with Mike was like eating with a cave ape who was seeing fire for the first time. He'd never shut up or stop snatching at things."

I laughed at that, but then sat up straight. David was right. The emotional churning, the words, the fights, and Mike's relentless window demolition had obscured some substantial social progress. Tonight was his umpteenth family dinner, and somewhere on the time line of Thanksgiving, Christmas, Easter, and a hundred other sit-downs, he'd acquired some social skill. Tonight he was composed and gracious—"Please pass the salad . . . yes, no . . . thank you"—ate very well, took modest portions, had seconds, handled his knife and fork with aplomb, helped clean up after dessert, thanked Susanne, and listened to the adult conversation. In fact, he joined in the conversation. A vast difference.

David stood up. "Want to take the coffee outside?"

Out on the porch it was dusk, orange, hazy, and hot. The traffic on the state route gone for the moment, the only noise the distant slam of a screen door down the street.

Then Mike joined us. "What's that sound?"

There was a faint chime of musical notes, and David listened for a moment, then said mischievously, "Ice cream truck!"

"What's an ice cream truck?"

"Aha."

We all piled into my pickup and tried to find it in the

spread-out network of roads. Finally we did track it down, and Mike bought Susanne a bubblegum-flavored ice cream bar.

Susanne said, trying to force a smile—she doesn't eat ice cream and hates the taste of bubblegum, "Why, *thank* you, Mike."

Later Mike was asleep on Susanne's couch, Brendan and Frank had taken off, Sue and Susanne were still chatting in the kitchen, and David and I returned to the porch.

"Mike is really starting to fit in," David said.

I looked through the doorway to where he was sleeping now in a quiet pool of light, a comic book open on his chest and Susanne's cat curled up under one arm.

David smiled again. "You don't have second thoughts?"

"Yes," I said helplessly.

"How so?"

"Well," I explained, "we're not changing our minds, of course, but we're beginning to wonder if our life will ever settle down with him in it. There was another scene this morning. We haven't had one for weeks, but there it was the moment we asked him to get moving. Sue squashed him like a bug, which is something new, and Mike was instantly contrite, but the fact remains that living with Mike is like having yourself permanently wired to a black box that zaps you with a zillion volts of electricity from time to time."

Seeing the puzzled look on his face, I tried to explain myself. "Dave, these scenes were the only device available to Mike when he wanted to get something or resist whatever it was he feared. There were no adults in his world who could be depended on to protect him. Now he's here with us, and on balance there's less in his life to be afraid of than there was before, so there are fewer scenes. But there still are scenes, so there's some one more thing that he feels compelled to push away at. And David, I don't think it's something we're ever going to be able to fix."

"What is it?"

"Something we just couldn't avoid. And *we* is not just Mom and me. It *is* us two, but it's also the boys, it's the social workers who took a chance on him, it's The Harbour Program, it's Susanne, and maybe, in a unique and special way, it's you."

"Me?"

"Look, Dave, Mike has been structured by the system for almost his entire life. He's never had to worry about the future. It was just presented to him, and he either fought it or went along. But now we expect him to think through the major elements of any task and then go out and put them together for himself. And it's not just major life decisions. It's the simple matter of getting ready for church in the morning or putting aside some time to do his room."

David shrugged. "He seems happy."

"David, most of the time Mike *is* very happy. He has his animals, his bike, his fishing pole. He has us leaving him alone, he has his room, the rest of the family—you, in particular—and he's come to love all of that. But he's been trained to be a spectator, and whenever we insist he get out of the bleachers and onto the field to do something for himself, he blows up. He zaps us with that zillion volts."

David flinched a little bit. "That sounds pretty childish."

Sue had walked out onto the darkened porch. "Dave, Mike might be twelve, but believe me, in a lot of ways he's twelve going on five."

David shook his head and looked back and forth between the two of us. "Lots of kids can't come up with any goals."

I huffed and scratched my back up against the doorpost. "And that's the other tail on this issue. Mike's got his feet in two camps. He's here with us, but he's also controlled by the system, and he knows it. He knows that if he does overcome his fears and invest in any plan, it could all vanish in an instant."

David put his hands up. "What do you do?"

"I don't know."

David thought for a long moment, smiled again, and then, ever the optimist about people, said, "Hey, look at it this way: a child so difficult now may just turn out to be a very, very special guy later on in life."

I sat back and sighed. "David, after raising six children, let me tell you the one bitter lesson we've learned. If a child's a pain in the ass when it's young, it's even more of a trial when it grows up."

David laughed then and wagged his finger at me. "Don't you dare compare Mike to Richard."

The next morning before he got on the school bus, Mike decided to release the bullfrog into the swamp. He stood there for a long time explaining to it why it couldn't stay in his room.

Sue took Mike to the orthodontist and the diagnosis was major work—there were baby teeth fused to his jaw and other problems. There would have to be something like nine re- movals. Sue carefully explained all this to Mike. But he wanted it done, and Sue said she'd handle her end if he could keep his up—after all, there would be a lot of discomfort and pain. We thought the state of his teeth was really a big thing with him, but he didn't want to admit it. Also, he saw Liam in the last stages of braces, went with me to pick him up from the ortho- dontist several times, and therefore, to some degree, viewed it as a rite of passage. "I can do it."

Mike wound up in a summer program—fortunately, with the same Mrs. Vandenburg. Today, though, he was off from school, and we went garage sale shopping—Sue, Mike, and I—in the pickup truck. A beautiful sunny, breezy day. Bought an antique (circa 1840) brass bed, lamps, rugs, etc. Then we all went home, ate a late lunch, and took a nap, even Mike.

The next day Sue and I went to see a therapist under contract to Harbour. We were after some strategies that would enable us to handle any future violent situations. Direct, no-nonsense guy, seemed to have a good command of his craft, quite well-spoken. This first session was spent, for the most part, in establishing the basis of our relationship with Mike and trying to ferret out what it would take to keep him in our home over the long haul.

Right away we came to understand that, while the therapist didn't think there was any silver bullet, he could provide us with a wider perspective and, without naming names, discuss a range of similar client behaviors and outcomes that we could learn from. That sounded a bit vague at first. Did he even know what we were dealing with? But then he changed our minds (and got us laughing) by using his experience to act out some chillingly accurate portrayals of Mike's behavior.

The idea of goals and direction for Mike was a nonstarter, however. "Keep on coming on and give yourself a break from time to time" was the bottom line. Something, someone might trigger him.

Since we were in Kingston, Mike was picked up from school by a friend who also has a child named Mike in the same school building. When we got to her house, Mike had just finished an hour or so of bike riding with her son. He was muddy, perspiring, and happy, and he kept the good mood through dinner.

The woman: "What a well-mannered boy. I wish my Mike was like yours."

Sue replied, "Hello?"

How many portentous conversations have begun with my walking into Sue's office—a hundred? A thousand?

"Sue, can I talk to you for a moment?"

"Sure. What's up?"

"I just talked to Richard on the other line. He's leaving the West Coast in a few weeks, driving cross-country. He wants to stay here for a couple of months while he sets himself up again in D.C."

"Oh, my God!"

I sat down with a thump.

"Why?"

"I don't know. Something happened, he thinks he can do better back in D.C., he's had a falling-out with somebody or a lot of people, a major change in his goals—I just don't know."

As solid, straightforward, and down-to-earth as our other sons are, Richard is emotional, sensitive, passionate, arrogant, and charming. They measure words as a miser counts ledger entries, while he is a raconteur, a wordsmith. And their lifestyles are far different. The boys are all jocks and essentially non- or light drinkers, while Richard inches up into a new suit size every year, smokes cigars, and drinks a lot of expensive whiskey. They—well, the contrasts go on and on. They're different people.

A gifted writer, Richard is most interested in hawking several proposals he's developed for television and radio, and spends eighty percent of his time and a hundred twenty percent of his money in logging thousands and thousands of travel miles each year. He's extremely bright, even brilliant, and we love him dearly, but from my perspective or Sue's or his brothers', Richard's center of gravity is anything but concentric to our spin.

To have him descend on us for a lengthy period of time meant major change around here. Major change. Richard is just raw force.

We didn't think Mike was ready for this guy. He was still paying for the theft of that knife. Frank was not often home, but on the few nights he was, Mike was in tears and we were letting the process proceed.

Later on that evening, Sue and Mike were cooking together in the kitchen. These are the happiest moments of his life with us. The boy loves to cook, follow recipes, and then serve what he makes with a flourish. Sue, so often prickly in other settings, thoroughly enjoys working with someone in the kitchen and relaxes and smiles and jokes a lot, so the kitchen is a demilitarized zone. I've never heard a harsh word or a confrontation begin there.

Mike does have some really good points. With two of our boys, in particular, if we didn't have roast beef for sandwiches in the house and purchased snacks when they had a field trip, they would make us feel like class-one socioeconomic failures. Mike, however, is more than happy with almost anything we do in the food department, and he makes do. Petty ingratitude and carping about details are not among his failings.

Dawn, and I was up on the mountain with the dogs. Very foggy. Huge flights of Canada geese just over our heads in the mist scared the bejesus out of me. The dogs took off howling, and I joined them.

All that morning, aside from one brief conversation, Mike was abnormally quiet and subdued. Sorting things out with deep, ragged sighs because Frank had called—he was coming home again tonight.

So, picking up on the contrite face he had on, Sue forced a final confrontation over the stolen fishing knife.

"Tell me what happened. I have had five boys. I will know if your story has the ring of truth. Then I'll have Frank back off."

"No one can make Frank leave me alone. He's too strong."

"I can. You have to trust me."

"I think Frank's friend Eric might have taken it."

"Uh, that doesn't have the ring of truth."

Mike, sort of sobbing: "I broke it, then got frightened and threw it behind the barn."

Sue, leaning way back and looking at him: "Ah, the ring of truth."

A Tuesday morning and my sister Patricia and a friend of hers named Karen were up from Florida. Three years before, in late July, Pat's daughter Laura, my niece, had been murdered along a hiking trail in Honesdale, Pennsylvania. The perpetrator was never apprehended. On each anniversary of Laura's death Pat spends a week or so in Honesdale, prodding the state police, meeting with the D.A., talking to newspapers, handing out fliers. She is determined by sheer force of will to keep the investigation going.

I am very, very proud of Patricia.

A student at Florida State, the year she was killed was Laura's second summer at Camp Cayuga in Honesdale. The first year we had driven her over and then picked her up for the occasional visit. But that year John, Patricia's husband, had gotten her a reliable car and she had driven herself. Then, at the end of July, on her Saturday off, Laura packed a lunch, a book, and left the campgrounds to hike to Tanner Falls, a few miles away.

The call from my older sister Harriet came midmorning on Sunday. Laura was missing in the woods at Camp Cayuga.

I called the camp and after discussing the situation with a staff member, the camp owner came on the line. His first words to me were, "Can we agree, Mr. Miniter, that whatever has happened I will handle all relations with the press?"

I hung up on him and told Sue, "No help there. We have to get moving."

"The boys are working," Sue said. "I'm calling around. You get some things together."

Ten minutes later I had a pack stuffed full of gear and was walking across the porch. "Do you think any of them will come with us?" I asked.

Just then the first vehicle skidded into the driveway.

"Here," Brendan said, running up to me. "Here are topographic maps Tony Tantillo threw at me. He said if you need anything else to call him—more maps, compasses, whatever." And then he turned and looked as Henry's truck made the turn in. In a few minutes more Susanne and David, Liam, and Frank showed up. Frantic packing, searching for more overnight gear, and then we were on the road.

I was never prouder of those guys than on that beautiful, sun-drenched, bleak-hearted Sunday morning when they stormed down the interstate in a convoy of vehicles to get Laura back.

But of course they couldn't.

By the time we reached the campgrounds, searchers had found her body and I identified her. I remember I could only stumble into the makeshift morgue, look down, and cry, "Oh, honey," and I touched her hair.

Then I called Patricia.

I would rather my right hand had been burned off.

Now Pat was here again, and I had to give her a hug big enough to last twelve more long months.

Karen, the woman with her, had been Laura's Girl Scout leader for many years. She has multiple sclerosis, and spends a good deal of time in a wheelchair, but still drives around with Pat and acts as her secretary and confidante, but mostly just keeps her going emotionally with a lot of warm support and encouragement. She is a grand lady, too, down-to-earth and determined, with two daughters of her own.

We sat and talked for a long time.

Mike came home from swimming in a pond and, already fed, didn't want to sit down to a roast beef dinner with adults. But he joined us later for cake. He exhibited excellent manners with the two women trying to feed him seconds.

"What a marvelous boy," Karen said. "I'd steal him in a second."

Mike went to bed still smelling like a pond, but happy and relaxed. We were having drinks on the porch when I walked into his room to say good night and Patricia peeked in behind me while he said his prayers.

"Good night, Mike."

"Good night, Aunt Pat," he said shyly.

Mike got up by himself this morning, glad he hadn't wet. He was well behaved in church, went to the bake sale afterward and bought himself four cupcakes. Later at home I repaired his bike outside in the sun, then greased it, and he took off on the country lane toward the mountain, white helmet on, his cat on the handlebars, dogs running after him barking, the iron hand that can squeeze his thoughts still gone. You could almost hear Mike think, *It's Sunday afternoon. Dad is going to cut the grass and take a nap, Liam is working, Mom is in the office doing paperwork. I'm out of here.*

And then later, in the misty, quiet summer dusk, a shiny black Mazda 626 with California plates and its headlights on bounced into the drive and came to a stop.

Richard was here.

The next morning I struggled out of bed at six o'clock to make coffee. Richard and I had stayed up late talking, drinking, and talking. "Ugh," I said, trying to hold my belly and my head at the same time. "I can't do this anymore."

The barroom was littered with Richard's stuff—a box of cigars, a notebook computer, a suit, newspapers, books, files. "Jesus," I said. "He's only been here twelve hours."

"You tried to stay up with him, didn't you?" Sue was walking into the barroom.

"We stayed up for a little while."

"Oh, it stinks in here from those cigars," and she started crashing open all the windows. "Rich, this will go on every night if you let it."

"Don't worry, I'm cured."

"You should have been cured years ago."

"Where's Richard?" We both turned around and looked. Mike had come downstairs.

"What are you doing up so early?"

"Richard got me up last night and told me he would take me running first thing this morning before I went to school."

Sue shook her head sadly. "Mike, you have to understand that when Richard says these things, he really means them. But there's little chance he'll be up before noon."

"Maybe I should wake him?"

Richard got in his car and took off for someplace, and after school I took Mike to get a videotape. At about eight o'clock at night Sue and I were weeding in the garden when Sue's cat Jerome was killed a few feet from her by a car speeding by on the road. The cat was Sue's constant companion for years—it followed her around the day long, sat with her hour after hour on the porch. At first Sue didn't believe it; it just happened so fast. Then she collapsed on the grass crying, and it took me ten or fifteen minutes to get her into the house. Mike watched the whole thing silently and hung back. But at dark I walked back to the spot to see if all was in order and found a flower transplanted onto Jerome's grave in the garden. Possible suspect, Mike.

About ten in the evening Sue and I were having a pot of tea, Sue still crying every so often over Jerome and I was more upset than I would have thought possible. Sue looked up and sniffled. "Where's Mike? I didn't see him or put him to bed."

"Dunno," I said and I trotted upstairs, then came right back down. "He's not in his room."

"What?"

But just then the storm door opened and the inner door after that. Mike walked into the barroom without his shirt and streaming with perspiration. Right behind him Richard stumbled in, looking even more whipped than Mike.

"Richard, what are you doing?"

He waved his mother off until he had caught his breath, then gasped out, "I promised Mike I would take him for a run."

"Richard, this kid has a bedtime, and he shouldn't be running along the road after dark."

"Mom, relax. I have to get in shape, and Mike chose to come."

"Why, Richard," I asked, very amused, "this sudden concern over getting in shape?"

"Well," he said, "I must get some direction back in my life. In order to do that I have to regain control over my body and my career."

"Since when have you been in control?"

"Ha, ha." He smiled, but his eyes were snapping.

"No offense, Richard, just joking."

Sue rushed Mike upstairs, and Richard pawed through some of his files. "Dad, I'm going to take a shower and start work. Great talking to you last night."

"I had a good time, too."

Then Richard said, almost as an afterthought, "I enjoy running with Mike. He listens to everything you say."

In the next few days a complex and curious symbiosis flashed into being between our educated and overweening eldest son and our abysmally uneducated, naive, and vulnerable foster child.

They actually like each other. They began running together each night after dark, and until then Mike would sit quietly in the barroom, watching Richard plug away on his computer. They even took meals together, Richard lecturing between swallows with one finger jabbing in Mike's direction as the kid nodded quickly.

"What's this all about?" I asked Sue.

"I don't know," Sue said. "The two of them are thicker than thieves. What do you suppose they're talking about?"

I shrugged. I couldn't think of one single thing they had in common.

"Maybe you'd better find out."

But I didn't follow up on my conversation with Sue and hence hadn't the foggiest idea of what was actually happening until Richard came into my room a week later.

"Dad."

"What?"

"Did you know Mike has goals and plans for himself now?"

"Richard, don't light that cigar in here, please."

"Yes, yes, of course," he said, ignoring me as he drew deeply against a lit match and then exhaled a cloud of pungent blue smoke. "But I'm trying to explain his goals to you."

"What? What goals?" I gave up on the cigar. *Goals?* Mike? What could Richard be talking about?

"Well, we worked things out on our run tonight," Richard said.

"Worked things out? What things?"

"His life, of course. His education and his career progression."

"What!"

"Well, for more than a few evenings now I've been detailing to Mike the new career decisions I've evolved, and tonight he actually changed tables. He began to tell me what he wanted to do and just how he was going to go about doing it."

I was stunned. "What is he going to do?"

Richard sat down in my leather chair and waved one hand in a trail of dismissive cigar smoke. "Oh, he thought he wanted to be a cook, that once out of high school he'd get a job in a restaurant and, as he tritely put it, practice."

"Thought?" I asked with a little pit opening in my stomach, "Thought? What did you say back? You *did* encourage him, didn't you?"

Richard waved that hand again and then jabbed the glowing tip of the cigar in my direction as he smiled indulgently. "Encourage him? Of course not, Dad. It's absurd, ridiculous. 'Don't you ever dare consider being a cook,' I said."

"What!"

"Yes, of course," Richard said expansively. "I told him a cook makes minimum wage plus five cents an hour at McDonald's. 'You, Mike,' I told him. 'You must be a chef.' "

"A chef?" I repeated weakly.

"Yes," Richard went on with the cigar marking his punctuation like a miniature skywriter in the air above him, "not only a chef, but a credentialed chef. Then I pointed out that to be such a thing he'd have to forget about on-the-job training in a local restaurant specializing in meat loaf and pizza and hamburgers. I mean, Dad, fish sauces alone take months to master. The degree of knowledge required is exquisite. And the state schools are out, too, I told him—they have no name at all, and you'd be mixing with people with far less aspiration. No, no. I explained to him that, barring, I assume, the Cordon Bleu in Paris, he'd have to attend the CIA, the Culinary Institute of America, or maybe the VCI, the Vermont Culinary Institute, or as a very last resort, the Cornell Hotel Management School."

I was at a total loss for words.

"Of course," Richard said, getting up and turning his back, "we'll have to keep him out of that retarded special-ed program and get him into a halfway decent high school, and his reading must pick up dramatically."

"Yes, of course," I said, looking at Richard like he'd grown two heads. "Of course."

"Fine," Richard said, stretching. "I'll get him a videotape on the CIA and make sure he has some better reading material."

"Thank you, Richard."

When Richard had trucked off, followed by a line of little blue clouds, I spun around in my chair and reassured myself out loud. "Well, at least Richard got him talking about the future. That's a step." But then I thought bleakly, *Yes, a step*. The kid came up with his first simple basic life plan, and Richard stepped right on it, crushed it, told him it wasn't good enough.

But then a comforting thought occurred to me. *Mike has known Richard for only a week. Richard couldn't exert a lot of influence after that short a period. Mike probably doesn't even pay any attention at all to what Richard has to say.*

Then, moved by that thought, I got up and walked inside to Mike's room.

"Mike, it's eleven o'clock. Why isn't your light off?"

"I'm reading."

I stared down at him. "Is that *The New York Times* you're looking at?"

"Yes," he said. "All the other papers are trash, except of course *The Wall Street Journal*."

"I see. Who told you that?"

"Richard."

"Yes," I answered softly. "Yes, of course," and then sat next to him on the bed. "And what are all those little circles you've drawn on the paper?"

"Those are the words I don't understand. Richard explains them to me. Richard says that is the way to improve my vocabulary."

"Okay," I said, touched in spite of myself, "but he can do that tomorrow. It's late. I want your light out in ten minutes."

"But I haven't done the Metro section yet, and Richard says the human body needs only four hours' sleep."

"Ten minutes, Mike."

"Richard says that arbitra . . . arbitra . . ."

"Arbitrary," I said, helping him.

"Yes, Richard says arbitrary time limits are a sign of weakness."

"I know, Mike, he used to say the same thing to me when he was twelve and I was putting *him* to bed."

"Richard says . . ."

"Mike, the light is going off in ten minutes."

"But Richard says . . ."

"Don't you dare quote Richard to me once more, Mike."

But Mike still had some prosaic issues left in his life, as well. The next afternoon he complained about our putting soda into his lunch Thermos. Apparently it shakes up on the bus ride and then blows the top off, soaking his lunch.

I said, "How long has this been happening?"

He said, "It happens every day."

Puzzled, I asked him, "Why didn't you tell us before?"

Mike just shrugged his shoulders.

"Well, I'll make sure you get fruit drink from now on."

"Never mind."

"Why?"

Mike shrugged again. "Today was my last day. I start at the elementary school in two weeks. Summer's almost over."

The next day I got Mike away from Richard and put him to some physical work, and that in turn led to another animal encounter.

We have a friend, Henry, who lives about five miles away. We're helping him get windows and siding on the house he's building. Henry and his wife Pat have a small farm where they raise horses. The weather was brutally hot, but Mike worked like a Trojan out in the sun with Frank and Liam, loading about three thousand pounds of steel scaffolding into Henry's horse van, then helping unload it at the building site.

Later, Henry took Mike into the paddock where the stallions were loose. The horses were chuffing, pawing the ground, and kicking from the sight and smell of strangers inside the fence. Mike was startled and hung back, but Henry looked at me. I nodded okay, and then he coached Mike on how to approach a big stallion from the front, breathe into his nostrils, and stroke his head. Mike then inched his way up to the enormous animal.

The technique Henry showed him worked like magic, and Mike was all smiles and laughing, hugging the horse and then turning back to us to show off. Henry and I clapped.

In the evening Richard, Mike, and I had a venison dinner (pan-fried with garlic and then drizzled with béarnaise sauce), the three of us quietly alone in the barroom, Richard and I drinking a bottle of wine, Mike with his Kool-Aid—the blue Kool-Aid that, being a budding connoisseur, he prefers with game. I don't like the color and think it has a distinct swimming pool bouquet, but he soaks up gallons of it.

The next night David and Susanne came over, and there was a long conversation among Richard, David, Susanne, Frank, Brendan, and Henry. A few minutes before midnight David came up to find me where I was working at my desk.

"You remember that concern you had with Mike having to work out some sort of future for himself?"

"Yes," I said. "I do. What about it?"

"Well," David chuckled, "it certainly looks like Richard nailed that for him. Before he went to bed, Mike talked and talked about becoming a chef and getting good marks in school."

I looked down at my desk. "I know. I was upset with Richard a few days ago, but now I'm cautiously pleased. I mean, Richard's a madman, but something about what he has to say actually clicked in with Mike. The kid's thinking about the future. More than that, he's a little bit more confident about his abilities, and we haven't had any sort of explosion out of the boy since Richard walked in the door."

"And when Richard walks out in a couple of weeks?" he asked with his eyes questioning, gauging my reaction.

"Oh, we'll handle it, I suppose. Something of Richard's confidence in him will stick. We'll try to fill in the blanks as we go."

"So you feel better now?"

I smiled. "Yeah, yeah, I do."

"Okay," then David smacked his hands together and rubbed them vigorously. "I wanted to get that out of the way. But that's not the real reason I came upstairs."

"No?" I asked.

"No. It's just midnight. Do you know what today is?"

I tried to think. "No."

"Follow me."

Curious, I walked out into the dark foyer, where I found Sue and the boys together in the dark, grinning.

"What's going on?"

"Sssh." David put his finger to his lips. He opened the door to Mike's room and tiptoed in with everybody else following, then flipped on the light. One boy grabbed Mike's arms and another his legs.

Mike woke up screaming, "Let go, let go." But David tickled him and then sprayed him with a bottle of beer or wine or something. "Congratulations, Mike."

They let go of his arms and legs. "Congratulations!"

"What?" Mike said, sitting up, his face flushed and angry. "What is everybody doing?" Then he screamed, "Leave me alone. Get out of here."

"Congratulations, Mike." David was grinning even wider.

"What?"

David chuckled. "It's the twenty-eighth of August, nineteen ninety-four," and then I understood what this was all about.

"So?" said Mike, even angrier.

"So, you little woodchuck," I said from the background, "you made it through a whole year with us."

Autumn 1997

"Mike" is still very much a part of this family, although legally he's vanished. Sue and I adopted him on the day before Thanksgiving 1996. Mike seized the opportunity to change his first name as well as his last and a long file of people appeared in family court in order to watch him go. Kevin and Kathy from the children's home were there, many other social workers besides Joanne and Gerri, Father Quinn from our parish, Susanne and David, and someone else who has become a major factor in our lives—Susanne's eight-month-old daughter, McKenzie Leola Warren.

Mike's taller than Sue now and even taller than I am. After that dramatic first year with us he transferred out of special education and into a small parochial school, where he tried, sometimes very successfully, to shed that detested "special" label.

There is only one dog in the house today—Pupsy has died—but Mike still has his bike and his fishing pole. He still cooks and wants to be a chef, plays basketball and soccer, and goes to church, and although he is boarding away during the week at a small high school, most weekends still find him and me bouncing around the countryside in my battered old pickup truck.

Yet life with Mike is still very much an emotional roller coaster ride because no matter how eventful any one year can be for a complex and reticent "special" child, there are always other issues, other years; good years and not so good years. But in looking back, Sue and I take immense encouragement from the fact that what that one year could do, it did do. It furnished Mike with a mom and dad, brothers and a sister, a brother-in-law, cousins, a niece, a church, dogs, legends, and, of course, a fishing pole. All the necessary appliances of life, one could say, and so most of what follows is up to him.

Joanne still stays in touch. Sue and I and Mike and she are old friends now with little left unsaid, and although she's taken on new and other children, it's hard to say good-bye forever. Paula is still director of The Harbour Program, it's still mostly women at the monthly meetings, and we still don't know who pulled strings and allowed Mike into Harbour in the first place.

Sue is still doing her business and more of it in a new office, and is still very much the central figure in this venture. Richard is back in D.C., still writing, and a radio show of his, "Enterprising Women," went up on satellite last spring. In a story about enterprising women, Sue and Richard were featured together on a national TV show. Susanne has her own technical writing business and is taking care of McKenzie. David, the best son-in-law in the world, is logging thousands of travel miles in setting up a new business. Henry, after graduating from Norwich, did become a Vermont state trooper, married Peggy, and then the two of them moved to Colorado. Frank graduated from Norwich, studied literature in Scotland, and is writing and taking awesome wildlife photos in Wyoming as the outdoor editor for a local paper. Brendan is a senior at George Mason in Virginia, tutoring "at-risk" children in reading, still soaking up the Civil War, and I still miss him dreadfully on quiet evenings. Liam has graduated high school, still runs in the moonlight, and remains very much my last light in the meadow. Matt and Kathryn left for Colorado even before Henry and Peggy, and so that autumn was perhaps the last time all of them had a chance to hunt together on Shawangunk. But my other niece, Melissa, has married an Army Ranger lieutenant named Steve, and when I heard him talk and plot and plan with our boys, I realized they won't ever be fewer in number in other years, on other mountains.

There are leavings, too. Sue's mother, Leola Tobin, who when staying with us, as the book described, made some of the shrewdest deductions about Mike, did pass away from her illness.

My sister came up on schedule the next two summers, raising again the issue of her daughter, Laura, in the town where she was murdered. This book is dedicated to Laura and through her, to her mother. When writing this story down, I cried again for her, for Laura, and for my sons, who tried so very hard to get to her on that terrible summer afternoon.

Me? I'm consulting on manufacturing planning and distribution systems, and whenever I can I walk up the mountain of a morning, down the country lane by the beaver pond, through our apple trees, past the lakes, and then way up on top, where I can look down and remember how Sue and I had decided to give up and let Mike go after all those appalling fights, and how the boy took one last walk up here with us, carrying a book on wildflowers, trying to stay brave.

ACKNOWLEDGMENTS

To my late encourager and friend, James J. McNamara, NYPD. It was on the day Jimmy was brought home behind bagpipes, into St. Peter's Church and schoolyard where he and his brother, my first five sons, and then finally Mike were boys, that I finally understood why he wanted me to write this story down.

To Christine M. Benton of Chicago, Illinois, for teaching me how to tell a story and for endless warm support.

ABOUT THE AUTHOR

RICHARD F. MINITER lives and works with his wife, Susan, a financial planner, in a country inn in upstate New York.